D1081870

To Be
Gifted &
Learning Disabled

Third Edition

To Be Gifted & Learning Disabled

Strength-Based Strategies for Helping Twice-Exceptional Students With LD, ADHD, ASD, and More

Susan M. Baum, Ph.D., Robin M. Schader, Ph.D.,
and Steven V. Owen, Ph.D.

PRUFROCK PRESS INC.
WACO, TEXAS

Library of Congress Cataloging-in-Publication Data

Names: Baum, Susan M., author. | Schader, Robin M., author. | Owen, Steven V., author.
Title: To be gifted and learning disabled : strength-based strategies for helping twice-exceptional students with LD, ADHD, ASD, and more / by Susan M. Baum, Ph.D., Robin M. Schader, Ph.D., and Steven V. Owen, Ph.D.
Other titles: To be gifted & learning disabled
Description: Third edition. | Waco, TX : Prufrock Press, Inc., [2017] |
  Revised edition of: To be gifted & learning disabled. Mansfield Center,
  Conn. : Creative learning Press, c2004. | Includes bibliographical
  references and index.
Identifiers: LCCN 2017019048 (print) | LCCN 2017021240 (ebook) | ISBN
  9781618216458 (pdf) | ISBN 9781618216465 (epub) | ISBN 9781618216441 (pbk.)
Subjects: LCSH: Gifted children--Education. | Children with mental
  disabilities--Education. | Attention-deficit-disordered
  children--Education. | Learning disabled children--Education.
Classification: LCC LC3993 (ebook) | LCC LC3993 .B39 2017 (print) | DDC 371.95--dc23
LC record available at https://lccn.loc.gov/2017019048

Copyright ©2017, Prufrock Press Inc.

Edited by Katy McDowall

Cover and layout design by Allegra Denbo

ISBN-13: 978-1-61821-644-1

No part of this book may be reproduced, translated, stored in a retrieval system, or transmitted, in any form or by any means, electronic, mechanical, photocopying, microfilming, recording, or otherwise, without written permission from the publisher.

For more information about our copyright policy or to request reprint permissions, visit https://www.prufrock.com/permissions.aspx.

Printed in the United States of America.

At the time of this book's publication, all facts and figures cited are the most current available. All telephone numbers, addresses, and websites URLs are accurate and active. All publications, organizations, websites, and other resources exist as described in the book, and all have been verified. The authors and Prufrock Press Inc. make no warranty or guarantee concerning the information and materials given out by organizations or content found at websites, and we are not responsible for any changes that occur after this book's publication. If you find an error, please contact Prufrock Press Inc.

Prufrock Press Inc.
P.O. Box 8813
Waco, TX 76714-8813
Phone: (800) 998-2208
Fax: (800) 240-0333
http://www.prufrock.com

Table of Contents

Part II: Neurodiversity
The Complex Minds of 2e Learners

Part III: Comprehensive Programming

Part IV: Strategies That Work

Appendices

Acknowledgements

This revision would not be possible without the wisdom, expertise, support, and comfort from those who have kept us focused on the idea that learning can be a joyful, rich process for twice-exceptional students. The privilege of being a part of the innovative and courageous Bridges community has deeply informed our practice and our vision. Thank you to the entire faculty, administration, specialists, parents, and students!

A special acknowledgement to our families, who have been our sounding boards and whose patience in reading, rereading, making suggestions, and—most of all—listening to us talk about our drafts, has been invaluable. And, many thanks to Edee Burke, who has been the inspired keeper of details.

Introduction

In an ideal world, school would be a wonderful place, full of exciting opportunities for learning and growth—a place that nurtures talents, cultivates interests, and helps each student understand and manage his or her individual patterns of strengths and weaknesses. Unfortunately, in many classrooms, lessons are apt to be taught in the same ways for all—and with student evaluations based on tests or other written products. Exciting curriculum is often reserved for that hypothetical time when students have mastered basic skills.

Within these classrooms are students who suffer in this type of learning environment because they cannot conform to what is expected, even though they have the capacity to contribute in exceptional ways in the classroom and, eventually, to society. When I wrote the first edition of this book in 1991 with Steve Owen, we titled the book *To Be Gifted and Learning Disabled* to specifically address students with learning disabilities whose intellectual and creative gifts were overlooked (termed GLD or GTLD), as well as gifted students whose learning disabilities were overshadowed by their advanced abilities (LDGT). By the time the second edition appeared in 2004, the field had expanded to include growing populations of students who, although intellectually capable, creative, and/or talented, are simultaneously burdened by a wide variety of learning differences that make traditional classroom approaches unsuccessful.

We now refer to these students as twice-exceptional (2e). In some areas they require learning opportunities that are beyond their grade level, and in other areas (cognitive, social, or emotional), they lack necessary age- or grade-level skills. When using the term *2e*, we include high-ability students who may have any mix of specific learning disabilities, attention deficits, executive functioning issues, anxiety, autism spectrum disorders, and social and behavioral issues. Throughout the book, we use that broad term, only including a more detailed label if it offers additional information.

Notes on This Edition

My experience and research with Robin Schader during the past decade at Bridges Academy, a private school for 2e students (grades 4–12) near Los Angeles, CA, has been a major influence on this edition. In addition to working with a group of 170 students each year, plus staff and administration at the school, both Robin and I are also involved with the 2e Center founded at Bridges, which provides research, professional development, and outreach efforts for those living and working with 2e students.

How This Book Is Organized

To help twice-exceptional students, their parents, educators, and other professional school staff with whom these students interact, we present both theoretical perspectives and practical strategies for school and home. Using case studies and authentic examples of strategies that work, we hope to inspire you to help others understand these wonderful students and feel confident about advocating for them.

The book is divided into four parts. The purpose of Part I is to introduce twice-exceptionality—both as a field and as it pertains to individual students. After reviewing specific mixes of twice-exceptionalities, we offer a fresh lens to explain the complexities of dual diagnosis and why those complexities are best served through a strength-based, talent-focused approach.

Part II explores the idea of neurodiversity and a range of factors that affect learning. Part III focuses on comprehensive programming, including identification. This section also introduces the Talent Centered Model as a basis for successful teaching and learning. Part IV is full of strategies for teachers, parents, and other professionals that will help them enhance students' intellectual, physical, and emotional growth.

You will also find larger, detailed versions of many tables and figures on the book's webpage at http://www.prufrock.com/tobegifted.aspx.

—Susan M. Baum

Part I

The 2e Basics

CHAPTER 1

Twice-Exceptionality

Evolving Definitions and Perceptions

How can some students appear "lazy" and "distracted" in the classroom, applying little or no effort to school tasks, but then successfully pursue demanding and creative activities outside of school without missing a beat? Why, despite years of research findings, do educators, parents, relatives, and other professionals have such a hard time accepting the idea that children can have both high abilities and learning disabilities? These questions emphasize that many students face not only an obstacle course of internal and environmental challenges that threaten their academic achievement, but also a host of widely shared beliefs at home and at school that can obstruct their progress. Exploring the realities underlying these attitudes can help us understand this unique group of children, nearly all of whom have been unable to successfully learn in a traditional classroom setting.

The Story of Neil

A turning point in the life of the first author of this book occurred when she crossed paths with a student named Neil in 1978. Susan was a learning disability "teacher consultant" specializing in "diagnosis and prescriptive teaching," which is what it was called then. Neil was a highly creative, unproductive, and troubled high school student with learning disabilities who had threatened suicide. It was at this juncture that Susan was called in to identify his learning issues and to help him with his academic productivity. The story of his roundabout journey to success has inspired an ongoing inquiry into the lives of students like him. Working with Neil led Susan to realize, for the first time, that many students with learning disabilities have exceptional abilities in certain areas, as well.

"School is like a basketball game, totally irrelevant to life!" muttered Neil in frustration. At the time, he was failing all of his classes as a high school sophomore. His observation was actually completely accurate. For him, neither school nor basketball was meaningful for neither connected with any of his needs or interests.

Convinced that Neil had the capacity to do better if only he applied himself, his teachers described him as lazy. "When I talk to Neil, he has so much to offer, but he just doesn't produce," one said. Neil's classmates, applauding his moments of cleverness, viewed him as the class clown. But Neil saw himself as a misfit. He was baffled and frustrated by the inconsistencies between what he knew he was capable of achieving and people's perceptions of him. What resulted were growing feelings of inadequacy.

Neil began to have academic difficulty in fourth grade. Each year, as he drifted upward, he accomplished less and less. Eventually, he was in such a depressed emotional state that weekly psychological counseling became necessary. His psychologist suggested an educational evaluation for Neil; the results indicated learning disabilities in writing, organization, and sequential tasks, such as those required in linear math.

With that knowledge, Neil's academic program was adjusted. He began receiving supplemental instruction from the learning specialist (Susan), and his teachers made special provisions for testing and assignments—procedures usually recommended for students with learning disabilities. However, unlike those students with disabilities who begin to feel better about themselves when they experience success through modified assignments or additional time, Neil's depression worsened. In spite of his improved grades, Neil discounted and dismissed his progress, attributing it to factors outside of his control—a less rigorous curriculum, accommodations, and extra support from a tutor. He clearly did not view his new academic accomplishments as personal successes.

Yet, although failing at school, Neil had independently amassed a wealth of knowledge about music, religion, psychology, and photography. He also pursued extracurricular interests with enthusiasm and commitment, running his own small business as a photographer. His photos won awards in amateur contests, and he was asked to photograph weddings and social events. Little wonder he was confused about the school's claim of impaired ability to learn when he was obviously learning so much through other channels. To add to the confusion, Neil's family placed a high priority on academic achievement that would lead to an eventual college degree. His father was highly accomplished, and the school identified his younger brother as a gifted student.

Neil best expressed his creative and insightful self through photography. The statements that he made with the camera were powerful and showed the depth of his feelings. Could using photography as a substitute for written schoolwork ease Neil's conflict? Surprisingly, when Neil was encouraged to submit photographic essays instead of written papers, he stopped taking pictures altogether, declaring, "Why can't I be like the piano player in Salinger's *Catcher in the Rye*, who used the piano for his own pleasure?" Photography was Neil's escape, an activity over which he had complete control. He didn't want teachers to use his work for their purposes or evaluate his photography by their standards. In essence, Neil was asking for attention to his strengths in their own right, not as a means to work through his weaknesses. Neil demonstrated clearly that the solution to overcoming the challenges of learning disabilities is not as simple as discovering and using the interests of these students.

We will return to Neil a bit later, but for now, the important message of his story is that it represents those of many other bright and creative students with learning, attention, and social issues. It is far from unique. Described as 2e today, young people like Neil experience frustration on a daily basis when trying to cope with the discrepancy between what they can and cannot do. Fortunately, continuing research has given us new ways of understanding these students, new terminology for describing them, and new approaches for helping them.

Twice-Exceptional: The Term and Its History

For many people, the terms *learning disabilities* and *high abilities* occupy opposite poles of a continuum of capabilities. The term *twice-exceptional* (2e) describes someone whose learning patterns have characteristics on both ends of the scale. On the surface, this combination might seem illogical for, as Assouline and Whiteman (2011) argued, the term *twice-exceptional* unites two seemingly disconnected special education categories. To resolve the apparent contradiction of thinking of someone as having both "high abilities" and "disabilities" simultaneously, let's look at a few notable observations from clinical psychologists, educators, and writers, some written prior to either the passing of special education laws or legislation on the gifted and talented.

Origins of Twice-Exceptionality in Education

The idea of public schools for all came to the forefront when Horace Mann founded *The Common School Journal* in 1838. In his adaptation of the industrial production model, there was an assumption that everyone should learn at the same pace within a classroom context, and children were placed in classrooms by age rather than ability. At that time, most "disabled" children (also described as "mentally defective" or "feeble minded") were institutionalized and were not included in public schools.

By the early 1920s, Leta Hollingworth (a psychologist, educator, and researcher known today primarily for her early contributions to the recognition and education of highly intellectually gifted children) had become interested in the distinguishing characteristics of students outside the norm. Her beliefs included the idea that schools should offer opportunities for all students to develop their abilities as completely and as rapidly as possible, and that included students who were highly advanced, as well as those who were below the norm. Hollingworth had started her work at the Clearinghouse for Mental Defectives and Bellevue Hospital, where she became the principal of the School for Exceptional Children. In her foundational work, *Special Talents and Defects: Their Significance for Education* (1923), Hollingworth explicitly included descriptions of students who exhibited both high abilities yet limiting deficiencies in areas such as reading, basic arithmetic, spelling, and handwriting. And she hinted at varying reasons why children of superior general intelligence might not succeed in school, stating, "All children cannot easily learn to read by the method that serves the majority" (p. 65). Providing examples such as a study of seven nonreaders with IQs ranging from 94 to 130, she wrote that all of them learned to read but through methods not regularly used in the classroom. She also noted, "Occasionally a very intelligent child is found who does not readily learn arithmetic, and on the other hand there exist children whose ability at calculation far exceeds expectation from other performances" (p. 114).

Not only did she observe and record examples of what is now called "twice-exceptionality," she also remarked on the need for personalized learning! She wrote,

> The most important single cause of truancy is that the curriculum does not provide for individual differences. . . . Not only is the curriculum not adapted to individual differences in general intelligence, but it is far less adapted to individual differences in special defects and aptitudes. (p. 200)

In the same vein, Samuel Orton (1925) tested a group of 88 students who were unable to learn to read. Using the Stanford-Binet IQ test, he observed a wide range of individual differences—from full scale lows between 70 and 80 to a high of 122. From this work, he questioned whether the IQ score always reflected true intellectual ability in students with reading disabilities. Describing a "typical case," he wrote:

> I was strongly impressed with the feeling that this estimate did not do justice to the boy's mental equipment, and that the low rating was to be explained by the fact that the test is inadequate to gauge

the equipment in a case of such a special disability. (as cited in Hallahan & Mercer, 2001, p. 3)

In the early 1940s, Austrian pediatrician Hans Asperger described and labeled a set of behaviors in patients he referred to as "little professors." They frequently showed intense, focused areas of interest and high-level, but rigid thinking processes. These children also had difficulty with environmental demands. Failing to read social cues, their play, as well as their speech patterns, appeared repetitive and pedantic. They were rarely educated in public settings (Asperger, 1944). Across the ocean, at Johns Hopkins Hospital in Baltimore, Leo Kanner first published the term *autism* and, in a 1944 issue of *Pediatrics*, outlined two characteristics of the condition—elaborate ritualistic behavior and autistic aloneness—but also noted "good cognitive potential" (as cited in Silberman, 2015, p. 184).

Strauss and Lehtinen (1947) wrote about children who exhibited "disturbances in perception, thinking, and emotional behavior either separately or in combination. These disturbances prevent or impede a normal learning process" even among children with at least normal intelligence (p. 4). Intelligence level, it was noted, was not a sufficient explanation for why a child was not able to learn conventionally. The focus, however, was on understanding or working with the neurological disorder(s) rather than developing the normal or high intelligence.

Dissatisfied with attributing mental retardation as the cause of learning difficulties in school, educational psychologists introduced new terminology to describe deficits in learning. For instance, in 1961, Cruickshank, Bentzen, Ratzeburg, and Tannhauser conducted a pilot study of educational options for children with brain injuries and hyperactivity, including those without brain injury but whose behaviors were considered typical of the brain injured. Their work opened the door to a distinct field of learning disabilities. The following year, Samuel Kirk published *Educating Exceptional Children* (1962), clarifying that a learning disability could interfere with academic learning, describing it as

a retardation, disorder, or delayed development in one or more of the processes of speech, language, reading, writing, arithmetic, or other school subjects resulting from a psychological handicap caused by a possible cerebral dysfunction and/or emotional or behavioral disturbances. (p. 263)

Other researchers were focused on understanding the development of giftedness. Terman and Oden published their first volume of *Genetic Studies of Genius* in 1947 but did not address the possibility of any learning disabilities among their subjects. However, when Mildred and Victor Goertzel (1962) reviewed the biographies of 400 eminent adults, they discovered that some of the highly accomplished individuals had negative educational experiences and even struggled with conventional learning. In their work, the Goertzels did not speculate about the reasons for these problems in school.

Continuing his work with children with brain injuries, Cruickshank (1977) noticed that descriptors used for hyperactive and problem students, such as distractibility or high energy could just as easily be applied to high-ability children. One of his observations from the study was that the multiattention and openness to stimuli of high-ability students appeared to increase their knowledge, as well as their experiences.

Even though repeated evidence of a co-occurrence of high abilities and disabilities in certain individuals appeared in the literature, the fields of special education and education for the gifted and talented continued to develop separately. Until the mid-1970s neither students with disabilities nor gifted students were entitled to special public school services and programming. If identified at all, gifted students may have received advanced curriculum and enrichment work, while those with "deficits" may have received only remedial support.

Legislation Paves the Way

In 1975, the Education for All Handicapped Children Act mandated several landmark provisions:

1. a free, appropriate public education for all children with disabilities,
2. due process rights for all of the children and families covered by the act,
3. a program of mandated Individualized Education Programs (IEPs), and
4. the introduction of the concept of Least Restrictive Environment (LRE).

Children identified as gifted and talented were not explicitly included in this legislation, however, in 1978, the Gifted and Talented Children's Education Act was passed. This act established a National Training Institute, a federal office of gifted and talented, and a definition. Six areas of giftedness were identified: general intellectual ability, specific aptitude, visual and performing arts, creativity, leadership, and psychomotor abilities (later excluded from the act). It was noted in the definition that students talented in one or more of these areas were entitled to specialized services, but there was no mandate to provide them.

Neither act addressed the fact that a student might be identified as gifted and also have a disability. Federal funding resulted in an increase in programs; however, many state policies did not allow schools to be reimbursed for a student in more than one category. This created a funding problem for schools with students requiring both types of support. It became apparent that there was a need for special services for these students, especially those who were struggling or failing in school despite their high intelligence. June Maker's influential work, *Providing Programs for the Gifted Handicapped* (1977), brought the issue to the attention of educators across the nation. Publications began to appear recognizing that gifted students with learning disabilities had a need for both learning supports and advanced programming (Baum, 1988; Meisgeier, Meisgeier, & Werblo, 1978; Whitmore, 1980). Notable public school programs were established in Westchester County, NY, and Montgomery County, MD, and became models for other school initiatives.

Advocacy efforts resulted in the founding of groups, such as the Association for the Education of Gifted Underachieving Students (AEGUS) in 1987 and the National Association for Gifted Children (NAGC), which created a division to focus on this special population of gifted students. Attention continued to grow in support of gifted students with disabilities at the federal level. The 1988 Jacob K. Javits Gifted and Talented Students Education Act established a National Research Center for the Gifted and Talented and funded grants for program development for underserved students, including gifted students with disabilities. Project High Hopes (ACES New Haven, CT, and Cranston, RI), which is described more fully in Appendix A, and the Twice-Exceptional Child Project (University of New Mexico and Albuquerque Public Schools) came from this federal initiative.

In the 21st Century

Opportunities for 2e students have continued to increase as their needs have become more widely recognized. The 2004 reauthorization of the Individuals with Disabilities Education Act (IDEA) included the student who is disabled and has "not failed or been retained in a course, and is advancing from grade to grade," which is important language that allows recognition of intellectually gifted students who do not thrive in school but might be able to survive (albeit at great personal cost). Finally, an avenue was available to address those with both high abilities and disabilities within the public system, giving credence to the existence of 2e students.

It is hard to estimate the number of twice-exceptional students. According to the U.S. Department of Education, there are approximately 360,000 twice-exceptional students in America's schools (National Education Association, 2006). It is also reasonable to assume that every school has twice-exceptional students whose unique learning needs must be met. The Oak Foundation (n.d.) noted that:

> Approximately 20 per cent of children (10 million students) in United States public schools have learning profiles that are not aligned with the expectations and teaching methodologies prevalent in mainstream school systems. Referred to as learning differences, this includes, but is not limited to: dyslexia; attention issues; and learning disabilities.

As a result, these students are often perceived as not being capable of performing well in school, unmotivated or just not trying hard enough. These students often disengage with school, perform poorly, and may not graduate from high school. Those who do graduate often choose not to pursue post-secondary educational opportunities. As adults, many are under-employed or can even end up in prison.

However, this is a loss of a critical resource in our society. Paradoxically, these learners bring the strengths of persistence, alternative problem-solving approaches and creativity along with their capable minds—to school, and later to the workplace and society. (para. 7–9)

Although twice-exceptional students can fall within this 20%, they may actually increase the overall numbers above 20%. Educated parents with sufficient financial means express their frustration in finding knowledgeable people, quality information, and services for their 2e child. For most others it is impossible. Low-income, non-English-speaking, poorly or minimally educated, and/or at-risk parents comprise a silent, but significantly large, group, which may be negatively impacted by lack of information about the possibility of twice-exceptionality as a diagnosis, and even more significantly affected by a lack of resources and options for help.

Currently, newsletters such as *2e: Twice-Exceptional Newsletter* and *Smart Kids With Learning Disabilities* concentrate on the special needs of these students and provide information for parents, teachers, and other professionals. Some states (Colorado, Idaho, Maryland, Montana, Ohio, and Virginia) have published policies and guidelines for identifying twice-exceptional youngsters.

Even as the field of twice-exceptionality becomes more recognized, some researchers continue to voice their concerns. They call for more substantive, empirical proof that this population of students exists, claiming that there is neither a research foundation for this field nor a precise, research-based, and operational definition (Cohen & Vaughn, 1994; Lovett & Lewandowski, 2006; McCoach, Kehle, Bray, & Siegle, 2001; Vaughn, 1989). As a response to these criticisms, Foley-Nicpon, Allmon, Sieck, and Stinson (2011) published their research, "Empirical Investigation of Twice-Exceptionality: Where Have We Been and Where Are We Going?" Their review outlined existing studies on identification, characteristics, and program strategies for three distinct twice-exceptional groups (gifted students with learning disabilities [GLD], Attention Deficit/Hyperactivity Disorder [ADHD], and autism spectrum disorders [ASD]). They concluded that there was no question "that gifted students can have a coexisting disability" (p. 13).

A New Definition: A New Basis for Action

In 2009, a national Joint Commission on Twice-Exceptional Students was formed to discuss the state of research related to 2e students and to adopt a new definition based on available research and scholarly discourse. The commission included the authors of this book, along with other researchers, practitioners, clinical psychologists, and educational therapists. The following definition emerged that underlies the approach taken in this book (Reis, Baum, & Burke, 2014):

> Twice-exceptional learners are students who demonstrate the potential for high achievement or creative productivity in one or more domains such as math, science, technology, the social arts, the visual, spatial, or performing arts or other areas of human productivity AND who manifest one or more disabilities as defined by federal or state eligibility criteria. These disabilities include specific learning disabilities, speech and language disorders, emotional/behavioral disorders, physical disabilities, Autism Spectrum Disorders (ASD), or other health impairments, such as Attention Deficit/Hyperactivity Disorder (ADHD). These disabilities and high abilities combine to produce a unique population of students who may fail to demonstrate either high academic performance or specific disabilities. Their gifts may mask their disabilities and their disabilities may mask their gifts. Identification of twice-exceptional students requires comprehensive assessment in both the areas of giftedness and disabilities, as one does not preclude the other. Identification, when possible, should be conducted by professionals from both disciplines and when at all possible, by those with knowledge about twice-exceptionality in order to address the impact of co-incidence/co-morbidity of both areas on diagnostic assessments and eligibility requirements for services.
>
> Educational services must identify and serve both the high achievement potential and the academic and social-emotional deficits of this population of students. Twice-exceptional students require differentiated instruction, curricular and instructional accommodations and/or modifications, direct services, specialized instruction, acceleration options, and opportunities for talent development that incorporate the effects of their dual diagnosis.
>
> Twice-exceptional students require an individual education plan (IEP) or a 504 accommodation plan with goals and strategies that enable them to achieve at a level and rate commensurate with their abilities. This comprehensive education plan must include

talent development goals, as well as compensation skills and strategies to address their disabilities and their social and emotional needs. (pp. 222–223)

As the commission's definition emphasizes, twice-exceptional students have unique characteristics that require alternative educational practices that take all of their exceptionalities into account. In general, once identified, students who demonstrate a substantial discrepancy between their performance and/or behaviors and abilities may receive remediation or support in deficit areas, but little or no attention is given to their strengths. Holding a spotlight on deficits can be counterproductive for a student whose special abilities are being ignored.

Even with a more inclusive definition, the proliferation of articles, the emergence of new private schools for twice-exceptional students, and pockets of recognition that students may have jagged learning patterns that include high abilities and learning disabilities, we find little current evidence that twice-exceptional students are receiving educational opportunities well-suited to their needs. Such youngsters appear to need both remediation and enrichment, as well as special counseling to help them understand the mix of conditions in which they must learn to succeed. With an ever-increasing emphasis on high-stakes testing and early reading and writing, traditional classrooms and instruction give these students little opportunity to shine. We firmly believe that 2e students require and deserve environments that incorporate options that address their individual learning patterns. To clarify, let's return to the story of Neil.

The Story of Neil, Continued

After working with Neil for a year, Susan was frustrated by his lack of improvement in terms of his academic self-efficacy and sense of self, even though he was making gains in achievement:

> It seems that all I learned in my undergraduate and graduate education in special education—and what to do for students with learning disabilities—seemed to backfire. Using interests, breaking down learning into manageable parts, and coaching how to organize and plan should have resulted in improved grades and self-concept. Why was that not happening with Neil?

Coincidentally, while working with Neil, Susan became interested in the education of gifted and talented students. The summer between Neil's junior and senior year, she attended 2 weeks of professional development at the University of

Connecticut (Confratute), which focused on enriched teaching and learning along with talent development. She said,

> Afterward, I was changed. I began to look for strengths, interests, and talents in students and how to develop them in their own right, not primarily as a means to remediate. When September came and I began working with Neil again, I began to view him differently. He had passed all his subjects the previous year and was counting off the days until graduation. His attitude seemed to be, "Let's just get through this year and get it over with."
>
> Shortly into the year, when we were studying for a history test, Neil continued complaining about school: "Why do I have to learn this?" He ranted on and on, and then asked me whether I was going to share his comments with his therapist, which I assured him was not my intention. Instead, remembering what I had learned during Confratute about creative productivity, I offered Neil an opportunity. I remarked that his feelings about school were important, and I was sure that these feelings were not unique to him. We talked about schools, curriculum, and how educational policies evolved and were transformed. One of those ways was through the press. So, I invited him to collaborate with me on an article. He reminded me that he didn't particularly like to write but perhaps he could create a photographic essay. (He had not taken pictures in months.) Our deal was made. I was amazed at what followed. He took the initiative to take new photographs. He used the metaphor of being on a train track following the straight and narrow path to frame his essay. I saw his excitement and willingness to stay in the struggle as he found just the right words as captions for the essay. (See Figure 1.1.)
>
> This was not only a turning point for Neil but also for me. I realized how important it was for me to pay attention to his strengths, learning styles, and interpersonal abilities. Learning was best for him when it was authentic, relevant, and contextual. The seeds that had been planted during this time have continued to develop as I have worked to understand the needs of youngsters like Neil and the special population he represents, and the kinds of learning that would be key to their success.
>
> Neil took a gap year before college that gave him time to explore and continue to pursue his interests. He included books about history in his reading and reported that now that high school was over he finally had time to learn. Entering a state college the

School is an ugly geometric existence.

I feel that school has turned its back on me.

For me, school is stepping-stone to nowhere.

Because it is irrelevant to life, it's but pieces of unconnected tracks, connecting nothing with nothing.

I know graduation is the light at the end of a very straight tunnel.

If I do make it out, what will I have gained? I feel like a barren tree, still reaching . . .

Figure 1.1. Neil's photographic essay, "How I Feel About School." From "Recognizing Special Talents in Learning Disabled Students," by S. Baum and R. Kirschenbaum, 1984, *Teaching Exceptional Children, 16,* 96–97. Copyright 1983 by Council for Exceptional Children. Reprinted with permission.

following year, he excitedly called upon completion of that first year. He said, "Susan, you are right, I do have a learning disability. I am smart but just need to work harder." And he boasted, "I passed all my subjects getting C's, but I did it on my own!"

Seeing 2e Through a New Lens

In the course of collaborating on the revision of this book, we discovered what we consider a fundamental new insight. In one sense it's a metaphor. But we believe it's more and can be much more. Consider looking at 2e students with this lens: In painting, green is a mix of yellow and blue. Similarly, twice-exceptional learners are those with distinguishing strengths (yellow) and complex challenges (blue). (See Figure 1.2. *Note.* This figure appears on the back cover in color.)

Although this two-dimensional representation of green risks the suggestion that each student is a static blend or type, the reality is that each student moves across the spectrum from yellow to blue at different times, in different circumstances, and in response to changing conditions. Because of the individual characteristics of their blues and yellows, 2e students come in a remarkable range of greens.

Like many other "green" youngsters struggling with a discordant mix of gifts and disabilities, Neil had been able to hide his learning difficulties through several grade levels—but eventually even his exceptional cognitive abilities could not sufficiently compensate for his deficits. Rather than admit he was having problems, Neil pretended his underachievement was caused by boredom. Although Neil's intellectual abilities had allowed him to mask his learning disabilities for a time, those very same high abilities coupled with his high personal standards served to negate feelings of success in what he perceived as a watered-down curriculum.

Working with a tutor, along with other accommodations such as extra time for tests and assignments, felt like cheating to him. In addition, what seemed to him like the "exploitation" of his photography led to the abandonment of his creative expression, an outlet so necessary for so many 2e youngsters. Puzzling complications such as these often aren't as readily observable when student needs are more clearly either blue or yellow. As we know from Kermit the Frog's classic song, "it's not easy being green," nor is it easy to teach, parent, or work with someone "green."

Green represents the intermingling of advanced abilities with challenging disabilities—both are exceptionalities—hence the term *2e*, which creates a paradoxical, often conflicting, yet sometimes symbiotic relationship within the individual. Understanding what can occur when working with combinations of exceptionalities is critical in meeting the educational and emotional needs of 2e learners.

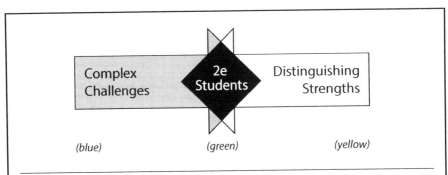

Figure 1.2. Making green. From *The 2e Center for Research and Professional Development* [PowerPoint slides], by Bridges Academy, 2013. Copyright 2013 by Bridges Academy. Reprinted with permission.

CHAPTER 2

The Yellows and the Blues of Twice-Exceptionality

This chapter provides an overview of the concepts, terms, and acronyms we will use in the subsequent chapters to describe 2e students. Twice-exceptional students all display an "e" of exceptional abilities and promise—a wide variety of gifts, talents, or in-depth interests in one or more specific areas. They also have another "e," an exceptionality of learning challenges, as illustrated in Figure 2.1. When students' high abilities, gifts, and talents are recognized within the educational community, they are frequently referred to as GT. The disabilities or learning differences may include (but are not limited to) specific learning disabilities (SLD) such as dyslexia and dyscalculia, Attention Deficit/Hyperactivity Disorder (ADHD), oppositional defiant disorder (ODD), general anxiety disorder (GAD), and autism spectrum disorders (ASD).

The First "e": Gifted and Giftedness, or What We Call "Yellow"

Acknowledging that a student who is twice-exceptional has both high abilities (gifts) and learning challenges (disabilities) can be difficult for many teachers and parents to reconcile. They often find it counterintuitive to believe that a child who can't read and write with ease could be considered "gifted" (GT). Yet it is essential to recognize

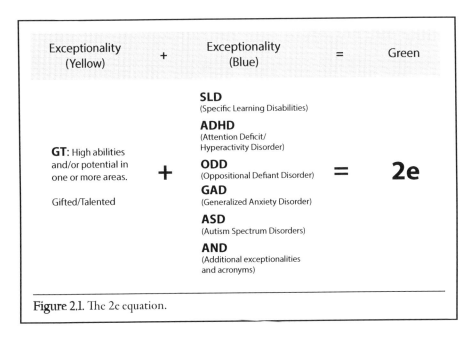

Figure 2.1. The 2e equation.

and include the exceptionality of a child's "gifts" or high abilities as a variable in the 2e equation.

The terms *gifted* and *talented* are emotionally laden and have been frequently misunderstood. Even today, the stereotype of a gifted youngster might still conjure up the image of the straight-A student who boasts an IQ of at least 130. And, unfortunately, in some schools, test scores continue to take precedence over gifted behaviors. Yet we know that more than a few of our civilization's most gifted individuals did not do well in the classroom—Pablo Picasso, Thomas Edison, Winston Churchill—and might very well be excluded from gifted programs by today's standards. Their abilities became known by what they produced, created, or performed, not by their grades in school.

Historical Perspectives on Giftedness

The shift away from assessing how a student actually performs or produces to using assessments and test scores as predictors of giftedness and potential success began in the late 19th and early 20th centuries. Sir Francis Galton started the transition. Influenced by his cousin, Charles Darwin, Galton was convinced that genius was an inherited trait and that intelligence was tightly related to the keenness of one's senses. He argued that tests of sensory acuity could effectively measure intelligence or genius.

At the same time, across the English Channel, the French Ministry of Education commissioned psychologists Alfred Binet and Theodore Simon to develop a test to identify children too "dull" to benefit from traditional schooling. After many unsuccessful attempts, they finally devised a scale based on specific skills that teachers felt students needed in order to achieve in school. They invented the concept of mental age to interpret test performance. The mental age concept eventually led to the first IQ (intelligence quotient). Binet warned against the overuse and sole reliance on a score to determine a child's capabilities, but the reign of the all-powerful IQ score began.

Before long, the idea swept across the Atlantic, generating further excitement and support. Most important to the field of giftedness was the test's effect on Lewis Terman, a professor at Stanford University. He translated and refined Binet and Simon's work and, in 1916, published the first form of the Stanford-Binet test of intelligence. From then until the 1950s, giftedness was simply measured with an IQ test. Characteristics of gifted students were based on the landmark study undertaken by Terman and his associates (Terman & Oden, 1947). They identified 1,400 students with an IQ score of at least 140 on the Stanford-Binet Intelligence Test and conducted a comprehensive, longitudinal study on the personality characteristics and the later creative accomplishments of these young geniuses. Early findings created the "Terman Myth"—"that gifted students are only those who excel in all areas of endeavor and score high on any achievement and aptitude test" (Whitmore, 1980, p. 13).

There were doubters about this talented-in-everything depiction. Witty (1958) asserted that "any child whose performance in a potentially valuable line of human activity is consistently remarkable" may be considered gifted (p. 62). The movement continued with educators and psychological leaders voicing new ideas and opinions. Hildreth (1966) argued,

> Today the simple formula of "giving a Binet" and deciding where to "draw the line" no longer suffices. If giftedness is viewed as developed capacities and unusual performance in a wide range of skills and achievements, the identification of the gifted and talented requires a many-sided study of the individual's intellectual abilities. (p. 147)

This shift in emphasis away from using a high IQ score as the sole indicator of giftedness was further supported by other research. Wallach (1976) found that test scores do not necessarily reflect a person's potential for creative productive accomplishments (as cited in Renzulli, 1978, p. 182). Getzels and Jackson (1962) and Guilford (1968) pointed to the importance of creativity as an ability to separate from intelligence. On the cognitive side of the debate, Guilford (1959) splintered intelligence into 120 separate skills. Pressure to broaden the view of human accomplishment eventually led to a revised definition by the federal government in the Gifted and Talented Children's Education Act of 1978:

> [The gifted are] children, and where applicable, youth, who are identified at the preschool, elementary, or secondary level as possessing demonstrated or potential abilities that give evidence of high performance capability in areas such as intellectual, creative, specific academic or leadership ability, or in the performing and visual arts, and who by reason thereof require services or activities not ordinarily provided by the school.

Although the federal definition allowed for a variety of superior abilities within specific fields, it failed to recognize nonintellective skills shown to enhance creative production (MacKinnon, 1965; Roe, 1953; Terman, 1959). In essence, according to Renzulli (2005), what seemed to be emerging were two different kinds of giftedness—"schoolhouse giftedness" and "creative-productive giftedness." Renzulli's distinction is essential to the understanding of students who can be learning disabled yet demonstrate behaviors of giftedness at the same time. Schoolhouse giftedness refers to students who are exceptional test-takers and talented lesson-learners. Their superior performance in school not only indicates high cognitive ability, but also their ability to learn in traditional ways or work within the system. On the other hand, he explained that creative-productive giftedness occurs when students use their knowledge and problem-solving abilities to develop original products and ideas. These products often grow out of students' individual strengths and interests in areas of personal relevance. (*Note.* What 2e students do well may not necessarily happen within the school environment. This theme will pop up again and again throughout the book.)

Using research on creative production, Renzulli (1978) provided a definition of creative-productive giftedness that emphasizes specific behavioral traits, both intellective and nonintellective. In his definition, giftedness or gifted behavior is viewed as the interaction among three clusters of traits: above-average ability, creativity, and task commitment, that are all brought to bear on a specific area (see Figure 2.2). When trying to identify students who have potential to demonstrate gifted behaviors, we look for signs of these traits and hope that our efforts in programming will result in bringing the rings together. For twice-exceptional students, we often find these traits are expressed in activities undertaken *outside* of the school setting where they are more able and likely to pursue interests in the ways they learn best. Some of these same traits come into play when 2e students use their gifts and talents to survive the school environments hostile to their needs rather than apply them to traditional classroom expectations (consider the child who has at least a thousand creative ways to avoid homework but freezes when asked to be creative in writing).

In the late 1980s, Congress authorized a small federal program on the gifted and talented, the Jacob K. Javits Gifted and Talented Students Education Act of 1988, which greatly expanded the definition of giftedness. A major goal of this act was to

Graphic Representation of the Three-Ring Definition of Giftedness

General Performance Areas

Religion	Visual Arts	Law
Mathematics	Social Sciences	Music
Philosophy	Language Arts	Physical Sciences
Life Sciences	Movement Arts	

Specific Performance Areas

Cartooning	Demography	Electronic Music
Astronomy	Microphotography	Child Care
Public Opinion Polling	City Planning	Consumer Protection
Jewelry Design	Pollution Control	Cooking
Map Making	Poetry	Ornithology
Choreography	Fashion Design	Furniture Design
Biography	Weaving	Navigation
Film Making	Play Writing	Genealogy
Statistics	Advertising	Sculpture
Local History	Costume Design	Wildlife Management
Electronics	Meteorology	Set Design
Musical Composition	Puppetry	Agricultural
Landscape	Marketing	Research
Architecture	Game Design	Animal Learning
Chemistry	Journalism	Film Criticism
Etc.	Etc.	Etc.

This arrow should be read as " . . . brought to bear upon . . . "

Figure 2.2. Renzulli's three-ring conception of giftedness. From "What Makes Giftedness? Re-examining a Definition" by J. S. Renzulli, 1978, *Phi Delta Kappan, 60*, p. 184. Copyright 1978 by J. S. Renzulli. Reprinted with permission.

identify students who traditionally would not be considered for gifted or talented programs. The legislation specified that federally funded demonstration programs be developed that placed special emphasis on economically disadvantaged youngsters, students with limited English proficiency, and students with disabilities who are gifted and talented. The act offered a broadened definition of gifted and talented with supporting guides for implementation:

> Children and youth with outstanding talent perform or show the potential for performing at remarkably high levels of accomplishment when compared with others of their age, experience, or environment.
>
> These children and youth exhibit high performance capability in intellectual, creative and or artistic areas, possess unusual leadership capacity, or excel in specific academic fields. They require services or activities not ordinarily provided by the schools.
>
> Outstanding talents are present in children and youth from all cultural groups across all economic strata, and in all areas of human endeavor.
>
> To put these definitions into practice, schools must develop a system to identify gifted and talented students that
> - Seeks variety—looks throughout a range of disciplines for students with diverse talents;
> - Uses many assessment measures—uses a variety of appraisals so that schools can find students in different talent areas and at different ages; . . .
> - Assesses motivation—takes into account the drive and passion that play a key role in accomplishment. (U.S. Department of Education, 1993, p. 26)

As a result of the Jacob K. Javits Gifted and Talented Students Education Act and the more inclusive definition of giftedness, programs appeared that focused on identifying and serving a wide range of students with unique gifts and talents in diverse areas. Finally there was a policy that not only acknowledged the existence of students who were twice-exceptional, but there was also money to develop programs that would identify and serve these youngsters.

Ongoing research continues to provide additional support for broadened and expanded definitions of intelligence, giftedness, and talent development (Gardner, 1983; Sternberg, 1997; Sternberg & Davidson, 2005; Subotnik, Olszewski-Kubilius, & Worrell, 2011; Winner, 1996), as well as less fixed views of intelligence (Dweck, 2000; Kaufman, 2013). Winner (1996) proposed that the term *gifted* be used for children with three "atypical characteristics"—early and rapid progress in a domain, independent acquisition of domain expertise, and "a rage to master," exhibiting an intense and obsessive interest along with intrinsic motivation and an ability to focus sharply (p. 3). Subotnik et al. (2011) explained that giftedness is about one's potential within specific domains that, with deliberate practice, can be developed into expertise. These broader and more inclusive conceptions of giftedness and talent development—allowing both potential and performance to be considered—along with the latest federal definition of giftedness have offered greater flexibility in identifying and promoting specific gifts and talents among students with learning disabilities. In 2010, NAGC approved a position paper, "Redefining Giftedness for a New Century: Shifting the Paradigm," that described gifted individuals as:

> those who demonstrate outstanding levels of aptitude (defined as an exceptional ability to reason and learn) or competence (documented performance or achievement in top 10% or rarer) in one or more domains. Domains include any structured area of activity with its own symbol system (e.g., mathematics, music, language) and/or set of sensorimotor skills (e.g., painting, dance, sports).
>
> The development of ability or talent is a lifelong process. It can be evident in young children as exceptional performance on tests and/or other measures of ability or as a rapid rate of learning, compared to other students of the same age, or in actual achievement in a domain. As individuals mature through childhood to adolescence, however, achievement and high levels of motivation in the domain become the primary characteristics of their giftedness. Various factors can either enhance or inhibit the development and expression of abilities. (p. 1)

Characteristics of Giftedness

Well-intentioned teachers, specialists, and parents may ignore or marginalize a 2e student's gifts, strengths, and talents because they are more concerned with the lack of success in school and the perceived pressing need for remediating learning problems. However, becoming familiar with the characteristics of high-ability students helps one see how easily some characteristics could be misinterpreted as pathology. For example, intense concentration and a desire to "stay in the struggle" of mastering something can be misread as perseveration. Or, an unusual sense of humor with a preference for doing things differently might be viewed as a form of oppositional defiance.

The characteristics of giftedness are well documented in the literature (Renzulli, 1978; Tannenbaum, 1983; VanTassel-Baska, 1992; Whitmore, 1980). Because gifted children vary in how they manifest their gifts and talents, they may not show all characteristics all of the time. As Renzulli and Reis (2014) pointed out, gifted behaviors can be found "in **c**ertain **p**eople, **a**t **c**ertain **t**imes, and **u**nder **c**ertain **c**ircumstances" (emphasis added, p. 13). The atom diagram (see Figure 2.3) is an important image to keep in mind because, as the adults in students' lives, we can help them discover and learn about the times and circumstances in which they can produce their best work. Conversely, each must also be aware of the times and circumstances that make it difficult, if not impossible, to function well.

Baum, Cooper, and Neu (2001) identified the following seven commonly observed characteristics of gifted students. We have added examples:

1. **A propensity for advanced content:** These students are obsessed with learning everything there is to learn about a topic such as dinosaurs, WWI, or robots. In their particular area of interest, they may know more specifics than the teacher, even in the primary grades.

2. **A desire to create original products:** An assignment to learn about the Spanish missions may result in a board game complete with replicas of each mission on a map of the state of California.

3. **A facility with and enjoyment of abstract concepts or playing around with the abstract:** Students are asked about their wishes for the year ahead. One responds with the provocative wish that planet Earth be larger, which leads to a discussion about how much space each person needs to live well and how people can learn to live peacefully together.

4. **Nonlinear learning styles:** Students may come up with creative solutions but not be able to explain where the idea came from. Or, students may refuse to write the steps used finding solutions because their thinking is not sequential.

5. **Task commitment in areas of talent and interest:** High levels of focus and energy can be seen in preferred areas, such as robotics, art, music, or sports, but regular classroom assignments or household chores are not completed well or at all.

6. **Identification with others of similar talent and interest:** Students may find "interest peers" more easily than age peers.

7. **A heightened sense of failure and injustice:** A strong sense of empathy and sensitivity can make it difficult to handle daily news stories or unachieved personally set goals (that may be unrealistic).

Additional lists of behavioral characteristics, such as those found in *A Parent's Guide to Gifted Children* (Webb, Gore, Amend, & DeVries, 2007), can help in the identification of high-ability children at home or at school. Gifted students may demonstrate:

- unusual alertness early in life;
- rapid learning and quick thinking;

Figure 2.3. An atom of optimal learning. From "The Schoolwide Enrichment Model: A Focus on Student Strengths and Interests" by S. M. Reis and J. S. Renzulli, in *Systems and Models for Developing Programs for the Gifted and Talented* (2nd ed., p. 326), by J. S. Renzulli, E. J. Gubbins, K. S. McMillen, R. D. Eckert, and C. A. Little, 2009, Waco, TX: Prufrock Press. Copyright 2009 by Prufrock Press. Reprinted with permission.

- strong memories and retention of information;
- large vocabularies and complex sentence structure for their age;
- understanding of advanced word nuances, metaphors, and abstract ideas;
- enjoyment of solving problems involving numbers and puzzles;
- self-teaching in reading and writing;
- unusual emotional depth, intense feelings, and reactions;
- abstract, complex, logical, and insightful thinking;
- sense of idealism and justice at an early age;
- concern with social and political issues and injustices;
- longer attention spans, persistence, and intense concentration;
- preoccupation with their own thoughts and daydreaming;
- impatience with self or others' inabilities or slowness;
- learning of basic skills more quickly with less practice;
- asking probing questions, going beyond what is being taught;
- wide ranges of interests (sometimes extreme interest in only one area);
- highly developed curiosity and asking of limitless questions;
- experimentation and doing things differently;
- putting ideas or things together in ways that are unusual or not obvious (divergent thinking);
- keen and sometimes unusual senses of humor, particularly with puns;
- organizing things and people through games or complex schemas; or
- imaginary playmates (in preschool) and vivid imaginations (pp. 11–12).

Unfortunately, the traits that indicate giftedness can be masked, offset, or complicated by deficits that impede students' success, particularly in classroom settings.

The most commonly reported problems for intellectually gifted students include poor reading and math skills, problems in spelling and handwriting, difficulties with expressive language, lack of organizational skills, inability to focus and sustain attention, limited capacity for social interaction, and poor self-efficacy and esteem (Baum, Schader, & Hébert, 2014; Reis, Neu, & McGuire, 1995).

The Second "e": Differences, Disabilities, or What We Call "Blue"

There are vast numbers of possibilities when considering a 2e student's "blue" exceptionalities. Consider the syndromes defined by the American Psychiatric Association (APA) in its Diagnostic and Statistical Manual of Mental Disorders (DSM-V, 2013) along with the disabilities described by the Individuals with Disabilities Act (IDEA, 2004).

IDEA[1] covers 13 disabilities. In this book we look primarily at four—specific learning disabilities (SLD), Attention Deficit/Hyperactivity Disorder (ADHD), autism spectrum disorders (ASD), and generalized anxiety disorder (GAD). To further illustrate the descriptions of the disabilities, we include brief sketches of 2e students we've met over the years. Each has suffered the consequences of being both bright and learning challenged, and each has felt the sting of school failure. In their stories you will see how the blends of yellow, blue, and green are neither clear cut nor do they manifest predictably. We selected these students because they were all able to eventually succeed—finding ways to develop and express their abilities, even though their paths were certainly not straightforward.

Specific Learning Disabilities

IDEA (2004) defined a specific learning disability as

> a disorder in one or more of the basic psychological processes involved in understanding or in using language, spoken or written, which disorder may manifest itself in the imperfect ability to listen, think, speak, read, write, spell, or do mathematical calculations.

This disability category includes "such conditions as perceptual disabilities, brain injury, minimal brain dysfunction, dyslexia, and developmental aphasia"

---

1   IDEA is the renaming of the Education for All Handicapped Children (EHA) legislation that existed from 1975–1990 and was updated significantly in 2004 and 2008, as mentioned in the previous chapter. The main elements of IDEA are: Individualized Education Program (IEP), Free and Appropriate Public Education (FAPE), least restrictive environment (LRE), appropriate evaluation, parent and teacher participation, and procedural safeguards. Wrightslaw (http://www.wrightslaw.com) maintains a website with information about IDEA, including updates of the pertinent key statutes and their impact on students.

(IDEA, 2004). Table 2.1 lists the diagnostic criteria and characteristics of SLD. Again, it is important to realize that many people with learning disabilities have average or above-average intelligence, even though there may be gaps between their potential and actual achievement, as noted by the Learning Disabilities Association of America (LDA, 2017).

The LDA (2017) explained that specific learning disabilities are problems with processing that are neurologically based. Signs of learning disabilities frequently come to the attention of teachers and parents once a child begins school because of problems with reading, writing, and/or math, as well as executive functioning skills such as organization, abstract reasoning, attention, planning, and time management. Because learning disabilities are "hidden," a person may look perfectly "normal" and seem to be very intelligent but show great difficulty with age-appropriate academic skills and/or social skills (para. 4).

Specific learning disabilities, an umbrella term, can include central auditory processing disorder (APD), dyscalculia, dyslexia, dysgraphia, language processing disorder (LPD), nonverbal learning disabilities (NLD or NVLD), and visual perceptual/visual motor deficit. Each disorder has its own signs and symptoms.

To be identified and served in school, students need to meet the criteria, as included in the 2008 update of IDEA (U.S. Department of Education, n.d.). A child may have a specific learning disability if

> the child does not achieve adequately for the child's age or to meet State-approved grade-level standards in one or more of eight areas (e.g., oral expression, basic reading skill, etc.), when provided with learning experiences and instruction appropriate for the child's age or State-approved grade-level standards; and (B) to add "limited English proficiency" to the other five conditions that could account for the child's learning problems, and that the group considers in determining whether the child has an SLD. . . .
>
> and (A) the child does not make sufficient progress to meet age or to meet State-approved grade-level standards consistent with Sec. 300.309(a)(2)(i), or (B) the child exhibits a pattern of strengths and weaknesses in performance, achievement, or both, relative to age, State-approved grade level standards or intellectual development consistent with Sec. 300.309(a)(2)(ii).

For the complete section, see http://idea-b.ed.gov/explore/view/p/,root,regs,preamble1,prepart1,D,72,.html.

Table 2.1

Specific Learning Disability (SLD) Diagnostic Criteria and Characteristics

DMS-V Diagnostic Criteria	Possible Behavioral Characteristics
• Exhibits difficulty learning and using academic skills; at least one symptom has persisted for at least 6 months. • Skills in the impaired area are quantifiably below those expected for the individual's age. • Presentations of SLD: impairment in reading, written expression, or mathematics. • Severity of SLD: mild, moderate, or severe. *Note.* Adapted from APA, 2013.	• Reads slowly or inaccurately; has difficulty understanding meaning; finds written expression challenging. • Has stronger verbal skills than reading, spelling, and/or writing skills; has difficulties with mathematical concepts that include calculation, time, and space, and memorizing facts or calculations that are out of context. • Is distracted by background noise or visual stimulation; has difficulty concentrating. • Displays poor organizational skills. • Has trouble taking notes while listening, poor handwriting, and/or difficulty putting ideas in writing. • Displays slowed information processing. *Note.* Adapted from National Center for Learning Disabilities (NCLD), 2007.

Debra

Nine-year-old Debra, identified as having dyslexia and other learning difficulties, appeared solitary and depressed. Although she was knowledgeable beyond her years in understanding the injustices of society and was preoccupied with world hunger, child abuse, and death, she had trouble making and keeping friends. Her dramatic flair in communicating her ideas only added to alienation from her classmates who were already confused by Debra's obvious inability to read and write. This sensitive, perceptive, young, would-be actress could only reach out to adults. Unfortunately, her overdependence on them further separated her from her peers. Debra's self-esteem was precariously low (at the third percentile on a widely used measure). Her teacher described her as defiant, distrustful, and easily hurt. She lacked confidence, concentration, and independence in approaching school tasks. Her short attention span, poor executive functioning skills, and sharp deficits in reading and writing, despite a Full Scale IQ score of 128 (verbal IQ = 119, performance IQ = 132) on the Wechsler Intelligence Scale for Children (WISC-III, 1991), pointed to a specific learning disability, in this case, dyslexia. Ironically, Debra had received remedial support in school since the first grade.

And, even though her basic skills improved somewhat, her emotional well-being in school withered more each year.

Her participation in a special enrichment program during fourth grade proved to be a turning point. In that program there were many ways of learning and communicating, so students who couldn't read or write easily could circumvent their disabilities. "I never thought I'd be able to create my own display. It's really going to be at the museum!" Her eyes sparkled as she recounted her role as a director, writer, and actress in her research work, "A Day in the Life of Jerusha Webster," a project she had attacked steadily for 10 weeks.

This project was inspired by her interest in a photograph album her teacher had brought into the classroom that documented the life of an unknown, unnamed family. Debra's curiosity was piqued. Who could they be? As part of the history exploration, the enrichment teacher had arranged a trip for the class to visit the Noah Webster House, located in Debra's town. Debra totally immersed herself in the museum, asking questions and carefully examining artifacts. Her intense interest was noted by the curator, who asked Debra if she might want to create an exhibit. Her positive response earned her a commission.

Both the curator and the enrichment teacher became her guides as she used the authentic methods of a historian to create a historical representation of the life of a young girl during the American Revolutionary period. Most of her research required interviews and looking at artifacts from that time period. Very little reading and writing was required. She kept notes by taking photographs and using her tape recorder. Later, the photographs became a storyboard that she used to tell her story as Jerusha Webster, one of Noah's five children. She rehearsed her visual script with her little sister until she felt comfortable with the performance. When she was ready to be filmed, the curator loaned her one of Jerusha's dresses and allowed the story to be filmed at the house itself. Her excitement in researching, acting, and producing this project resulted in a sense of pride, confidence, and accomplishment. Debra's classmates were astonished with the finished project, resulting in new respect for her. Most importantly, Debra finally seemed to believe in herself.

Debra, like many bright students with dyslexia, was identified first with a specific learning disability. Although she had advanced interests and undertook creative pursuits at home, she failed miserably in school. Her high levels of sensitivity made her acutely aware of her inabilities. Coping with the contrast between what she could do at home and couldn't do at school caused anxiety. Her failure to learn to read and write overshadowed her advanced interests and talents. She viewed school as a hostile environment in which she had to survive, and to protect her fragile self-concept she became defiant and distrustful. These negative behaviors diminished in fourth grade when she was identified for the special enrichment program for gifted students with learning disabilities. Students in the program were encouraged to explore their interests and talents without the requirement of reading and writing. In that setting, Debra could succeed. There, she felt valued and accomplished.

Attention Deficit/Hyperactivity Disorder

Because a great majority of children and adolescents with ADHD demonstrate significant characteristics of both inattention and hyperactivity-impulsivity, an older diagnosis—Attention Deficit Disorder (ADD)—was renamed. The change reflected the position that the primary symptoms of the disorder are hyperactivity, along with problems in sustained attention and controlling impulses. A core aspect of ADHD is that an individual's pattern of inattentive or hyperactive, impulsive behaviors is exhibited with *more frequency* and *intensity* than in others at comparable developmental levels. Table 2.2 lists the diagnostic criteria and characteristics of ADHD.

To explain various combinations of behaviors and traits characterizing ADHD, three subtypes have been identified: ADHD Combined Type, ADHD Predominantly Inattentive Type, and ADHD Predominantly Hyperactive-Impulsive Type. Although parents and teachers may be tempted to use the term ADHD when describing an active, inattentive child, only trained healthcare professionals can diagnose the presence of ADHD.

Most children with ADHD are eligible for special education services under IDEA's "Other Health Impairment" or "Specific Learning Disabilities" categories (Wright & Wright, 2007). The legal definition of *other health impairment* is

> having limited strength, vitality, or alertness, including heightened alertness to environmental stimuli, that results in limited alertness with respect to the educational environment, that . . . is due to chronic or acute health problems such as . . . attention deficit disorder or attention deficit hyperactivity disorder. . . . (as cited in Wright & Wright, 2007, para. 10)

Some students with ADHD do not qualify for specialized instruction under these requirements but still require accommodations, such as more time for tests, note-taking services, or support on the playground. Schools can provide students with appropriate support services using Section 504 of the Rehabilitation Act of 1973, a civil rights law ensuring nondiscriminatory access to education. It is not unusual for gifted students with ADHD to receive accommodations through a Section 504 plan.

Jimmy

Jimmy flopped down next to his dad and declared, "I'm going to start a campaign to get kids to wear bike helmets. I know it will be hard, and some days I won't feel like working, but it's such an important project." He had been inspired

Table 2.2

Attention Deficit/Hyperactivity Disorder (ADHD) Diagnostic Criteria and Characteristics

DMS-V Diagnostic Criteria	Possible Behavioral Characteristics
<ul><li>Displays a "persistent pattern of inattention and/or hyperactivity-impulsivity that interferes with functioning or development."</li><li>Has symptoms presenting in two or more settings (e.g. home, school, or work).</li><li>Symptoms negatively impact social, academic, or occupational functioning.</li><li>Several symptoms were present before age 12.</li><li>Presentations of ADHD: combined, inattentive, hyperactive/impulsive.</li><li>Levels of ADHD: mild, moderate, severe.</li></ul>*Note.* Adapted from APA, 2013.	<ul><li>Is easily distracted or forgetful.</li><li>Does not pay attention to details; makes careless mistakes in schoolwork or other activities.</li><li>Has trouble keeping attention on schoolwork or play activities; does not follow through on instructions or fails to finish assignments.</li><li>Does not seem to listen when spoken to directly.</li><li>Has trouble organizing activities; loses things needed for schoolwork and other activities.</li><li>Avoids activities that require mental effort (e.g., classwork, homework, etc.).</li><li>Appears restless: fidgets or squirms in seat, gets up when remaining seated is required, and/or runs or climbs excessively when not appropriate; appears "on the go" or "driven by a motor."</li><li>Has trouble doing activities quietly.</li><li>Often talks excessively, blurts out answers, and/or interrupts or intrudes on others/has trouble waiting one's turn.</li></ul>*Note.* Adapted from Center for Disease Control, 2016.

after a helmetless classmate was seriously injured while biking in town. On that day, Jimmy started on the path of becoming a practicing researcher.

A fourth grader, Jimmy had been diagnosed as "mentally retarded" during his preschool years. His parents were told that his cognitive development was delayed, and his potential was uncertain. When Jimmy started school, results from retesting indicated strong intellectual ability, but he had great difficulty learning to read. A thorough assessment by a team of educational specialists showed that Jimmy had ADD (now called ADHD) as well as problems in reading and writing. Unexpectedly, his Full Scale IQ was 134 on the revised Wechsler Intelligence Scale for Children (WISC-R, 1974) with a verbal IQ of 133 and performance IQ score of 129.

Jimmy hated school and often complained of headaches and stomachaches to avoid completing tasks or even going to school. In school, his concentration was so limited that he was distracted by everything and everyone. He was constantly doodling, appearing not to pay attention. He claimed he already knew what the teacher was teaching and school was just boring.

His research interests came to light in a special program that focused attention on strengths and interests. Throughout the 6 weeks of the enrichment project, the teacher helped him plan a project that would include statistics about where bicycle accidents had occurred in his town and a survey to learn how people felt about wearing helmets. His teacher connected him to a professor in measurement and evaluation at a local university so he could learn the basics about making surveys. Jimmy followed the professor's suggestions to add some open-ended questions and include adults in his sample. He visited the map library and studied traffic patterns in his town. Who knew he could attend so long and engage so deeply? Jimmy's parents and teachers reported positive changes in his attitude, motivation, and achievement that year. His classroom teacher noted that "Jim finally feels that he has the ability to achieve and is putting forth greater effort in reading and writing." His parents could not believe how differently Jimmy felt about school, especially on Wednesdays, the day of the special program: "We don't even need to set the alarm on Wednesdays! He's up early, prepared, and eager to get to school."

Jimmy is a prime example of how confusing it is when disabilities hide abilities. He was first identified by his disruptive behaviors and inability to learn to read and write. He attended special education classes until identified for the special enrichment project. It appears that his high IQ fueled much of his hyperactivity, as he sought stimulation to offset boredom. Project-based learning and engineering and design were talent areas for him. Unfortunately, these kinds of activities are rarely available for students in lower grades, who spend the majority of time learning to read and write—the areas especially difficult for Jimmy.

Autism Spectrum Disorders

Temple Grandin, accomplished researcher, professor, writer, and one of the world's best-known adults with autism, explained, "autism is not a one-size-fits-all diagnosis" (Grandin & Panek, 2013, p. 107). Instead, *autism spectrum disorders* (ASD) and *autism* are umbrella terms for a group of complex disorders of brain development. In short, the symptoms of one person with ASD can be very different from the symptoms of another person with ASD—in both the set of behaviors as well as the severity with which they manifest. The DSM-IV categorized autistic disorder, Asperger's syndrome (AS), and pervasive developmental disorder not otherwise specified as separate diagnoses (APA, 1994). All have been subsumed under the single category of ASD in the DSM-V (APA, 2013).

There are two overarching diagnostic criteria for ASD: (1) persistent deficits in social communication and social interaction across multiple contexts, and (2) restricted, repetitive patterns of behavior, interests, or activities (APA, 2013). Prior to 2013, intellectually gifted students with ASD were most often diagnosed with AS. In the DSM-IV, delay in language development was the primary difference between those diagnosed with AS (no delay) and those diagnosed with autism (significant delay; Grandin & Panek, 2013).

Students who meet the diagnostic criteria for ASD (see Table 2.3) qualify for special education services under the auspices of IDEA (2004), which defines ASD as

> a developmental disability significantly affecting verbal and nonverbal communication and social interaction, generally evident before age three, that adversely affects a child's educational performance.... Other characteristics often associated with autism are engaging in repetitive activities and stereotyped movements, resistance to environmental change or change in daily routines, and unusual responses to sensory experiences. The term autism does not apply if the child's educational performance is adversely affected primarily because the child has an emotional disturbance . . .

Bill

Bill, a high school senior, smiled with pride as he described "The Wounds that Glow," an award-winning project he and his friend had completed. As Bill explained, "I'm a Civil War buff, and my buddy loves science. We thought if we could team up, we would improve our chances of winning an award in one of the competitions coming up." These two young men impressed the judges enough to claim two first-prize awards, one in the Siemens Westinghouse Competition and one in the Intel International Science Fair competition. Like other students we've described, several roadblocks obstructed Bill's journey to these triumphs. School was not always an ideal environment for him. Problems surfaced as early as preschool for poor peer relations, inappropriate social behaviors, cognitive rigidity, and reluctance to complete written assignments dominated his early childhood years, even though he had been identified as gifted by the district and placed in a gifted magnet elementary school. His parents requested a psychoeducational assessment of Bill when he was in fourth grade, but the psychologist who conducted the assessment declared that the discrepancy between his performance and ability was not large enough to merit special education services.

Fortunately for Bill, his fourth-grade teacher was sensitive to his needs and skilled in working with youngsters who had learning and social differences. Her highly enriched classroom—truly a learning laboratory—was often transformed into a museum-like setting, mirroring Ancient Egypt or China or some other venue from the curriculum. In this particular class, simulations, arts integration,

Table 2.3
Autism Spectrum Disorders (ASD) Diagnostic Criteria and Characteristics

DSM-V Diagnostic Criteria	Possible Behavioral Characteristics
• Displays "persistent deficits in social communication and social interaction across multiple contexts." • Has difficulty with social situations that require reciprocity such as back-and-forth conversations and initiating appropriate social contact or responding to others. • Lacks socially communicative behaviors; poor eye contact. • Lacks understanding of gestures and facial expressions. • Fails to develop, maintain, or understand relationships. • Displays "repetitive behaviors, interests, or activities." • Has intense interests that are highly restricted and fixated. • Insists on routines; has difficulty transitioning; displays rigid patterns of thinking. *Note.* Adapted from APA, 2013.	• Sticks to routine and ritualized patterns of communication; resists change. • Has issues developing skills with nonverbal communication, such as eye contact, facial expressions, and body language. • Lacks empathy. • Displays difficulty making friends with age-mates; little interest in sharing enjoyment or activities with others; preoccupied with certain topics; focuses on pieces (e.g., plays with parts of toys). • Displays problems with learning to talk or never learns to talk; struggles with starting and carrying on conversations; repetitive use of phrases (echolalia); unable to understand perspective or implied meaning. • Displays motor behaviors such as rocking and hand flapping. *Note.* Adapted from WebMD, 2017.

and project-based instruction allowed children to learn in ways that best suited them, and knowledge was measured in many ways in addition to writing.

When Bill first arrived in her class, he would hide under the desk and act out inappropriately, especially when confronted with writing assignments. Although she recognized him as troubled, she also saw his considerable talents as he engaged in creative projects. She arranged for the enrichment coordinator to work with Bill and several other boys with learning problems in small groups. They built models with LEGOS and dug for dinosaurs on the school playground during recess. Concerned about these boys' difficulties with writing, the teacher also arranged for them to have assistance in developing their fine motor skills. Bill was finding success in her classroom. When this teacher transferred to another school, however, the support came to an abrupt halt, and Bill began a rapid decline.

The IEP Team (classroom teacher, school psychologist, and guidance counselor) described Bill as "just lazy," very "quirky," and recommended academic remediation as well as social skills classes. Then, a number of things happened: His parents paid for a private evaluation; his scores on the various WISC-IV (Wechsler, 2003) subtests ranged from the fourth to the 99th percentile; a psychiatrist diagnosed him as depressed; and finally, Bill was transferred to a school with a gifted program where he also received support in organization, learning strategies, and social skills support. Later, he joined the ROTC program where he thrived in the highly structured, predictable setting.

To ensure continued support from the school, Bill's parents, along with Bill, agreed that he needed to be classified. With an increasing discrepancy between his ability and his performance, the team formally labeled Bill as having pervasive developmental disorder not otherwise specified (PDD-NOS; now ASD). With the classification, Bill was able to attend a resource class for academic support throughout middle school and high school and was permitted to take AP courses. Plus, his high school offered a special counseling component for twice-exceptional students, which provided both academic and emotional support.

Even in this adaptive environment, the quality of Bill's work was patchy. Listening to lectures and writing papers were difficult for him, and often he was discouraged and withdrawn. At those times, Bill and his family found outside activities to enrich, inspire, and re-energize. He participated in a leadership program, and during his high school years, he attended college classes in the summer, which built his self-efficacy and eased his depression.

The award-winning science inquiry was extracurricular for both Bill and his friend. The two boys had conceived and conducted their research after school and on weekends in Bill's mother's laboratory. Having the tools of the practicing professional at their fingertips and the opportunity to experiment on a topic of their choosing enabled them to pursue their passion with commitment and creativity. Bill observed the irony: "My teachers have no idea what I can do. I was afraid they would laugh at me if I told them I was entering these science competitions."

During his senior year, Bill began to make decisions about his education. He decided to take 5 years to complete high school. He used his fifth year to earn elective credits as a teaching assistant in a chemistry class, to complete his English requirements by enrolling in an Internet English course, and to continue his research and leadership activities.

Bill's journey mirrors many students whose gifts and challenges mask each other. He was not failing sufficiently to warrant special education, but his struggles kept him from being recognized as a student with high abilities. His depression seemed to be the result of not fitting in at a school where he had no friends. School personnel were aware of his deep interest in the Civil War; he amused himself by studying the Civil War, reading every book on the topic, going to reenactment camps, and watching all of the movies he could. Yet the Special Education team saw this as a sign of cognitive rigidity and hyperfocus, noting that all school projects in any subject area revolved around some aspect of the Civil War. That obsession, however, led to a project that received national and international first-place science recognition.

If Bill had been viewed from the perspective of gifted education, the scenario might have been different, for his in-depth interest in the Civil War would have been seen as task commitment and encouraged as a way to develop his academic skills and involvement. We know that young children with high abilities who are diagnosed with autism spectrum disorders often have in-depth interests that can make it very difficult for them to have friends their age. Talent development activities such as those Bill's parents discovered helped him form friendships by finding intellectual and interest peers rather than age-mates. Looking at behaviors in isolation, without considering the whole child, makes it easy to get things wrong. It's not easy seeing green.

Generalized Anxiety Disorder

According to the Anxiety and Depression Association of America (2016), those with GAD are marked by persistent, excessive, and uncontrollable worry. Although the things they are anxious about may be small and insignificant, suffering from GAD makes everyday events and activities highly stressful. This type of worry is disruptive, can be paralyzing, is difficult to control, and may manifest in physical symptoms such as headaches or general fatigue. For students, the concerns often focus on their abilities and school performance. It is not unusual to also have related challenges such as obsessive-compulsive disorder, panic disorders, social anxiety disorders, depression, and even selective mutism. Although generalized anxiety disorder can appear at any age, it commonly begins during childhood or adolescence. See Table 2.4 for a list of diagnostic criteria and characteristics.

Under IDEA (2004), students with GAD can receive special education services. GAD can be found within the category of "Emotional Disturbance," which is defined as,

> a condition exhibiting one or more of the following characteristics over a long period of time and to a marked degree that adversely affects a child's educational performance:
> a. An inability to learn that cannot be explained by intellectual, sensory, or health factors.
> b. An inability to build or maintain satisfactory interpersonal relationships with peers and teacher.
> c. Inappropriate types of behavior or feelings under normal circumstances.
> d. A general pervasive mood of unhappiness or depression.
> e. A tendency to develop physical symptoms or fears associated with personal or school problems.

Students who are eligible for special education services under this category often have a specific mental health diagnosis like depression, anxiety disorder, or oppositional defiant disorder; however, it is not required that a child have a disorder

Table 2.4

Generalized Anxiety Disorder (GAD) Diagnostic Criteria and Characteristics

DSM-V Diagnostic Criteria	Possible Behavioral Characteristics
• Displays "excessive anxiety and worry" about events or activities at work or at school. • Has anxieties that persist more than 6 months, with more days of worry than not. • Has difficulty controlling the worry. • Exhibits worries that are associated with at least one (for children) of the following six symptoms: shows restlessness or edginess; is easily fatigued; has difficulty concentrating; is irritable; suffers from muscle tension; suffers from sleep disturbance. • Symptoms cause significant distress or impairment in social or occupational functioning. • Symptoms are not attributable to another medical condition or medications. *Note.* Adapted from APA, 2013.	• Worries or obsesses persistently about concerns in ways that are out of proportion to the actual event. • Shows difficulty letting go of a worry. • Is unable to relax; appears on edge. • Displays restlessness. • Has difficulty concentrating. • Shows distress about making decisions and fears making the wrong decision. • Shows perfectionistic tendencies. • Considers multiple options in a situation and then imagines how each could conclude negatively. • Finds it difficult to handle uncertainty or indecisiveness. • Appears to lack confidence. • Requires reassurance about quality of performance. *Note.* Adapted from Mayo Clinic, 2017.

diagnosis to meet the IDEA criteria. If a child's disturbance is so significant that it prevents him from learning, it could qualify and an evaluation should be recommended (IDEA, 2004).

Many 2e students experience high levels of anxiety; however, it is not always clear if the anxious behaviors are due to an anxiety disorder or result from other causes, such as the angst sensitive students can feel from being out of step with others.

Kyle

Standing at 6'4" and touting a 10-gallon hat, Kyle earned a standing ovation with his impressive rendition of Johnny Cash's "I Walk the Line." The performance would have been impressive for any high school senior lucky enough to be singing for a packed audience on a rainy winter night at a Los Angeles venue. But for this young man, this stage event—along with other accomplishments during his senior year—marked the end of a 6-year transformational journey.

Kyle had performed poorly in public school, despite having an IQ in the superior range and standardized achievement test scores above the 98th percentile in all subject areas. He had been identified as gifted by the district and was placed in a gifted program. Because he didn't speak and he didn't produce work, he was soon removed from the gifted class. His anxiety increased and he refused to go to school.

He moved to an independent school for 2e students as a shy, fragile seventh grader who often cowered in the hallway between classes. When he felt stressed, he folded his arms over his head to shield his face and withdrew. Often, before he entered a classroom, he would stand at the door with hands over his ears and require several minutes to settle himself. His parents feared that their exceptionally bright and talented son might give up on school altogether. They saw his pronounced shyness and "shut-downs" as signs of increasing stress, worrying that Kyle would become "the brilliant dropout who ends up pumping gas," as his mother said, never able to go to college.

The new school provided engaging, intellectually rich content in areas that interested Kyle. Teachers and staff carefully structured his social environment— understanding that his anxiety and shy temperament affected every aspect of his life, both at school and at home (his parents revealed that performance anxiety had caused him to discontinue music lessons, which he loved). Some of the strategies included giving Kyle the time he needed to transition to class and allowing him to communicate with others through e-mail. Kyle was able to take advanced classes and independent studies, including online college courses. In addition, he participated in an invitation-only writer's group and took rock band and Shakespeare boot camp as his winter session courses (student-chosen classes with special topics that are held for the 2 weeks between semesters). On another occasion, Kyle was invited to team teach a design course with the school's web designer. In each of these enriched opportunities, Kyle became more social and outgoing.

As Kyle matured, he collaborated with his peers and faculty on projects as the tech expert. As knowledge of his abilities spread, he was hired by a financial firm to work with a top team on a special computer project. Later, in his college essay, Kyle wrote, "I couldn't believe that talented adults thought I had something to offer. Their confidence in me helped me outgrow my shyness, as did my participation in winter session opportunities."

Gifted students with high levels of anxiety can experience trait inhibition. Feeling too anxious to speak or to produce blocked all evidence of Kyle's brilliance. The high expectations shown by those who had earlier identified him as gifted only served to intensify his anxiety. With no attention paid to his crippling disability in his earlier school, Kyle began a downward spiral. Luckily, the second school dealt with both his gifts and his disabilities simultaneously. They provided a safe, highly enriched, and less stressful environment for him, one that allowed his anxiety to dissipate.

Throughout this chapter we addressed the characteristics of yellow and blue as separate entities and then followed each learning disability with a story to illustrate different combinations of advanced abilities with disabilities. Table 2.5 summarizes

Table 2.5
Student Profiles

Student	Full Scale IQ Score on the WISC	Advanced Abilities and Interests	Disability	Complexities of Coincidence
Debra	128	Drama, human rights, history	Dyslexia, SLD	• Depressed, low self-concept, defiant, lonely • Failed to be identified as gifted until fourth grade
Jimmy	134	Mechanical skills, highly spatial	ADHD, SLD	• Hyperactivity may have been due in part to high IQ • Failed to be identified as gifted until fourth grade
Bill	133	History, science, military, engineering	Asperger's Syndrome (now ASD)	• Passions seen as obsessions • No friends of his age • Not identified until middle school (eighth grade) for either disability or ability • Depressed • Anxious
Kyle	112	Technology, engineering, music, writing	GAD, executive functioning and productivity	• Disability not identified until seventh grade • Selective mutism • Social anxiety • Lack of friends

these examples. The heading of the fifth column ("Complexities of Coincidence") hints at a deeper concern. The mix of abilities with disabilities can create an overlay of other issues (anxieties, depression, and loneliness, etc.) that obstruct development.

As convenient as it might be to deal with one "e" at a time, considering the yellows and blues apart from each other results in an incomplete understanding of the confusing complexities of twice-exceptionality. Note that each of the four students found opportunities to work in their area of ability and each story had a happy ending. This, however, is more the exception than the rule. In the next chapter, we discuss why being green isn't easy.

CHAPTER 3

Complexities of Green

People ask us to define 2e, but in truth there are so
many different combinations . . .
—Zucchini, *2e: Twice Exceptional* (Film)

Twice-exceptional students encounter barriers and hazards on a
daily basis. As noted, the contrasts between what they can and cannot do lead to difficulties that are often quite distinct from those faced
by students with high abilities (without learning challenges) or those
identified with a disability of some sort (but not displaying gifted
potential). In this chapter, we discuss the complex and frequently confusing dynamics of twice-exceptionality and we explore why "being
green" isn't easy. Specifically, we consider these main topics:
- recognition of twice-exceptionality,
- understanding the psychological impact of being 2e, and
- the paradoxical needs of a 2e learner.

Twice-Exceptional Students: Three Groups

Recognizing the mix we call green is not a straightforward
endeavor—but it is an important one because the ways an individual
child's abilities and disabilities co-occur will impact how they are identified for either "e" and what services are afforded to them.

Let's look at three different groups of students. First are those who are noticed because their intellectual abilities or talents are outstanding. The second group is made up of students who are noticed when their disabilities and challenges clearly stand in the way of success. The third group includes students neither recognized by their abilities nor by their disabilities.

2e Students Identified by Gifts With Undiagnosed Disabilities

These 2e students are noticed for their achievements and/or high IQ scores. Because of high grades and obvious high potential, they may be in programs for the gifted. However, over time, the discrepancies between their anticipated and actual performance can widen. These students may charm with their oral facility, impressing others with their insights or knowledge, but their spelling, reading, or math skills may contradict this image. When facing particular tasks, these seeming "experts" can be forgetful, sloppy, and disorganized. (Of course, the same could be said about many preteens or young adults. But this group is different.) By the time they reach middle school or junior high, the students whose executive functioning abilities are underdeveloped begin to fall behind noticeably. With longer writing assignments and heavier emphasis on comprehensive, independent reading, or the need for time management and organizational skills, these students find it increasingly difficult to maintain their previous high levels of achievement. Students with ASD can become intellectually paralyzed when assignments become more abstract and require inference and synthesis. And students who cannot read because of dyslexia or other issues are no longer able to hide behind their excellent memories or compensate through grueling hours of painstaking study.

Well-intentioned teachers, guidance counselors, and parents often lament, "If James or Tisha would only try harder. . . ." Although some students may be able to put forth more effort, it is unlikely to improve the situation in many cases because trying harder does not address the real issue: These students simply do not have the learning strategies necessary for them to be successful. Like Neil in Chapter 1, they may first blame the curriculum—it's boring, they say—or they turn into class clowns to divert attention from their lack of success in the curriculum, or they simply "check out" and refuse to participate. Eventually, they become depressed, confused, and discouraged about their inability to meet classroom requirements and begin to doubt themselves. After all, when those around them appear to function without too many problems, why can't they? Over time, if the learning issues are not identified, social-emotional problems can grow to accompany, or even eclipse, the existing learning, attention, or executive functioning issues.

Because below-grade-level achievement is the usual signal that triggers a psychoeducational screening for possible learning disabilities, very bright students with problems are often passed over. They have been too smart to fail. But consider the resources (prodigious effort, lots of time, plus support from family) it takes to for these students to maintain passing grades. In many schools, a C average is not a reason to refer a student for testing even though that same student may demonstrate well-above-average learning potential in some areas. Identifying the learning issues underlying these students' inabilities to work up to expectations would help these students, their parents, and their teachers better understand the situation. More importantly, once recognized, professionals could offer learning strategies and compensation techniques to help these twice-exceptional youngsters deal with the dualities of their learning behaviors.

Note that just because a gifted student is not "achieving to potential" (as it's often put), he or she is not necessarily twice-exceptional. There are several other reasons why bright students do not meet academic expectations, and it is essential to rule out other possibilities before assuming a disability is present. Perhaps teacher or parent expectations are unrealistic. Excelling in science, for example, is no assurance that high-level performance will also be found in other areas. Motivation, interest, efficacy, beliefs, and specific aptitudes influence the amount of effort students apply to a task and the quality of their subsequent performance. In some instances, the student's self-expectations are so high that a task is not—and cannot ever be—finished to perfection. As these students become aware of the struggle between perfectionism and impossibility, procrastination may become an escape route from the anxiety of the moment, although even that route usually leads to other conflicts.

Underachievement can also result when a student perceives the curriculum to be unchallenging or irrelevant. Some bright students do not subscribe to the school's apparent value system. Also, highly capable students may perceive grades as inconsequential, and these bright youngsters search out other rewards in other forms and environments.

If the curriculum was unchallenging, well beneath ability level, and not interesting in the elementary grades, these students may have had little occasion or incentive to learn how to study or apply themselves when given assignments that require more memory, organization, and planning. Or, if the curriculum is not stimulating and novel, highly creative students may have a difficult time attending to the task and focusing on their work. In essence, one must ask whether the behavior is a signal of curricular-related issues or indicative of a learning disability, ADHD, or other neurological or emotional issue. And the best way to begin answering this question is by engaging in honest, open conversations in which a student feels he or she is not risking punishment by telling the truth about what he or she feels or does. Students can help us help them tremendously, if we adults appear ready to listen carefully and nonjudgmentally.

2e Students Identified Only for Special Programming or Accommodations

Another 2e group can be discovered within an identified special education population. Unlike the first category of 2e students (those noted as high ability or gifted, but with undiagnosed learning disabilities), children in this group are often failing in two or more subjects and/or they manifest behaviors interfering with their ability to succeed in school. They are first noticed by school personnel for what they *cannot* do—and they are *not* noticed for their particular skills and interests. These students are at serious academic risk because of the implicit message that accompanies a special education label. When sensitive 2e students respond to the emphasis placed on their disability, or if their education is managed only through accommodations, they experience genuine feelings of inadequacy. Their poor sense of self-worth can then overshadow any positive feelings connected with their areas of high ability. Regrettably, the school system all too often reinforces these negative, pessimistic attitudes because there is no place for the student to shine.

Typically, the emphasis is on addressing the disability until a student is "up to grade level" or "fixed" before any attention is paid to the gifted potential or talent area. This practice values acquisition of basic skills and appropriate adherence to classroom procedures over creative productive behavior. Reading, spelling, writing, and math take precedence over a student's ability to engineer bridges, program robots, use art to explain conflict, or campaign to save endangered species. Even if the child's high abilities are noticed, they may be misused or exploited, as with Neil's photography in Chapter 1.

We believe the prevalence of high abilities among students with special needs is higher than many realize and is related to how school districts identify their special education students, especially those with learning disabilities. There may be as many as 180,000 students with learning disabilities and above-average IQs in American schools, and about 10% of high-IQ children are reading 2 or more years below grade level (Winner, 1996). Even though a 1985 study examining the traits of high-ability students with learning disabilities indicated that nearly one third of a group of students identified with learning disabilities also had superior intellectual ability, we can find no evidence that concerted efforts have been made to discover and program for high-ability students within special education (Baum, 1985). In fact, recent researchers note there are numbers of students receiving services for special education who need gifted services but have no access (Crim, Hawkins, Ruban, & Johnson, 2008; Kaufman, 2013).

Students Not Identified With Either High Abilities or Special Needs

The third subset includes students who have neither been identified nor are receiving any special services (gifted or special needs), for each of their "e"s can disguise the other until the learning load becomes too heavy.

In an ongoing personal tug-of-war, their intellectual abilities hide their disabilities, and their disabilities disguise their areas of giftedness. These students are difficult to spot because they are academically inconspicuous and do not grab attention with exceptional behaviors. The signs of their hidden gifts can emerge in specific content areas or when they are with a teacher who uses more creative approaches in the classroom. Sometimes a talent emerges in a particular learning environment in which written production is minimized in favor of projects, drama, debate, and discussion and in which less traditional teaching methods are favored.

Often a hidden disability is not discovered until college or adulthood when the individual happens to read about stealth dyslexia or attention deficits, or hears peers discuss learning difficulties. By that time the student may be discouraged about school and learning and have little confidence in his or her abilities. For the past decade, Brock and Fernette Eide (2011) have devoted their practice to researching and advocating for individuals with dyslexia who have significant strengths and talents in specific areas. The Eides argued that notable successes in the careers of dyslexics were due to the intellectual strengths brought on by their "different" brains. Annually, the Eides bring together a conference of people who are talented entrepreneurs, filmmakers, and scientists whose abilities were not nurtured in school.

Dynamics of a High Abilities/Learning Disabilities Mix

Research over the past 20 years indicates that 2e students are distinctly different. In their review of the literature, Foley Nicpon et al. (2011) identified studies where cognitive and nonintellective traits of 2e students were compared to both students who were gifted (but not with identified disabilities) as well as to students with disabilities (but not with above-average abilities). In all cases, the behaviors of the 2e group were different from the other populations.

It is the merger of high abilities with disabilities that affects how behavioral traits manifest in the student. Reis, Baum, and Burke (2014) explained that this combination can impact these students' behaviors in three different ways:
1. increased intensity,
2. inhibition, and/or
3. the emergence of new behaviors.

Increased Intensity

When students' specific behaviors appear on both "yellow" and "blue" lists of characteristics, the manifestations can be greatly intensified. For instance, as Budding and Chidekel (2012) discussed, with issues of "giftedness and ADHD comorbidity," the curiosity shown by highly creative students that leads them to take risks and seek stimulation can also ramp up the impulsivity characterizing their ADHD. It is common for students with ADHD to blurt out answers and have difficulty waiting their turn. For high-ability students, the lack of impulse control is more problematic because intellectually gifted students have a greater knowledge base and rapid assimilation of information. This magnifies the difficulty of waiting their turn. In some students, the impact of their competing yellow and blue traits can result in a demonstrated stubbornness that borders on defiance. For example, Ellen Winner's (1996) discussion of the "rage to master" exhibited by some gifted children described a persistent and intense focus on a specific area of interest. This trait can interact with an ADHD trait of hyperfocus or the difficulty in shifting focus and sustaining effort when the student is asked to switch to a less desirable activity. Students may stubbornly refuse to shift focus when engaged passionately in a task.

Trait Inhibition

In some cases, the advanced abilities or learning disabilities can obscure the other exceptionality, resulting in students who do not receive appropriate attention or services (Kaufmann, Kalbfleisch, & Castellanos, 2000; Webb et al., 2005). For example, we might see a highly verbal student demonstrating complex understandings of concepts but simultaneously displaying difficulty in organizing ideas on paper because of slow processing speed and limited working memory. Learning difficulties block students from expressing their ideas, and they suffer from the inability to communicate their insights at an appropriate intellectual level. The competing behaviors often result in minimal production (Baum, 2004; Reis et al., 1995) and may explain why gifted students with learning disabilities or attention issues underachieve and/or act out (Minner, 1990; Reis et al., 1995; Senf, 1983).

Emergence of Additional Traits

A third consequence of dealing with twice-exceptionality is the appearance of new behavioral manifestations because of the co-occurring traits. The emotional overlay of being 2e can cause difficulties in motivation, academic self-efficacy, anxiety, and behaviors resulting in oppositional behavior, anxiety, obsessive compulsions, and depression—a finding that has been noted since we first started looking at this population of students. Schiff, Kaufman, and Kaufman (1981), for example, found these students to feel powerless and more emotionally unhealthy, vengeful, and troublesome than expected. Reis et al. (1995) confirmed these observations through research with college-aged gifted students with learning disabilities, discovering that many were already disruptive and off-task in elementary school and that they also exhibited low feelings of self-worth. Mendaglio (1993a) argued that these differences might suggest that 2e students need to receive differentiated counseling and support services.

The Paradoxical Needs of a 2e Learner

The third difficult dynamic for 2e learners is their enigmatic, individual set of learning needs. A dual diagnosis brings along yellow and blue sets of traits simultaneously; thus the two must be considered simultaneously, as well. For instance, if a middle school student is reading at a third-grade level, the solution is not giving him a third-grade text (in which the ideas are too simple). Instead we must find ways for him to access the information at his intellectual level—sophisticated information without complex reading passages. Consider the following examples of "green" dichotomies.

1. **Creative and sophisticated ideas *but* difficulty putting them down on paper.** High-ability students' depth of knowledge can be extensive. In areas of interest, these students may convey surprising and detailed knowledge, especially if they are allowed to communicate in a mode that does not require written production.

2. **High-level comprehension (a need for sophisticated content) *but* with reading limitations.** Twice-exceptional students who have difficulty decoding often have a wealth of knowledge that they have collected through other kinds of experiences (verbal interactions, films, and documentaries, etc.). Because their ability to grasp abstract ideas, verbal vocabulary, and depth of interests is out of sync with their reading levels, they can be humiliated by having to read low-level readers. Using poetry, graphic novels, and listening to books on tape can be helpful options.

3. **Task commitment and times of sustained engagement *but* difficulty attending to task when things lack novelty or sophistication or require listening and auditory processing.** Motivation, concentration, and persistence can be observed when twice-exceptional students are involved in creative-productive activities outside of school. These students often demonstrate their potential for high achievement by engaging in enterprises that align with personal strengths and interests. At these times and in these circumstances, they persevere. They become "at one" with the activity, sometimes even giving up a meal in order to complete a model or finish an art project. Unfortunately, this absorption with an area of interest is sometimes misunderstood as *hyper*focusing or obsessing; thus this area of interest is not reinforced in the school setting. In traditional school lessons where seatwork involving listening, reading, and writing is required, many of these students appear restless, often do not complete tasks, and may behave as though they have attention deficits. Attention requires novelty, and if there is no novelty or new information, attention will wane. If the lesson goes too slowly, attention may wane. If the teacher is too verbal, attention may wane. It is important to make sure that the learning environ-

ment is attuned to both the speed and instructional levels of the students and the lesson, as well as the mode of delivery.

4. **Potential for expertise *but* difficulty learning novice skills and/or developing automaticity.** Performing tasks at different levels of thinking is another conundrum. Some 2e students are excellent at higher level thinking and problem solving but, at the same time, show a deficit in lower level skills where automaticity is required, such as spelling, memorizing math facts, and handwriting. Unfortunately, many schools subscribe to the belief of hierarchical learning—a fixed sequence of learning that assumes that mastery of basic facts must occur before the more creative, higher level applications can occur: "You can't do science if you can't read, and you can't follow math applications unless you have memorized the times tables."

5. **Desire to fit in *but* little social awareness and sense of appropriateness.** Many 2e students have difficulty making friends and displaying appropriate social skills. One reason for this is that they have not found an appropriate peer group with whom to engage and relate. Once they are with others who share their interests (interest peers), they can learn social skills and image management in ways that are meaningful.

6. **Towering standards for success *but* turn in sloppy and incomplete assignments.** Quality of work can be especially inconsistent for 2e students. They can be perfectionists, especially when pursuing areas of interest, but then are often apathetic about quality when completing mandatory school assignments. If these young people find tasks too threatening and feel that even their best efforts may result in work beneath their personal standards, they may opt to "lose" their completed work or simply not do it.

Understanding the confusing, seemingly contradictory presentations of these students will enable us to find appropriate methods for helping them succeed. Dual diagnoses do indeed require dual differentiation (Baum et al., 2001), a topic we will return to in Part IV of this book.

A Very Green Tale: The Story of Olivia

The story of Olivia points out the need for understanding the whole person—not just the pieces. This story is another example of the complexities of "being green."

Diagnosed with Asperger's syndrome (now ASD) and ADHD, Olivia had great difficulty focusing her attention in class and getting along with others. However, she was extremely intelligent. In elementary school, her scores on the WISC-III (Weschler, 1991) ranged from 155 in verbal abilities and 147 in perceptual reasoning, to 88 in processing speed and 69 in freedom from distraction. Her extraordinary verbal abilities allowed her to be witty and creative, and she was adept at using those abilities negatively and positively. An avid reader, Olivia would contribute insightful comments to class discussions when motivated. However, when uninterested she was masterful in bringing things to a halt by arguing with others, being disrespectful, and putting down her classmates. She tried in any way she could to "hog the attention" in the classroom. In addition, Olivia stubbornly refused to produce anything in writing or to participate in math class.

Everyone who met Olivia knew she loved art. In school, she often entertained herself by making families of miniatures, and, when she needed to listen to discussions or to her teacher, she would fill a paper with creative images and doodles.

Her school realized that, for Olivia to be successful, she would require support and attention for both her abilities and disabilities. Her school's pupil personnel team, consisting of her classroom teachers, a learning specialist, and the curriculum coordinator, met and developed what they believed was a plan to address her needs. They first identified her strengths and challenges (see Table 3.1).

To support her advanced verbal abilities, especially in reading, the team placed her in an advanced reading class. Simultaneously, they enrolled her in the district's social skills class for students with ASD and provided occupational therapy for handwriting. Because there was no time in her schedule for any extra art lessons (a scheduling conflict with social skills class), they suggested that her parents enroll her in art classes outside of school. In addition, she was given accommodations in class that included more time to complete tests and a scribe to take notes and help her produce some written work.

At first glance, this plan may seem appropriate—and one that might be typical of those used by some schools that attempt to meet both sets of needs. Unfortunately, this approach failed as miserably with Olivia as it would with many others with a similar learning profile. First of all, placement in advanced reading also meant more note-taking and a host of writing assignments, the very things that were among the most problematic for her. Even though Olivia did participate in class discussion, the advanced reading teacher had no patience for her lack of productivity. She suggested that Olivia did not belong in the class and proposed a less rigorous section.

Olivia had no tolerance for the occupational therapy class in handwriting. Using a pencil wasn't the problem. It was the ordeal of trying to put her ideas into writing. As Olivia explained, "I think in paragraphs, speak in sentences, but write in words." Her ideas were often too complex to describe easily. Trying to simplify the ideas and write the words down in coherent paragraphs slowed her down to the point that, in the end, the most she could manage were a few phrases and simple sentences.

The social skills class did not work out well either. Olivia had trouble relating to the other students in the social skills class. They were not her intellectual peers nor were they as verbal as her. These factors led to an unhealthy group dynamic that grew worse over time.

Table 3.1

Olivia's Strengths and Challenges

Strengths	Challenges
• High verbal abilities • Advanced reader • Interests in art	• Nonproductive—will not put anything in writing • Oppositional defiant • Severe attention issues • Poor social awareness and lack of social skills • Refuses to participate in P. E.

Olivia's situation graphically demonstrates the complexity of being "green." The plan looked first at Olivia's gifts (yellow) and then her challenges (blue). The yellow and blue were addressed separately. The idea of dual differentiation (concurrently paying attention to both abilities and disabilities) is often overlooked by professionals working with 2e students. For example, a student like Olivia would have benefitted from participation in a book club where advanced readers discussed the piece of literature without needing to produce written work. Likewise, teaching Olivia social skills in the context of an appropriate intellectual or interest peer group could have been more successful.

When Olivia moved to a new school, the faculty and staff understood her dichotomies and provided a program more reflective of her needs. She was placed in classes with other students of similar abilities. All of the students were given options for how they would communicate what they had learned; all students were allowed and encouraged to use technology to help them put their ideas in writing; all children were offered enrichment opportunities where they could mix with like-minded peers and, within that context, develop social skills.

In Olivia's case, the English teacher allowed her to doodle during classroom discussions. She would create visual metaphors, showing her understanding of the material. Profoundly rich writing resulted from the sketches—her preferred form of what many schools now help students explore as "prewriting." Her chemistry teacher applauded the comic books she created to show the characteristics of the elements. She had opportunities for art every day, and her art teacher (a professional artist herself) became her mentor. Not only did Olivia work to overcome obstacles that she felt were holding her back in art, but she also used her art to work through emotional difficulties. For example, she learned to manage her stress by retreating to a quiet space in the art room where she could be alone, uninterrupted, and immersed in her work.

Olivia thrived in a school environment where students were defined by what they could do rather than by their failures. Olivia succeeded when she was in an environment sensitive to yellow, blue, and green. Chapter 4 provides a rationale for such a learning environment.

The Case for Strength-Based, Talent-Focused Education

What 2e Students Need

> Treatment is not just fixing what is broken; it is nurturing what is best. (Seligman & Csikszentmihalyi, 2000, p. 7)

The belief that 2e students' deficits must be remediated before attention can be given to their abilities and interests often results in little or inappropriate attention to students' gifts or talents. Moreover, because the remediation techniques usually lack the characteristics high-ability students require for successful learning, many remedial attempts are unsuccessful (Baum, Owen, & Dixon, 1991). Also, twice-exceptional students who are eligible for—and invited to—advanced classes may then discover there is little tolerance for their learning differences. Even when it is acknowledged that a particular student has a dual set of needs, meeting those needs in productive ways is complicated. A strength-based, talent-focused approach can provide a successful entry to meeting the needs of these students.

Research Pointing to the Benefits of Starting With Strengths

In their 1997 review of the issues facing gifted children with learning disabilities, Brody and Mills included descriptions of a variety of systems, models, and teaching strategies appropriate for 2e children.

They reported a need for flexible programming that includes high-level learning opportunities in areas of strength, developmental instruction in average areas, and remedial services in areas of disability. Throughout Susan Baum's long history working with and conducting research examining effective ways to meet the needs of 2e students, she has found that talent development can be both a viable means of intervention and the basis of a new learning approach for 2e students not thriving in the regular classroom. Results from several of her studies provide the framework for the ideas discussed in this book.

Susan's initial research in the 1980s asked whether it was possible to distinguish between three groups of students ($n = 120$):

1. those with high cognitive ability (non-learning disabled with IQs 120 or more and identified as "gifted" by their district);
2. students with learning disabilities (LD) average cognitive abilities (with IQs 90–119 and diagnosed learning disabilities); and
3. students with learning disabilities and high cognitive ability (with IQs 120 or more).

If it was possible to distinguish between the groups, what did that say about the students' needs (Baum, 1985)? She used a variety of instruments to assess and compare cognitive and motivational patterns in the three groups and found that there were striking differences. As might be expected, the high-ability, nonlearning-disabled students were markedly distinct from both learning-disabled groups. Teachers rated the high-ability students much higher on creative traits than they rated either group of youngsters with learning disabilities, which accounted for most of the differences between groups. Predictably, these high-ability students also felt more confident about their ability to do well on academic tasks (academic self-efficacy). Teachers viewed the students with LD and high cognitive ability as more creative than their average peers with LD, and these students also self-reported higher levels of interest in creative extracurricular activities than did their LD-average peers. However, of the three groups of youngsters, they were also the most disruptive and frustrated in school. This group (who would now likely be known as 2e) felt that school offered plenty of opportunities for failure and, interestingly, often ascribed their academic failures to shyness.

Twice-exceptional students were found to have learning, motivational, and perhaps emotional patterns different from those of their peers. Overall, as a group, the students with LD and high cognitive abilities showed high creative potential coupled with low levels of academic success and a tendency toward disruptive behavior. The profile of high ability, high creativity, and high interest coupled with failure, low self-efficacy, and a tendency to disruptive behavior led Susan to hypothesize that this type of student might benefit from a positive approach—one which would accentuate gifts, talents, and interests, as opposed to a focus on remediating weaknesses.

Following up on the hypothesis, Susan received a grant to study the impact of using enrichment with seven identified gifted learning-disabled (GTLD) students (Baum, 1988). Prior to the study, the students were in general education classrooms with resource room support for their deficits. After the students participated in a yearlong, 2.5-hour-a-week enrichment program that had been originally designed for identified gifted students, both qualitative and quantitative data supported findings that included improved attitudes about school and self, improved self-regulation and independence in learning, and the ability to produce creative products judged to be comparable to those of the gifted students without any learning issues. In addition, there were unanticipated academic gains.

Next, Susan and her colleagues extended this approach to see if it was possible to discover whether talent development opportunities would affect underachievement in gifted students (Baum, Renzulli, & Hébert, 1995). They used individual and small-group investigations of real-world problems based on the Enrichment Triad Model (Renzulli, 1976) as an intervention with gifted underachieving students. Many of these gifted underachievers had ADHD, social and behavioral challenges, or what appeared to be undiagnosed learning disabilities. The most compelling findings were the gains made by students after completing the intervention. Eighty-two percent of the students improved in achievement—reversing their pattern of underachievement during the course of the year or within the following year. Along with academic gains, there were also improvements in attitude or behavior.

Following this line of research, during the next 5 years, Susan collaborated with Barry Oreck on two Javits grants—Talent Beyond Words and New Horizons—that focused on identifying students with abilities in music, dance, and theater, and providing special classes designed to develop their talents (Baum, Owen, & Oreck, 1996, 1997). Instructors were professionals from the particular talent discipline. The majority of students identified were at-risk academically due to economic or family issues and were performing significantly below grade level in reading and math. Some students were also identified with specific learning disabilities or attention deficits. Students identified in the Talent Beyond Words project were studied through high school to understand how talent development impacted their lives. Results indicated that the process of artistic talent development bolstered their abilities, skills, and confidence. The students emerged with a sense of purpose, poise, independence, and determination that carried over into their academic and personal lives (Oreck, Baum, & McCartney, 2000).

The New Horizons project emphasized reading and math curriculum development and classroom instruction based on students' strengths to improve academic achievement. In addition, the at-risk students received additional academic support. For the experimental group, this support integrated the arts into the instruction. The comparison group was taught using traditional remediation. After 3 years, the talented at-risk students showed significant gains as compared to other equally talented students who did not receive arts integration programming within the core curriculum (Baum, Owen, & Oreck, 1997).

A separate study, Project High Hopes (Baum, Cooper, Neu, & Owen, 1997), served students with special needs in grades 5–8 at nine sites, including six public schools, a private school for the learning disabled, and two schools for students who are deaf or hearing impaired. This project focused on the identification and development of potential talent in students with disabilities in the domains of engineering, performing arts, the sciences, and visual arts. A major goal was to discover the ways in which these students learn best and the effect of talent development. Over the course of the study, students showed dramatic improvement in their identified talent areas. In fact, when compared to neurotypical students talented in similar areas, the Project High Hopes students performed equally as well, and, at times, their work surpassed the performance of their nondisabled peers.

An interesting finding was how well the 2e students were able to attend and produce when working with the professionals who mentored them in the specific areas. Project researchers noted that there was limited discussion between the mentor and the whole group of students in domains such as engineering and visual arts. Talking most often occurred when the professional sat next to a particular student, providing content and feedback as the student continued to work. They were able to discuss what was happening and carry on conversations—not necessarily making eye contact with each other. In the project, the students and mentors were speaking each other's language in ways authentic to the domain of practicing professionals. This is a very different approach from a typical lecture or question-and-answer format. (*Note*. More details about this project can be found in Part III, and a full description of the program can be found in Appendix A.)

The commonality among these studies is a focus on talent development that supplemented the more traditional approach of providing compensation strategies, remediation, and social skills classes for students with learning challenges. Although the elements in the traditional approach may be necessary, findings from these studies suggest the need for a shift away from remediation as the primary emphasis to a model that includes "talent focus" as an integral, essential component.

New Evidence for Using a Strength-Based Approach[2]

The various findings confirmed the success of using a strength-based approach in grant projects and specialized programs; however, there had been no studies that looked at the impact of a full-time program for 2e students. To that end, Baum, Schader, and Hébert (2014) looked at the ways a cohort of 10 students attending a

---

2   Material in this section has been adapted from "Through a Different Lens: Reflecting on a Strengths-Based, Talent-Focused Approach for Twice-Exceptional Learners," by S. M. Baum, R. M. Schader, and T. P. Hébert, 2014, *Gifted Child Quarterly, 58,* pp. 319–322. Copyright 2014 by National Association for Gifted Children. Adapted with permission.

strength-based, talent-focused school was able to grow and the factors that contributed to growth. Figure 4.1 defines what we mean by a strength-based, talent-focused approach.

Growth

All students showed positive development across 11 categories in three developmental domains—cognitive, emotional/behavioral, and social—as shown in Figure 4.2. Each category formed its own continuum from negative to positive indicators.

Cognitive growth. When entering the independent school, these students had been defined by their deficits. They showed little motivation or confidence in their abilities, and were not completing assignments. "I was overwhelmed, disorganized, frustrated in school," explained one student. Similar sentiments were echoed by all of them. At the time of application, no student was having a positive school experience. Their sixth-grade teacher said it was "a fight to get them to produce anything." As a group, these youngsters were initially rigid in their thinking, each to varying degrees. The students identified as having Asperger's syndrome (now ASD) and those who were classified as obsessive-compulsive were especially prone to this behavior. They tended to be rule-bound and easily upset by changes in routine or procedures. When a certain student was asked to make any adjustment, "he would explode," explained the high school director.

Over the 6 years at this school, these same students became more productive, especially when working in their areas of interest and strength. Those talented as writers became part of a writing group and produced publishable pieces; the artists created portfolios; the musicians played in jazz festivals; the actors shone in performances; and the computer whizzes programmed. Although not nearly as obvious, the students began to participate and produce in their other classes. One young man marveled at his growth, "I now write papers that I never would have started. I even complete projects on time." Another said he learned that to be productive, one needs to "utilize the tools the teachers give you and be proactive. Teachers can only help you as much as you let them."

Emotional/behavioral growth. In middle school, many of the students were highly anxious and depressed. They spoke of feeling hopeless and different from their age-mates. As the teachers recalled, these students were an oppositional and defiant group. They disliked each other and often refused to cooperate under any circumstance. The middle school director commented that the emotional turmoil of this cohort in its early years at the school had a profoundly negative effect on the students' learning:

> At times our resources were just exhausted. All of the energies of
> the therapists, teachers, and staff were spent on dealing with behav-

- **"Strength-based"** is defined as curricular and instructional approaches that are differentiated to align with students' cognitive styles, learning preferences, and profiles of intelligences.
- **"Talent-focused"** involves on-going identification and recognition of a student's advanced abilities as well as budding interests, along with explicit options for exploring and expressing those abilities and interests within and beyond the curriculum. *Talent focus* is used as an overarching term that includes "talent development."
- **"Talent development"** refers to encouragement and support of identified talents and abilities that are nurtured in their own right—neither as an opening for remediation nor as a reward or motivator for achievement.

Figure 4.1. *Definitions of terms.* From "Through a Different Lens: Reflecting on a Strengths-Based, Talent-Focused Approach for Twice-Exceptional Learners," by S. M. Baum, R. M. Schader, and T. P. Hébert, 2014, *Gifted Child Quarterly, 58,* p. 312. Copyright 2014 by National Association for Gifted Children. Reprinted with permission.

	Upon Entry to School	**At Graduation**
Cognitive	Defined by deficits	Defined by abilities and talents
	Unproductive	Productive
	Unmotivated	Goal directed, self-initiated
	Cognitively rigid	Willing to experiment, see possibilities
Emotional/ Behavioral	Anxious	Confident
	Without hope	Optimistic about future
	Defiant/aggressive	Cooperative
	Feel different	Identify with others
Social	Unaware, oblivious	Self-aware
	Alienate others	Tolerate and accept others
	Have few or no friends	Part of a community

Figure 4.2. *Growth continua.*

ioral issues. There wasn't time to teach content. It was a struggle to understand that the time spent dealing with these issues during these early years would be productive down the road.

Manifestations of anxiety varied across the group. For some, it was extreme inhibition, as one student explained in his college application essay:

> When I was younger, I never spoke a word to anybody . . . I wanted to talk, but simply found myself unable—it was a huge handicap. . . . At the time, I had no idea how to change this. Years later, I'm a thousand times more outgoing. Looking back on how this came to be, it now looks a lot like a set of scenes from a delightfully corny inspirational drama.

For some, the anxiety manifested in a sense of hopelessness. A student commented,

> I was a mess with no future. I had just been released from a psychiatric hospital. I didn't want to go to school. Learning was not for me. I was a social recluse who escaped by reading and playing video games.

By graduation, these students were confident, hopeful, and looking forward to the next phase of their lives. When asked how he would describe himself now, this same young man responded,

> Accomplished. I have accomplished things I never thought I would. And I know I will continue to accomplish. My mom is really proud of me now . . . because I was able to come from where I was 5 years ago to where I am now . . . a mature and developing young adult who can handle responsibility.

Social growth. Most students revealed they did not have friends, often felt isolated, and did not adhere to social conventions prior to attending this school. Those with ASD were particularly limited by their inability to understand and navigate the social world. The difficulties seemed to center on being unaware of their place in the world and how they fit into it. They frequently alienated those around them. One young woman used the word "oblivious" to describe herself prior to coming to the school:

> I was not born with knowing how to interact with other people. And I didn't know what to do. I didn't know how to play with the other kids. I didn't even know that I didn't know how to play with them.

The students also talked about how much they disliked each other initially. Their individual behaviors (i.e., arguing, criticizing, screaming and yelling, being sarcastic and opinionated, even bullying) served to keep them separate. "The kids were angry with each other much of the time. No one liked anyone very much," explained one student. Another described the class as "a fray of excited, nervous kids. We were all wary of each other." But changes among the group began to be noticeable as they entered high school. Several reported making a conscious decision to get along: "We all hated each other at first because we were so similar and so different. We began to lighten up in eighth grade. In ninth grade we started to gel." Over time, the group became a tightly knit community, highly supportive of each other.

Factors Contributing to Growth

Five critical, interconnected factors were essential for student growth along the continuums—and they were found to work in concert:
1. a psychologically safe environment,
2. tolerance for asynchronous behaviors,
3. time (allowing for changes to take place without rushing or demanding),
4. positive relationships (with faculty, staff, peers, family, and professionals), and
5. a strength-based, talent-focused environment (based on a growing awareness of each student's individuality).

Psychologically safe environment. Students described their prior school experiences using words such as "shamed" and "excluded." At the new school, they began to feel safe. As one student pointed out, "We were treated badly in other environments. [This school] allowed us to get our confidence back." Another described the school as "like other high schools but more relaxed. It provides a friendly place to socialize and grow with other people. It lets you blossom into what you can be."

The cohort's sixth-grade teacher talked about creating a welcoming environment. She noted it was important for students to find self-acceptance:

> Children come here with baggage and you need to give them the opportunity to look at their issues. At [this school] we find out what the students need and then deliver it.

Tolerance for asynchrony. Creating a psychologically safe environment required that teachers embrace tolerance and patience, especially for the students' asynchronous behaviors. Asynchrony is a term used for the uneven developmental rates of a child's intellectual, emotional, social, and motor skills. For example, a student demonstrating highly advanced intellectual abilities may have social or motor skills that lag substantially behind. Asynchrony is confusing for the student, parents, and teachers. A female student explains the dilemma,

> Mentally I'm probably 2 or 3 years ahead of most kids my age, but socially I'm probably 2 or 3 years behind. So I'm stuck in this sort of weird time warp thing where I'm at the same time younger and older than kids my age. I mean, socially I've come much closer, but still, I needed those years to catch up. And that's what a lot of kids at this school are like. They need those few breathing years. It's like you need those healing years.

Most of the teachers talked about the need for patience in working with these students. They said it was important to remember to meet the students as they are at any given moment and to keep remembering that the students need time for growth.

Time. Time was critical to the students' development. By allowing for growth to take place without rushing, or pushing for students to perform at grade level, the students were able to come to terms with extreme anxieties and developmental asynchronies. "The main thing about [this school]," recalled one young man, is that "it gives you time to grow socially and learn how to control your whatevers."

The music director explained that when he was first hired, he was told he would need to practice patience with these students, understanding that, over time, as they began to trust the environment, they would then be able to develop at a rate commensurate with their abilities. He explained that this advice had served him well over the years, and gave an example of a student in seventh grade during drumming class. This youngster would sit in the circle with his arms over his head and turn himself into a ball with his face down on his lap. His anxiety kept him from being an active participant. Even though he improved somewhat, he was not ready for the class's year-end coffee house live event, but he did want his work to be there. He composed his own piece of music, recorded it on techno track, and sent it in so it could be played in public. Years later, this same student performed on stage in front of a live audience of more than 100 people. It just took time.

Positive relationships. Patience and understanding by teachers helped forge positive relationships with and among students and parents. Parents commented on how well the faculty related to this population of students and also seemed to like them. The high school history teacher explained, "These kids are quirkier, they're more interesting. Some of the things they come up with are out of left field, but often times brilliant."

Students acknowledged how easy it was to talk to the teachers about problems: "Greg was my advisor, and he was always there for me. He could tell when I was having a bad day."

Strength-based, talent-focused environment. Finally, awareness of the strength-based, talent-focused philosophy echoed throughout the interviews with parents, teachers, students, and staff. The school's approach was openly discussed in team meetings. The focus on student capacities offered hope for parents, as described by a mother after her first meeting with the school's admissions director:

> It was very clear that they were looking for the strengths of the kids . . . I fell apart and started to cry because nobody had. Everybody had pathologized [my son] and said what was wrong with him. We needed a place that would say what is right with him.

Although recognition, encouragement, and opportunities to grow and refine abilities were shown to be critical in student development, learning how to integrate a student's talents, strengths, and interests respectfully within the curriculum proved to be of equal concern and importance. Students also commented on the strength-based philosophy:

> The school tailors curriculum around your strengths. It helps you grow your mind in every way. You may not do well in one area but then there will be a class in an area of strength like programming, art, or music.

When students feel that their contributions are appreciated, they will show fewer negative issues. In the right environment, they fit; they're productive. Yet, if they were taken out of that environment, the problematic behaviors, etc., would likely reappear. We tend to forget the importance of the environment in a student's ability to focus, learn, and be productive. And, again, it's about a match (or fit). When a student is thriving, there is a tendency to believe that student has been "fixed."

An effective program creates educational contexts that suppress students' problematic behaviors, while simultaneously encouraging the emergence of more positive gifted traits.

The effect of talent development. Talent development refers to the encouragement and support of identified abilities that are nurtured in their own right. Talent development opportunities (TDOs) were found to be valuable in the students' lives in several ways. By the end of their senior year, more than half of the students had received notable awards or acknowledgement for their accomplishments. For example, one artist's work was shown at a recognized invitational exhibit, another received an internship working with distinguished scientists, and a musician was offered a recording contract.

TDOs provided an environment in which students could be a valued part of a social group. For example, during middle school one student had alienated most of his peer group by his oppositional defiant behaviors. Although talented in music, he was never willing to stay in the struggle when lessons required practice and perseverance. Instead, he would just quit. In ninth grade, however, an opportunity to participate in Jazz Band gave him a way to be with peers whom he admired. To assure getting into the group and holding up his musical responsibilities to others, this young man practiced hard and began to be appreciated. Soon, he and his classmates were jamming together, which eventually extended to other social invitations. His parents remarked that this was the "first time he ever stuck with something." His Jazz Band experience not only provided a social group in which he could hone his communication skills, but it also offered opportunities for authentic performance among the band members. As his father explained,

> So now suddenly here are all of these kids who can't seem to get along, who are not only having to cooperate as part of a band together, but they are writing together. They are coming up with collaborative pieces. They're having to appreciate what each person brings to the group. None of these kids have done this before.

For those students whose abilities and interests took hold prior to graduation, the TDOs opened mentor relationships that facilitated growth along possible career trajectories. For example, the music teacher talked about his relationship with a young, musically talented student:

> Many of the kids [at this school] can communicate through music, but this student rocked. In other classes he struggles. In music the guy is a rock star. I made him my course assistant, my right hand man. . . . I know someday I will say, I knew him when.

For some of these youngsters TDOs appeared to be key in helping them overcome emotional issues blocking their development. In his college essay, one young man described events during his high school years that contributed to overcoming his shyness and anxiety:

> Very early in high school, my school offered a 2-week stand up comedy class during intersession. The final product was to be a

comedy routine delivered to the entire school. Throwing all common sense to the wind, I entered that class. One might argue that a kid so shy he was practically mute might not be an ideal candidate for a class on public performance. I, however, refused to let something as silly as a complete inability to speak stand between me and sweet, sweet comedy. In place of a vocal performance, I programmed my laptop to act as a ventriloquist dummy using text-to-speech software. I wrote a routine for it to perform, in which it told jokes, made horrendous puns, and viciously mocked me and my silence. The audience loved it. I didn't speak a word, but I sure did communicate.

Another example was how a student's art talent provided a way for her to confront social issues. As the art teacher commented,

> She told me that because of her Asperger's, she had always had a hard time making eye contact with people. She noticed that progress in her art had reached a plateau as none of her drawings or sketches included people with eyes. She has struggled with it and has tried to force herself, but with difficult results. To improve her art, as well as confront a weakness, Beth decided to start drawing eyes realistically, from observation, as a way to learn about eyes, and their importance to expression.

The retrospective study showed positive influences on cognitive, emotional/behavioral, and social growth. Not only did the students grow in their talent and interest areas, but they also overcame many of their challenges. The focus on what they could do resulted in self-confidence and a positive sense of self. Recent contact with these students confirmed their success experiences in college and their subsequent entry into careers, all of which reflect their individual profiles of strengths, interests, or talents.

The studies discussed in this chapter offer evidence that 2e learners respond well when a strength-based, talent-focused approach is carefully implemented and used. Twice-exceptional students require a learning environment that supports their physical, intellectual, and emotional needs. Such an environment provides dually-differentiated educational experiences that assure appropriate challenge, while offering specialized instruction, accommodations, and compensation strategies that minimize the effects of learning, attention, and behavioral difficulties. Finally, it is important to have counseling and advocacy support available both within and outside the school setting.

Part II

Neurodiversity: The Complex Minds of 2e Learners

CHAPTER 5

2e Students and Learning

In the chapters of Part I, we painted a picture of twice-exceptional learners using the metaphor of "green" to underscore that it is the *combination* of high abilities and learning challenges that makes them not only unique individuals but also, as a group, different from successful mainstream students. Now we bring in the concept of neurodiversity, for, as discussed earlier, there are many, many shades of green.

What is neurodiversity? In 1998, Australian Judy Singer posted the following comment on *The Atlantic*'s interactive Word Fugitive column by Barbara Wallraff, noting:

> We need a word for people whose bodies and/or minds have some slight flaw or impairment, and thus do not conform to our ideas of 'normal,' and whose lives are made difficult by invidious comparisons with this norm.
>
> The word would need to be less strong than the dramatic word 'disabled,' which draws all attention to the few things that these mildly impaired people can't do, instead of the multitude of things they *can* do. It would be stronger than 'different,' since everyone is different. It would need to express 'deviating from the norm,' but not with all the negative connotations of perversion that the word 'deviant' has. And

it would be less mawkish and awkward than the oft lampooned 'differently abled.' We need this word desperately, because nearly every one of us suffers prejudice of some sort, some of the time, for not embodying a supposed 'normality,' that is in fact a rarely achieved 'ideal.' (para. 1–2)

By following threads on an autism listserv, Singer discovered journalist Harvey Blume, and they began phone conversations about the concepts of "normal" and "neurological pluralism." It was through those discussions that the term *neurodiversity* was born (Silberman, 2015). Blume (1998) then wrote an article titled "Neurodiversity: On the Neurological Underpinnings of Geekdom," in which he gave nod to the Institute for the Study of the Neurologically Typical (ISNT), created as a parody of the attention given to studying autism as an abnormality. He wrote,

Until recently, NTs [neurotypicals] have had the privilege of believing that their form of wiring was the standard for the human brain. ISNT wants to make it clear that this will no longer be held to be self-evident . . . Neurodiversity may be every bit as crucial for the human race as biodiversity is for life in general. Who can say what form of wiring will prove best at any given moment? (para. 2–3)

Expanding on the idea, Singer (1998) wrote in her undergraduate thesis:

The rise of Neurodiversity takes postmodern fragmentation one step further. Just as the postmodern era sees every once too solid belief melt into air, even our most taken-for-granted assumptions: that we all more or less see, feel, touch, hear, smell, and sort information, in more or less the same way, (unless visibly disabled) are being dissolved. (pp. 12–13)

In his book, *NeuroTribes: The Legacy of Autism and the Future of Neurodiversity*, Steve Silberman (2015) wrote that thinking in terms of human operating systems is a clear, simple way to understand the concept of neurodiversity:

Just because a computer is not running Windows doesn't mean that it's broken. Not all the features of atypical human operating systems are bugs. . . . The main reason why the Internet was able to transform the world in a single generation is that it was specifically built to be "platform agnostic." The Internet doesn't care if your home computer or mobile device is running Windows, Linux, or the latest version of Apple's iOS. Its protocols and standards were designed to work with them all to maximize the potential for innovation at the edges. (p. 471)

Since 2000, the term *neurodiversity* has found wide acceptance in the autism community; however, we believe its relevance extends across environments and is especially pertinent for 2e learners. With that in mind, we will next look at some qualities of 2e students—considering the ways they learn, where and how learning might break down, patterns of motivation, regulation, along with profiles of intellectual and personality strengths. When we accept that their brains are "wired differently" and also embrace the belief that they have valuable contributions, we can then design optional educational environments for 2e students.

An Information Processing Model: Explaining Learning

To understand how the learning process can be difficult for 2e students, we must first understand how cognition typically takes place. Cognition encompasses the mental processes of thinking, memory, and learning—that is, how we acquire, store, and use information. Even external behaviors—movements—reflect cognitive activity because they are planned, observed, and evaluated in the brain. At the highest levels, often called *metacognition*, mental activities involve awareness and personal control of various strategies to learn and to perform.

Interest in cognitive psychology and computational psychology (Pinker, 1997) grew as professionals became dissatisfied with the behaviorist movement. They recognized that behaviorism fell short in explaining thought and memory, for it depends on observable behavior that can be objectively and scientifically measured. Yet thinking and knowing continue to be unobservable and difficult to measure. Cognitive researchers, in contrast, wanted to understand how people learned, and approached the topic through inferences about the mental processes underlying the behaviors.

The information processing model, an offshoot of cognitive psychology influenced by computer programming, offers a basic way to look at learning. Just as the computer manipulates sets of data, the brain transforms information to solve problems. The brain, of course, does much more, fashioning new, original ways of processing information. Its plans are not as rigid as computer programs. It is flexible and insightful. And it makes errors. In the information processing view, humans seek information, interpret it, organize, transform, and process it into memory. They also merge the information with other data already stored in their heads and act on the basis of it. Figure 5.1 presents a simple snapshot of the process.

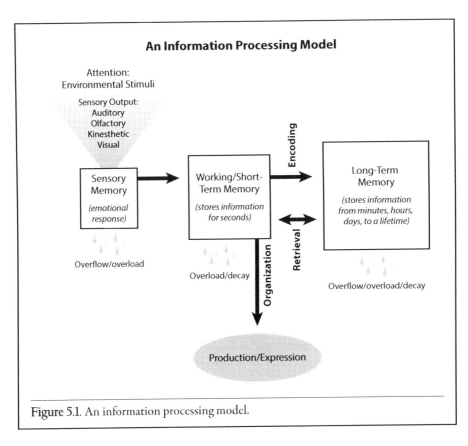

Figure 5.1. An information processing model.

As a staggeringly complex computational system, the brain is believed to have some 100 billion neurons, connected by an estimated 100 trillion synapses, which offers quite a bit of storage space. In fact, a recent study from the Salk Institute for Biological Studies estimated the brain's capacity to be around a quadrillion bytes (Bartol et al., 2015). In a lifetime, ordinary people store billions of items of information in their memories, including some 50,000 words and an even greater number of images. Although it is convenient to think of memory's three distinctive storage systems (sensory, working [also called short-term], and long-term) as separate, it is more likely that they are related levels of a single, coherent memory structure we call learning.

Attention, Sensory Input, and Sensory Storage

Learning begins with attention. What we pay attention to, how well we can control our attention, and what influences our attention are caused by many factors. Great quantities of information in the form of environmental stimuli bombard us and enter the sensory storage system. Experimental evidence suggests that sensory storage holds accurate images of incoming stimuli while the brain searches for familiar features or patterns. When recognition occurs (almost instantaneously), information is passed to working memory for short-term storage. The irrelevant information decays, and the sensory storage busily attends to new stimuli.

Can sensory storage attend to all incoming stimuli? Probably not. Researchers believe there must be a filtering mechanism that sifts through the information, and there are several hypotheses about this filter. Although there is little agreement, a popular theory promotes something called an *attenuated filter* (Triesman, 1964). This filter includes a threshold that may be set at high or low levels, depending on the intensity, novelty, relevance, and emotional connectedness of the stimulus. In ordinary settings, the filter lets only some of the stimuli through for examination. Certain important stimuli, such as your name, will leap over the threshold and demand immediate and conscious attention. Other stimuli are let in the perceptual door (to different areas of the brain depending on whether they are visual or verbal, for instance), but are not awarded such high status. A stimulus may sneak through consciousness and into behavior without the person being aware of it, unless we happen to think about what we are thinking or doing. Awareness, though, and intentional control of memory's behavior is the foundation of self-regulated learning, and therefore an important skill for high-ability students with learning differences to develop.

Working Memory/Short-Term Memory

Working memory is a term used to refer to a multicomponent temporary memory system. Awareness of thinking or behavior seems to takes place in working memory (also called short-term memory). It also has a major role in controlling attention, thinking, and monitoring learning (executive function). In fact, working memory and control of attention are inseparable (Klingberg, 2010). Ironically, though short-term storage performs extremely important functions, it doesn't have a large capacity.

Short-term memory holds information just long enough to sort it out and determine whether or not it merits keeping. If we remembered everything that happened to us, every ordinary conversation along with all of the significant ones, our minds would soon be cluttered with trivia. In short-term storage, we aim to dismiss the trivia and pass on the worthwhile data to long-term storage. If you were asked what you have just read, you probably could not reproduce each word. The image has already decayed. But you could relate the general meaning of the words, thanks to the encoding process and the ability of working memory to summarize.

A good working memory is vital for learning and productivity because it is where the multiple parts of an activity must be stored long enough for the activity to be completed. Active working memory has four specific tasks (Levine, 2002):

1. providing the space for developing or combining ideas (so you can remember the beginning of a conversation while listening to more of it);

2. providing a place to hold together the parts of a task while doing the task (so that as you're cooking, you can remember where you last had the paring knife);

3. creating a "workspace" for getting short and long-term memories together (so you can remember the question while searching for the answer); and

4. serving as a holding space for multiple immediate plans and intentions (such as remembering to sharpen your pencil, get a glass of water, and grab a dictionary as you head toward your desk to finish an assignment; p. 100).

In general, short-term storage has only a maximum of 20 or 30 seconds to sort and encode. When a lot of information is competing for attention, it may last only 4 or 5 seconds in short-term memory. After that time, information is either passed to long-term storage or lost from the system. Because of this limited capacity, there is only so much mental energy available to be expended on mental problem solving or following directions. Automaticity is key for working memory to be efficient. It refers to an action or knowledge so well practiced that it can be carried out without conscious effort. For instance, when given a math word problem to solve mentally, one must remember the facts of the problem, the procedure to help solve the problem, how to perform the procedure, and then be able to calculate the answer. If the basic steps have become automatic, the learner does not have to think about each one, and the working memory's capacity can be used in answering the problem.

Passing From Working Memory to Long-Term Memory (Encoding and Retrieval)

Working memory connects to long-term memory through the processes of encoding and retrieval. Encoding refers to the ways information moves into long-term memory, assigning meaning to pieces of information and creating links to other pieces of information that are already in long-term memory. Memories are transferred as pictures, sounds, and meaning, and some researchers include touch. (*Note.* There is an interesting perspective from animal scientist/engineer Temple Grandin in her 2006 book, *Thinking in Pictures: My Life with Autism.*) Through encoding, working memory constructs meaning by seeking patterns, making associations, and building inferences about the importance of the information. It then conveys the information in such a way that it can connect to schema already encoded or form new memory traces (Baddeley, 2001).

The other role of working memory is to initiate the retrieval process. Retrieval refers to processes that enable individuals to search memory and access information for active processing back into working memory. Information can be coded using different symbol systems and thus stored in various areas of the brain. The efficiency of both these systems depends on how well information is organized during the storing process.

Long-Term Memory

The role of long-term memory is as a repository for all different kinds of knowledge. Unlike sensory and working memory, the capacity of long-term memory is seemingly endless, and its contents can last over a lifetime. Recently, interest has turned to two major features of long-term memory—the types of information represented and the organization of information. Researchers agree that information is encoded into qualitatively different kinds of symbol systems (feelings, words, pictures, etc.). The key issue is in understanding how these bits of information are categorized and organized.

One of the simplest and most widely used explanations is the two-part system suggested by Cohen and Squire (1980), who argued that information may be coded as declarative knowledge (knowing what) or procedural knowledge (knowing how). Declarative knowledge can be broken down into two subcategories: (1) semantic memories, which consist of facts and ideas, and (2) episodic memories, which have contextualized and personalized information within events. For example, if you spent an afternoon at a newly opened science museum, you would store the facts you picked up through reading the displays or listening to lectures about the exhibits. In addition, this experience would also be stored as an episode (how it felt to walk into an unfamiliar space, what the freshly completed building smelled like, the other people you noticed in the lines waiting to get in, the unexpected thunderstorm, the joy of seeing live macaws, etc.).

Semantic and episodic memories communicate with each other in interesting ways. When asked about your afternoon, you might first recreate an image of the building, remembering the event and your reaction to it. This memory could then trigger more specific details about the exhibits and what you learned.

In contrast, procedural memory is about the skills of how to do something. Stored as knowing how to do something, it is not conscious. For instance, once one has learned how to ride a bike, tie a bow, or to read fluently, these processes are then likely automatic and done without much (if any) thought.

These different categories of memory do not necessarily work in isolation with each other but may actually complement each other. For instance, when trying to learn a new skill, we talk our way through it, reciting information that may have been stored as declarative information. Once the skill becomes automatic, the semantic knowledge of it is no longer necessary.

Although neuroscientists are learning more and more about these systems and where the brain stores different kinds of information (sensory, emotional, or coded in different symbol systems), little mention is made about individual differences in thinking that can also affect what is remembered and how it may be organized. We know that some people see details and can produce accounts that include any number of specifics about a topic or situation. Others take a broader view that focuses on the big picture, and can make inferences or draw conclusions but have a difficult time with exact details. Some people seem to have better memory when it comes to concrete information, while others remember more abstractly, creatively, or metaphorically. The same holds true for how we organize our thoughts. Some of us think of information as webs, knowledge trees, or lists and ladders. Understanding our preferences may be helpful in understanding exactly what kind of a thinker we are. With a clearer idea of learning, we can experiment with and develop strategies to enhance our individual abilities to encode and retrieve information.

Long-term memory, however, is not a passive storage device—it is active and complex as it merges, creates, and modifies information. This constructive view of long-term memory presents something of a paradox. On one hand, it is an astonishing strength. It allows the formation of useful knowledge from the inside and the creation of new ideas by merging others. It also permits, somehow, the comprehension of novel arrangements of information, such as a sentence that you have never read or expressed before. As memories are stored, new information changes and deepens understandings. Each revisit of an idea, concept, or memory will form new neural pathways allowing deeper understandings and more opportunities for retrieval.

Unfortunately, the activity of long-term storage can also blend data into faulty concepts or inaccurate information. As an example of long-term memory's constructive activity, Loftus and Palmer (1974) showed adults a film of an auto accident, then gave each participant one of two questionnaires. One questionnaire asked, "About how fast were the cars going when they *smashed* into each other?" The second asked, "About how fast were the cars going when they *hit* each other?" (emphasis added). The subjects who had been given the "smashed" question estimated the speed of the cars at 30% greater than did those who had the "hit" question. A week later, all subjects were asked, "Did you see any broken glass?" Of the subjects who had responded to the questionnaire using the word "smashed," 32% said they had seen shattered glass. Only 14% of the other group claimed to have seen broken glass. In reality, *no* glass had been broken in the mishap. This sort of creative but unintended restructuring has led some researchers to question the accuracy of eyewitness testimony in criminal trials (Loftus, 1996).

In short, evidence indicates that we pull together information from several areas of the brain to construct a "memory" of an event and may employ, in retrieving from memory, information beyond our actual experiences. Long-term memory is a process that is highly active. We organize ideas and facts as we gain information, even if the information is incompatible with our experience.

Because working memory and long-term memory are connected by encoding and retrieval processes, the more we help students organize, conceptualize, grapple with, and provide a wide variety of experiences with information, the more pathways there will be to retrieve information when needed.

Acting on Information: Production/Expression

Production is a highly complex cognitive task. Success in production relies on the ability to attend, understand and follow directions, search long-term memory for relevant information, and then organize the information according to the guidelines needed to craft an appropriate response. Production also assumes that the student possesses adequate automatic motor skills (knowing how to use a pencil, keyboard, or some artistic tool without having to think about it). Additionally, success will rely on the degree to which the student has stored procedural information (i.e., how to add numbers, write a sentence, or spell a word without having to expend mental energy on those processes). Too many demands on memory will interfere with higher levels of thinking possibly needed for production.

The information-processing model that looks at attention and memory for explaining learning is helpful in understanding why some students have difficulty achieving in school. However, it doesn't cover other aspects of learning such as organization and self-regulation—in other words, ways that learning is governed.

Prior to the existence of functional magnetic resonance imaging (fMRI), clinicians noticed that adults with damage to their frontal lobes frequently were able to perform within the normal range on tests of memory, learning, reasoning, and language, but they had notable difficulty with organizing their daily lives, problem solving and developing strategies, accomplishing multistep tasks, and, in some cases, moderating their emotions. Goldstein, Naglieri, Princiotta, and Otero (2014) hypothesized that there must be an "overarching system responsible for coordinating these other cognitive resources that appeared to be working inefficiently" (p. 6). This system has been called the *executive function*, and there are many arguments for why it is such an important construct for understanding learning.

Executive Function and Self-Regulation Skills

Among the multiple definitions, executive function has been described as a separate branch of the attentional system (Posner, 1975), a supervisory system (called "the central executive") for manipulating information in short-term memory (Baddeley, 1986), and a "single phenomena, conceptualized as the efficiency with which individuals go about acquiring knowledge as well as how well problems can be solved across nine areas (attention, emotion regulation, flexibility, inhibitory control, initiation, organization, planning, self-monitoring, and working memory)" (Goldstein et al., 2014, p. 4). Dean Delis (2012), who authored the Delis Rating of

Executive Function, wrote, "executive functioning is the sum product of a collection of higher level skills that converge to enable an individual to adapt and thrive in complex psychosocial environments" (p. 14).

The term *executive* as applied to the functions of the brain's prefrontal cortex (PFC) has been attributed to Karl Pribram (1973), who stated, "the frontal cortex is critically involved in implementing executive programmes where these are necessary to maintain brain organization in the face of insufficient redundancy in input processing and in the outcomes of behavior" (as cited in Barkley, 2015, Sec. 1, para. 10). Indeed, current imaging studies point to the PFC as necessary for executive functioning capacity. Good executive function and self-regulation skills depend on the coordination of three interrelated brain functions: working memory, mental flexibility, and self-control (Center on the Developing Child, Harvard University, 2017).

As noted earlier in this chapter, working memory governs our ability to retain and manipulate pieces of information over short periods of time. Mental flexibility enables us to sustain attention—or shift attention—depending on the varying demands of the environment. It also allows us to apply different rules in different settings. Self-control is what helps us set priorities and resist impulsive actions or responses. These functions develop over time (usually reaching peak at around 25 years of age) and are believed to result as the PFC region of the brain develops. Interestingly, the PFC is the last portion of the brain to mature, and it is not unusual for 2e students, particularly those with high IQ and those with ADHD, to experience prolonged delay in development of the PFC (Shaw et al., 2007, as cited in Thompson-Schill, Ramscar, & Chrysikou, 2009). Slow development of the PFC in 2e students means that many will suffer from executive functioning and self-regulation difficulties during their school years—just when those skills are needed to succeed (although Thompson-Schill et al. [2009] contend that the slow maturation may likely carry benefits, as well).

When Learning Becomes Difficult

There are any number of areas where 2e students might have difficulty in learning and producing. Identifying the possible causes of the breakdown will help find appropriate strategies to use with individual students in overcoming or compensating for their weaknesses—as well as develop self-knowledge that can help with advocacy and self-regulation.

Problems With Attention and Sensory Input and Storage

Three major types of issues can interfere with the very first stages of learning, especially in terms of attention.

Attention. We know that a stimulus needs to be noticed for someone to pay attention. As we mentioned earlier, novelty, relevance, intensity, and emotion all help focus and sustain attention. Let's look at these four elements with 2e learners in mind.

Novelty. Ingredients to focus students' attention would include new, interesting information delivered through fast-paced lessons that are intellectually engaging. For many students with high cognitive abilities, this may happen rarely. Inattentiveness, hyperactivity, and impulsivity are natural responses when lessons are perceived as repetitive, routine, and dull. Often these learners already know what is going to be taught (Reis, Renzulli, & Burns, 2016). And, even if they don't, they usually do not need as much practice to grasp new information. Maintaining attention during lectures, classroom discussions, and assignments can be painful if students must routinely wait until everyone in the class understands the lesson.

Relevance. When 2e students are not interested in the topic at hand, it can be challenging for them to override their problems with attention. Students with autism spectrum disorders focus best in an area of interest, and this is also true for students with attention deficits. Sometimes, in an attempt to stay engaged in class, bright students try to make a lesson relevant for themselves. As a way to participate, they pose questions or make observations that, on the surface, may appear unrelated to the topic or are too complex for others in the class to comprehend. Sadly, these questions are often rebuffed and, even more disturbing, may cause ridicule from their peers. For example, when asked to describe a ceiling, a kindergartener responded that it "seals up a room," playing off the sounds of "*ceil*ing" and "*seal*ing."

Relevance can also be a problem when students are drawn in by many different elements of the environment. To focus on what is relevant to the lesson or discussion may be difficult, especially if students are also gifted and creative. Their divergent thinking abilities along with their curiosity can create connections from what's going on in the environment that they see as relevant to the topic. Cruickshank (1977) found that seeking out novelty and making creative connections are part and parcel of giftedness.

Intensity. Some 2e students, especially those with ASD and finely tuned senses, may be oversensitive to environmental stimuli. The buzzing of fluorescent lighting, the feel of the chair, or the presence of scents can be so intense that they cannot pay attention to the lesson or assignment. Some highly gifted students experience the same sensitivities (Dabrowski & Piechowski, 1977) as those with ASD (see Chapter 7).

Emotion. As discussed earlier in this chapter, emotions connect to memory and learning (Immordino-Yang, 2016). When students view an experience as positive, fun, and interesting, their attention is enhanced (Willis, 2007). Likewise, anxiety is a damper on the availability of minds to learn. The challenge is like a Goldilocks story—too much emotion or too little emotion negatively affects learning.

Sensory input and storage. This relates to both the modality through which students are being asked to learn as well as the content (visual, verbal, musical, mathematical) being processed. Depending on the intellectual strengths and weaknesses of the student, any one kind of learning might be problematic. If students must read (visual and verbal) to access the curriculum, listen to a lecture (auditory and verbal), or participate in an activity (kinesthetic), and any of those are areas of weakness for the learner, some information may not move into the working memory phase.

Working Memory/Short-Term Memory Difficulties

Working memory deficits are common among twice-exceptional learners. When automaticity in basic processes has not been developed (like memorizing math facts, spelling words, or other basic academic tasks), there is limited cognitive capacity available to perform more complex mental operations. For example, students who still need to sound out words when asked to read may not have sufficient mental energy to also comprehend the passage. Consider tasks like note-taking. To perform this task, students must simultaneously listen, sort for important information, and write, but if they need to consciously think about how a word is spelled or how to form the letters, they become lost easily.

Many 2e students have difficulty processing auditory information, especially if they are visual learners. Too much material flooding in causes them to break down. We have found that our young architects, filmmakers, and artists have difficulty in attending and following verbal discussions, but are much more able to organize information and solve problems mentally when the content is more visual and/or spatial.

On the other hand, those with nonverbal learning disabilities may fail to process visual information well. They often agonize when solving math equations as the symbols can be confusing and they may not be able to organize the information perceptually. For them, verbal scaffolding or self-talk can guide them through a procedure.

You can extend working memory's available space by reentering and rehearsing the information—reading, looking at, saying, or hearing the information again (and again). You can even rehear it silently by thinking of it. Information can also be chunked for more efficiency. In short, because we know that working memory can be a bottleneck for these students, we must provide strategies to help them encode and organize information, as is discussed in Chapter 13.

Problems Passing Information From Working Memory to Long-Term Memory

Learning might also hit barriers as information passes from working memory to long-term memory, either in the encoding or retrieval stages, or both.

Encoding. Encoding information involves changing the information being encountered for storage. Once encoded it enters long-term memory. A typical problem for 2e students is that they may or may not grasp the essence of a lesson; therefore, what is encoded may be quite different from what the lesson intended. For example, when the teacher is discussing proteins in the DNA molecule, Laurie could be fantasizing about building an origami molecule. When Laurie actually starts fiddling around with a page torn from her notebook, her inattention becomes obvious. To the teacher, Laurie is locked in a cycle—the less she pays attention, the poorer her learning, and the poorer her learning, the less she pays attention. However, one might also ask whether Laurie is doing anything useful with her memory when she appears inattentive. The answer is that she probably is, but the material being coded and rehearsed diverges significantly from the task at hand. The challenge for the teacher is to motivate Laurie to approach rather than disengage from the classroom work.

For students with attention deficits, the topic at hand can be encoded very creatively in no particular linear order. The students' mental drumbeats get them marching out of step with the lesson. The student may be following a jazzy improvisational line, skimming here and dwelling there. Meanwhile, the teacher is trying to keep a methodical, even beat. For example, a discussion about the Wright brothers' first manned flight in Kitty Hawk may set off imagery about strapping a jet propulsion engine onto the original rickety craft. Or it may stimulate a mental spin into a different area of long-term memory, resulting in private analogies. For example, the child might wonder why flying animals do not use propellers or jet engines and why planes must. If the student makes the analogy public, an unprepared teacher will probably have difficulty fitting the analogy to the lesson plan. Because bright minds crave knowledge and often feed on imagination, it becomes difficult for many of these students to keep their mind focused on the topic at hand and to keep it from straying.

Students with ASD may have the opposite issue. When connections are not made between and among concepts, it then becomes difficult to connect these details to find more abstract meaning. For example, a fact about dogs having evolved from wolves should connect in long-term memory to the idea of canine class, other domestic animals, and where they might have come from. For many people, that fact may then connect to evolution, survival of the fittest, or even questions about what kind of dog makes the best pet. But, for students with ASD, just knowing details about the dog being described may be sufficient and stored only as "dog" facts.

Retrieval. If the encoding process sends wild kinds of information with no clearly defined pathways, the information could then be difficult to use again, especially if it was encoded differently than intended. The teacher may be asking about DNA, and the needed particular fact about DNA can't be found. Also, retrieving all of the thoughts connected with a concept makes it difficult, if not impossible, for the working memory to sort back out again.

Long-Term Memory Problems

As for long-term memory, the information stored is stunningly varied. We know that some students have remarkable facility with details but lack conceptual understanding. Many students with ASD excel with semantic and procedural knowledge. Their storage system seems to be organized more linearly with fewer connections between and among pieces of information, making transfer to new areas more difficult. These students are more likely to show their knowledge by providing all of the details and are rather adept at "lecturing" to all who are willing to listen.

Other students are more conceptual in how they organize information. They are able to generalize across content areas and understand universal concepts. However, remembering lots of details could be difficult for them—for example, knowing names, dates, math facts, or the correct spelling of words. These students tend to think and learn more contextually with information stored episodically. Knowing individual strengths or styles of organization can help provide strategies that support areas of weakness.

Problems With Production

The most common complaint about 2e learners is their inability to produce timely or complete responses to assigned tasks—yet they can be so knowledgeable, have creative and insightful ideas, pursue in-depth interests, and may even be productive outside of school. What is it about the school environment that makes production so problematic? As explained above, production involves automaticity and efficient working memory function. Retrieving information and organizing it to produce a product or to express an idea involves a search and reconnaissance mission. Students must be able to recall relevant information that addresses the task at hand and organize their ideas in a logical manner in order to craft a thoughtful response. To understand the cognitive complexity of production, Marcy Dann, an educational therapist, listed cognitive tasks involved when a student is asked to write a paragraph or essay (personal communication, March 17, 2014). The student must:

- activate and sustain attention during the brainstorming and writing process,
- understand the writing prompt,
- have an inner experience or knowledge of the topic,
- keep the audience in mind,
- remember the rules and conventions of writing,
- clearly organize thoughts in sequence,
- describe visual imagery,
- use specific vocabulary, and
- set a tone.

All of this can be further compromised by students' lack of automaticity in spelling and handwriting, making the task of written production excruciatingly difficult.

Simply allowing more choice in how students are allowed to express learning would greatly improve productivity. Many of these students are builders, actors, and artists. Their talent and evolving expertise in these areas will allow production to occur more easily without as much strain on executive function and working memory.

Executive Functioning Problems

In her ongoing practice, Leslie Packer (2017) proposed that neurologically-based executive dysfunction is frequently overlooked as a possible cause of learning difficulties. This is her description of what might be observed:

> Think of an academic activity such as writing a big report—a common source of frustration for many students. The student who has Executive Dysfunction will have difficulty picking a topic, planning the project, sequencing the material for the paper, breaking the project down into manageable units with intermediate deadlines, getting started, and completing the activity. And because these students frequently underestimate how long something will take, they'll generally leave the project until the night before it's due.
>
> Now consider another academic activity: conducting a laboratory experiment. In the laboratory, the student has a list of supplies that are needed to run the lab and a set of instructions. If the student begins the lab before lining up all the supplies, she may find herself having to run to get something at a time when timing was critical. If she cannot follow sequential steps, she may skip a step and ruin the lab. . . .
>
> How many of us watched these children suffer day after day and never thought to get a neuropsychological assessment of their executive functions? It's not a motivational problem—he really can't seem to organize himself. (para. 18–21)

Fortunately, those with poor executive functioning can learn, develop, and apply strategies that can help regulate their behavior academically, socially, and emotionally. Packer (2017) suggested that we let students recognize their problems and ask how we can help, assuming the best—that they want to be responsible and organized. Often, she noted, their ideas or strategies may be better than anything we might suggest, and, because they are the authors of the plan, they are more likely to give it a try.

Issues With Anxiety

Good memory processes are inhibited by anxiety and stress, particularly those of the working memory and executive functioning (Goleman, 1995). However, anxiety and stress can serve as positive motivators, as well. Consider the benefits of just the right amount of anxiety (arousal)—the feeling of being stimulated and excited. This type of positive response actually activates and engages higher order thinking centers, providing energy to meet challenges and excel. Too much anxiety or stress, on the other hand, makes a student feel out of control and threatened. This affects the brain by limiting the capacity to learn. It is as if the stress and anxiety short circuit neural pathways in the prefrontal cortex (executive functions) and, as such, halt the processes of reasoning, memory, self- and impulse control—the very skills that are essential to successful learning. Some studies indicate that cortisol even has the ability to flip a switch in stem cells so that they actively will inhibit the forming of new connections in the prefrontal cortex, while hardening pathways that run between the amygdala and the hippocampus (as cited in Levy, 2014). This is especially concerning when thinking about 2e learners who feel as though they are in difficult, threatening environments, because when students experience repeated stress, their brains repeat the same negative anxiety and stress responses again and again, thus strengthening the neural pathways that control the stress and fear responses. In these instances, brains learn to jump to a stress response quickly and/or stay stressed. This is why it is so important for students to feel psychologically safe, and why it is counterproductive for anyone to expect good learning can take place when students are in survival mode.

Twice-exceptional learners could need more time to process information, even if each of the stages described above is intact. Think about how, at times, your computer is slow when you are trying to access information or produce work. The sluggishness might be because there are too many files or web browser tabs open. Or, you may spend time looking for saved information that wasn't filed efficiently. And, it's possible to "freeze" your computer when running too many programs.

Likewise, for 2e students, the ability to deal with new information, make connections, or complete complex tasks can put their minds on overload. Simply stated, these students can become frustrated and anxious, further slowing down their ability to process information and to stay in the struggle. For these students, providing more time to think and process information is critical.

With knowledge of how learning breaks down for these students, we can offer interventions and strategies to help them overcome their challenges. These are discussed later in book.

CHAPTER 6

Multiple Intelligences and Personality Preferences

There are other ways to look at how individual minds work and how to explain distinctive dispositions, zones of comfort, areas of excellence, and "islands of competence" (Brooks & Goldstein, 2012, p. 13). In this chapter, we will look at two—multiple intelligences and personality preferences.

Multiple Intelligences

In looking at the 2e learner, there are a number of models of intelligence that add useful information to understanding cognitive differences and intellectual patterns. Traditionally, psychologists and educators rely on traditional tests of intellectual functioning, such as the Wechsler Intelligence Scale for Children and the Stanford-Binet Intelligence Scales, to measure cognitive skills and functioning. These tests result in a Full Scale IQ score and provide quantitative estimates of a learner's intellective strengths and weaknesses, such as quantitative and verbal reasoning, memory, and processing speed. However, there are other cognitive strengths these tests don't measure but are useful to us in better understanding learning patterns of a 2e learner.

Howard Gardner (1983) and others (Goleman, 1995; Sternberg, 1995, 1997) argued that traditional views of intelligence limit our explanation and understanding of human potential and talent. When Gardner introduced his theory of multiple intelligences (MI), it was against a backdrop of the widely held belief that intelligence is a unitary trait that can be adequately measured and explained through an IQ score (Gardner, 1993). In at least two significant ways, MI theory challenges that idea. First, MI theory claims that we have several intelligences at work, not just one. And, secondly, Gardner (1999) defined *intelligence* as

> the bio-psychological potential to process information that can be activated in a cultural setting to solve a problem or fashion a product that is valued in one or more community or cultural settings. (pp. 33–34)

Intelligence is not how well an individual performs on a narrow set of short-answer questions. MI theory argues that there are many ways to be smart and that an individual's abilities are expressed in performances, products, and ideas.

Using evidence from brain research, human development, evolution, and cross-cultural comparisons, Gardner (1993) initially arrived at a set of seven intelligences: linguistic, logical-mathematical, musical, spatial, bodily-kinesthetic, interpersonal, and intrapersonal, and later added an eighth intelligence, naturalist. We have provided a short description of each intelligence, careers that require advanced abilities in a particular intelligence, and examples of famous people who exemplify a particular intelligence in Table 6.1.

Multiple intelligences has been confused with the concept of learning styles. Learning style theories focus on identifying modality preferences—the *senses* we prefer to learn new information, remember that information, indicate that we have learned, and the conditions that are optimal for our learning (i.e., visual, auditory, etc.). Multiple intelligences is fundamentally different. It does not address modalities. Instead, the eight intelligences represent capacities that reside in each person, the particular *content or symbol systems* a brain must interpret (i.e., verbal, spatial, emotional, or musical).

Understanding MI aids in understand how 2e students can have extraordinary abilities in one domain yet suffer in others. For instance, we know that some 2e students have difficulties with linguistic information, but when the information is spatial, they can perform at high levels. Gardner (2000) explained this dichotomy as *fruitful asynchrony*: "a deficit in one cognitive or affective area (intelligence) may go hand in hand with the capacity to develop strengths in another" (p. 196). In fact, recent ongoing work with individuals with dyslexia indicates they have considerable strengths in spatial abilities (Eide & Eide, 2011), giving them advantages in fields such as architecture, storytelling, filmmaking, and entrepreneurial endeavors. Findings to support the idea that "wiring" differences in a particular domain create cognitive advantages in others have been put forth consistently over the years, espe-

Table 6.1
Gardner's Multiple Intelligences

Intelligence	Abilities	Related Careers	Famous People With Advanced Abilities in the Intelligence
Linguistic	• Can perceive or generate spoken or written language. • Favors communication through words.	Poets, journalists, screenwriters, teachers, salespeople, orators.	Emily Dickinson, Mark Twain.
Mathematical-Logical	• Can understand a causal system. • Can manipulate numbers, calculations to explain a phenomenon. • Can quickly explain cause and effect through numbers and equations. Because they represent the world through numbers and equations, words can get in the way.	Accountants, statisticians, computer programmers, budget analysts, math teachers, engineers, physicists.	Albert Einstein, Marie Curie.
Spatial	• Can visualize space mentally. • Can understand spatial relationships, navigate unfamiliar places, see visual patterns, and recreate details visually. • Can represent concepts through the visual arts. Because they think in visual images, words can get in their way.	Architects, graphic artists, engineers, sculptors, painters, fashion designers, topographers, illustrators, set designers, filmmakers.	Coco Chanel, Steven Spielberg.
Musical	• Can think in music and tends to hear music in one's mind when experiencing feelings or events. • Can remember tunes easily. • Can represent ideas, maps, and concepts like a rainstorm through music. Because they think in music, words can get in the way. (Not about writing lyrics or having music on in the background.)	Musicians, composers, conductors, sound editors, music critics, soundtrack composers, piano tuners.	Carly Simon, Franz List.

Table 6.1, continued.

Intelligence	Abilities	Related Careers	Famous People With Advanced Abilities in the Intelligence
Bodily Kinesthetic	• Can use body to communicate an idea, solve a problem, or create a product. • Can control bodily movements to provide concise ideas and understanding, to perform precise motor tasks, and to create two- or three-dimensional models. • Because their knowledge and skills are in their muscles and body, words can get in the way. (Not about hyperactivity, which is uncontrolled movement, not a means of communication.)	Performing artists, gymnasts, sculptors, ballet dancers, athletes, car mechanics, plumbers, brain surgeons.	Auguste Rodin, Serena Williams.
Interpersonal	• Can understand other people, mood, and emotion. • Can use this ability to teach, persuade, negotiate, and lead. • Can use other intelligences and symbol system to convey meaning. It does not mean an extrovert personality.	Teachers, performing artists, counselors, psychologists, managers, negotiators, salespeople, politicians, community organizers, clergy.	Mother Theresa, Barack Obama.
Intrapersonal	• Can understand oneself in terms of strengths and weaknesses, preferences, and the kind of environments one needs to be successful. • Can set appropriate goals, make good decisions, and regulate their behavior. Being successful in life requires that one knows oneself and is clear about motive. (It does not mean they have an introverted personality.)	Debaters, philosophers, politicians, leaders, activists, therapists, editorial writers.	Martin Luther King Jr., Ayn Rand.

Table 6.1, continued.

Intelligence	Abilities	Related Careers	Famous People With Advanced Abilities in the Intelligence
Naturalist	• Can see patterns in the natural world, which allows for discriminating among living things (plant and animals). This ability undergirds how we evolved as humans—hunters, gatherers, and farmers. • Can see relationships among species and can offer classification systems for the living and nonliving world. • Can use other symbol systems to represent their ideas.	Botanists, geologists, chefs, fishermen, forest rangers, zookeepers, aroma therapists.	Jane Goodall, John Audubon.

Note. Adapted from "The First Seven . . . and the Eighth: A Conversation With Howard Gardner" by K. Checkley, 1997, *Educational Leadership, 55*(1), pp. 8–13.

cially in terms of individuals with dyslexia or specific learning disabilities (Dixon, 1983; Schneps, 2014; Silverman, 1989; West, 1997).

Gardner (2000) also speculated that certain intelligences naturally encode information in symbol systems, such as numbers, pictures, musical notation, and scientific formulas. Thus, those who may be strong in a particular intelligence may be able to use the symbol system of that intelligence yet still experience difficulty with other symbol systems. For example, a student who lacks skill at decoding written language may easily be able to decipher the symbol system used in music, which is spatial.

In contrast to traditional conceptions of intelligence, MI theory argues that intelligence is not the same in all situations. Rather, thinking, learning, and problem solving demand fluid situational and task-specific approaches, and each individual taps different intelligences in different combinations to work through problems. MI theory also suggests that intelligences do not work in isolation. Any adult role requires collaboration among intelligences. For example, playing the violin in an orchestra certainly requires musical intelligence, but it also demands bodily-kinesthetic ability to master the physical demands of bowing and fingering, and enough interpersonal intelligence to work with a conductor or audience. Therefore, how intelligences operate is best considered in the context of a specific domain—that is, in the world of real problems.

Intelligences also include subabilities. One is not merely "musically" or "linguistically" intelligent. One's musical intelligence may manifest in the ability to compose (musical composition), hear and distinguish patterns of harmony (musical perception), or improvise while keeping time with other musicians (musical collaboration). In the case of linguistic intelligence, one's ability may emerge through creative expression (as in a story), the descriptive language of a presentation, or in subtle and deep understandings of narrative passages.

This view of intelligences fits well with what we already know about 2e students, who often excel at solving problems and fashioning products in particular domains that tap their strengths and interests, especially in contexts outside of school. These domains often involve intelligences and symbol systems outside of linguistic and logical/mathematical intelligences. For example, the purpose of Project High Hopes (see Appendix A) was to identify and nurture specific abilities within a special education population. The talent areas chosen were visual and performing arts, science, and engineering because these are the domains in which many adults who had experienced difficulties in school have later found remarkable success.

In short, MI theory offers an authentic description of intelligence as it operates in the real world and provides insight for school practitioners and parents in understanding individual students (Baum, Viens, & Slatin, 2005). Looking at students through MI theory can help educators identify the circumstances in which

2e youngsters perform at their personal best and isolate those areas where they may need support.

Applying Information About Multiple Intelligences

MI information can help with programming and educational approaches to curriculum and instruction as well as be useful for counselors and parents. Observing students and noting when they are at their personal best (intelligences at promise) versus times when they are struggling (intelligences at risk) alerts us to how these students process information. For example, if a student is on task, communicating knowledge, and demonstrating higher level thinking when engaged in an improvisational activity, one might guess that he or she is strong in both bodily kinesthetic intelligence and the personal intelligences, especially in the domain of acting. Researchers have found that such students write better when they are allowed to become "the character" in order to describe the character's personality and motivation (Baum, Cooper, Neu, & Owen, 1997; Baum, Owen, & Oreck, 1997). It is not that the students' ability to write improved; rather, changing the context to fit the student's strengths and interest allowed him or her to process and organize his or her ideas with more ease. In addition, using authentic assessment within specific domains, as Gardner (1983) recommended, allows us to identify many students in the special education population as also having gifts and talents within particular areas not noted through traditional intelligence tests.

Personality Preferences

Identifying individual personality preferences, as first introduced by Carl Jung's archetype theory (1939), is another way to note how people are wired differently. He claimed that individuals are born with a proclivity toward the ways they think and feel. Reactions represent certain personality types and are predictive of human behavior. Since then, theorists have speculated that all people have certain personality traits such as introversion, optimism, and trust, which suggest characteristic ways of behaving. During the 1980s, educators began to look at personality traits to help understand how learning occurs for different style preference (Gregorc, 1982; Silver & Hanson, 1996; Silver, Hanson, & Chu, 1982; Silver, Strong, & Perini, 1997). Confusingly, personality preferences can also be called learning styles in education. These preferences help educators understand ways students organize their worlds, including the kinds of environments for which they are best suited and the kinds of lessons they like. Gregorc (1982) offered a four-style model categorized by how people perceive their world (concrete or abstract) and how they organize their world (sequential or random). Silver et al. (1997) chose to organize types of learners by looking at how they perceive their world (sensing or intuiting) and how they judge their world (thinking or feeling). Once teachers could identify the preferences of their students, they could align learning environments. Each of these theorists identified strategies most suitable for each type of learner.

In working on a grant, we could not find a tool to gather information about personality preferences in students, so we adapted existing ideas to construct a system that pertains to children, as well as adults—the *Baum-Nicols Quick Personality Indicator* (Nicols & Baum, 2003; Baum & Nicols, 2015). Based on Gregorc's categories of perception and organizational preferences, we named four types of personalities—Practical Manager, Learned Expert, Creative Problem Solver, and People Person. The tool contains 10 forced-choice statements that are each rated from one to four. No matter how the four personality types are scored, the total of all of the ratings will add up to 100 (it's important to remember that the most anyone can earn in any single style is 40 points, with the least at 10 points). Some of us will show definite preferences while others will score more evenly across all four styles. Although a high score in a particular style area can indicate a talent for tasks requiring that type of personality trait, those who score more uniformly across styles may be more adaptable to a wider variety of environmental demands. When the environmental demands (such as working in a busy, noisy, highly stimulating room) or the expectations of teachers or parents (such as calling out fluid brainstorming responses, working cooperatively with others, or completing a worksheet in sequential order) do not align well with particular personality profiles, the resulting student behaviors could appear falsely as symptomatic of a learning or attention issue, such as ADHD or lack of social skills.

Personality Preferences and the Twice-Exceptional Learner[3]

Consider the story of Jane. At 11 years old, she rarely completes any task in a timely manner. According to her mother, she can't focus on the task at hand. Her mother, a highly organized professional, who prides herself on running her home and family with precision, is frustrated by her daughter. For example, Jane's job is to clear the dinner table and load the dishwasher—a task her mom has estimated should take 10 minutes. For Jane, it usually takes three times the allocation. Why? Highly verbal Jane has turned this boring, predictable task into a creative opportunity by inventing a novel way to clear the table. She carefully varies the sequence according to innovative categories. One night she may remove all of the dishes that contain vegetables first and then those that are perfectly clean. She may decide to collect the silverware by taking one spoon, two forks, three knives, and then reverse the pattern. She carries on a lively discussion during this process as if she were teaching young children to categorize. Placing the dishes in the dishwasher offers more

---

3   Material in this section has been adapted from "The 2e Profile: Multiple Perspectives" by S. Baum, C. Novak, L. Preuss, and M. Dann, 2009, *2e Newsletter, 36,* p. 13. Copyright 2009 by S. Baum, C. Novak, L. Preuss, and M. Dann. Adapted with permission.

creative opportunities. Jane often pretends that she is acting in a commercial, trying to sell the detergent, the dishes, or the dishwasher. This commercial may include jingles, dances, or rhymes. Jane's mom does not find this amusing and fails to enjoy Jane's creative talents. After all, she still has homework to finish and bedtime is looming. Her mother wonders whether Jane may have ADHD, and if so, would medication help her focus? It is apparent that Jane's mother values how quickly the task is accomplished rather than whether it is accomplished.

The truth is that Jane and her mother have two distinct ways of interacting with the world—two different personal styles. All of us possess different degrees of personality traits that make us unique. Some of us seem to prefer order and predictability. We feel comfortable when we work on a schedule. A good day is when we can check everything off our to-do list, yet others of us are more spontaneous and become bored when things are too predictable. These distinctions help to explain the differences in Jane and her mom. Is one better than the other? The answer, of course, is that it depends on the situation. In the best of all worlds, we would be able to spend the majority of our time in environments that allow us to function in ways that align to our personal style. However, there will be times when we need to be flexible and accomplish tasks and be able to adapt to the demands of the environment. The secret is balance. If Jane spends most of her time in an environment that requires a rigid schedule and strict adherence to rules and specific directions, she may act out or shut down. On the other hand, if she continues to disregard the times when she needs to be more focused and act in a timely manner, she may keep herself from accomplishing important goals.

Four Personality Patterns[4]

The *Baum-Nicols Quick Personality Indicator* (Nicols & Baum, 2003; Baum & Nicols, 2015) identifies four styles. Each of us possesses all of them but in different quantities, giving each of us a unique profile. We may be balanced across all four or show clear preferences. Difficulties can occur when students have an extremely high score in one area with quite low scores in the other styles. In those instances, it is a clue for further investigation that would include gathering other learning information about the student.

The categories are shown in Figure 6.1 and then explained in more detail below.

Practical Managers. Students who have strengths as Practical Managers (see Table 6.2) have a gift for organizing people and things. Their rooms or desks are neat, clothes are usually hung up, and possessions put away in an organized fashion. They appreciate and follow rules, and make sure others do the same. Socially, they are happier with one or two friends who share their interests and talents.

---

4   Material in this section has been adapted from "The 2e Profile: Multiple Perspectives" by S. Baum, C. Novak, L. Preuss, and M. Dann, 2009, *2e Newsletter, 36,* pp. 15–18. Copyright 2009 by S. Baum, C. Novak, L. Preuss, and M. Dann. Adapted with permission.

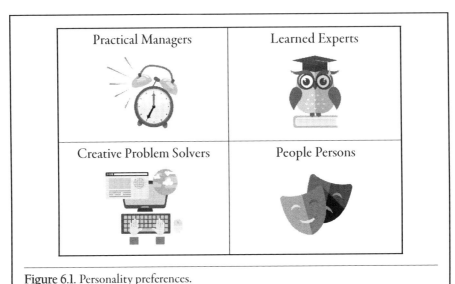

Practical Managers	Learned Experts
Creative Problem Solvers	People Persons

Figure 6.1. Personality preferences.

Table 6.2

Characteristics of Practical Managers

Gifts	Needs	Possible Problems
• Pay attention to details (love deadlines, timelines, punctuality) • Create to improve products or ideas • Have finely tuned senses • Keep others on task	• Orderly, predictable environment • Structure, clear expectations, and detailed directions • Opportunities to elaborate and add detail	• Perfectionism • Rigidity • See the world in black and white

Note. From "The 2e Profile: Multiple Perspectives" by S. Baum, C. Novak, L. Preuss, and M. Dann, 2009, *2e Newsletter, 36,* p. 15. Copyright 2009 by S. Baum, C. Novak, L. Preuss, and M. Dann. Reprinted with permission.

Life works well for these Practical Managers when they know what is expected and how they will be evaluated. The more events unfold as planned, the more comfortable they are. Quiet, orderly environments help them learn. They enjoy having a plan and checking off tasks as they are completed.

All positives have a flip side. Although Practical Managers can be excellent with details, they may become over-focused on them at times. Some can appear to be obsessive compulsive or exhibit perfectionistic characteristics. Easily upset when things are out of place or when the routine changes, they can become overwhelmed and overstimulated. With their finely honed senses, they may be highly sensitive to light, sound, and textures. They can become stressed when they're not certain of the requirements of a task or situation, when there is too much chaos, or when no one seems in charge!

Learned Experts. Learned Experts (see Table 6.3) have a talent for scholarly pursuits and often become class experts on complex and abstract topics. They love to hypothesize and synthesize. These students value knowledge and satiate their curiosity about how the world works by reading nonfiction, watching documentaries, and listening to interesting and informed people. As one 8-year-old explained about his thirst for knowledge, "I crave knowledge like a tiger stalks his prey" (personal communication with a student, 2005). In fact, these Learned Experts often would rather read or hear about the adventure than experience it. They may not like crowds of people or freezing temperatures. The field trip might just take too much time. Viewing a TED Talk would be more expedient. These individuals often possess advanced vocabularies and can express themselves eloquently. They usually earn good grades and enjoy class discussions and writing research papers. They are very logical and enjoy and are good at verbal debate—often arguing to play "devil's advocate."

Learned Experts are most fulfilled when engaged in some sort of intellectual pursuit or interacting with others whose abilities they admire. They engage fully when allowed to give their opinion and make their points of view known.

Learned Experts may be found with book and flashlight in hand as they prepare for bed. These students are often stressed when curriculum is not complex or the lessons move along too slowly. In fact, Learned Experts may enjoy the pursuit of knowledge to such an extent that they can be unwilling to end the research aspect of a task. Learning environments that don't offer advanced explorations of topics and issues or limit the opportunities for these kinds of students to be with one another inadvertently obstruct the development of their bright minds, often causing behavioral problems.

Here's the dark side. Because of their advanced vocabulary and argumentative nature, their comments may be sarcastic and seen as put-downs by others. Some of these students are in the need of image management and coaching, as they are often unaware of how they appear to others.

People Persons. People Persons (see Table 6.4) have a talent for human relations and creating harmony. People Persons live in a world of feelings and feel the emotional climate of the room as soon as they enter. These youngsters have many friends, enjoy social interaction, and are often talented in the creative arts.

People Persons shine when allowed to connect meaningfully with others inside and outside of school. They perform well in group activities and can contribute to the process by helping others get along. They flourish when given an assignment that allows them to respond emotionally, such as one that integrates the visual and performing arts. Because they are eager to please, they like special jobs.

Table 6.3
Characteristics of Learned Experts

Gifts	Needs	Possible Problems
• Very knowledgeable • Can synthesize ideas and create theories and models • Outstanding vocabulary • Excellent debaters	• Intellectually stimulating environment • Games and activities that require strategizing • Opportunities to research, discuss, and hypothesize	• Intolerance of others less smart • Using sarcasm • Being opinionated • Being argumentative

Note. From "The 2e Profile: Multiple Perspectives" by S. Baum, C. Novak, L. Preuss, and M. Dann, 2009, *2e Newsletter, 36,* p. 16. Copyright 2009 by S. Baum, C. Novak, L. Preuss, and M. Dann. Reprinted with permission.

Table 6.4
Characteristics of People Persons

Gifts	Needs	Possible Problems
• Creating harmony • Colorful, dramatic • Social skills • Attuned to feelings	• Colorful, social environment • Opportunities to interact with others • Opportunities for creative expression	• Disorganization, lack of attention to details • Repressing own needs to keep the peace and avoid conflict • Being overly sensitive

Note. From "The 2e Profile: Multiple Perspectives" by S. Baum, C. Novak, L. Preuss, and M. Dann, 2009, *2e Newsletter, 36,* p. 17. Copyright 2009 by S. Baum, C. Novak, L. Preuss, and M. Dann. Reprinted with permission.

On the flip side, People Persons don't pay much attention to details. Thus, they can seem disorganized or forgetful. They become stressed when things in their social-emotional world are not going well and respond poorly to criticism and conflict. They need to feel special and count on the people in their lives to appreciate them. These students can be overly sensitive, experience meltdowns—dramatizing and exaggerating events when they feel neglected or undervalued. In these circumstances, they shut down and may not be emotionally available to learn.

Creative Problem Solvers. Students like Jane, introduced in the initial scenario, are best identified by their talent for innovation. They are the Creative Problem Solvers (see Table 6.5) of the world, energetically leaping from one idea to another. Never satisfied with the status quo, they can always find a better way to do anything and, in fact, would much prefer to do it their way. Unlike those with more sequential styles, Creative Problem Solvers understand that rules can be bent and exceptions made for the good of the cause. They may appear impulsive as they leap first—for

Table 6.5
Characteristics of Creative Problem Solvers

Gifts	Needs	Possible Problems
• Divergent thinker who can generate many ideas • Flair for adventure and spontaneity • Empathetic • Life of the party, fun	• Creative environment • Options • Opportunities for multiple projects	• Disorganization, lack of attention to details • Difficulty following directions • Stubbornness, having own agenda

Note. From "The 2e Profile: Multiple Perspectives" by S. Baum, C. Novak, L. Preuss, and M. Dann, 2009, *2e Newsletter, 36,* p. 17. Copyright 2009 by S. Baum, C. Novak, L. Preuss, and M. Dann. Reprinted with permission.

they tend to see the end result before identifying the steps they need to get there. This group is always taking risks if there is a chance for fun and adventure.

Creative Problem Solvers thrive when they are given choices and can work on multiple projects at once. They prefer open-ended assignments and opportunities to be creative. They do best when allowed to pursue assignments or tasks their own way with few and general guidelines. Creative Problem Solvers enjoy discovery learning, spontaneous lessons, mild competition, use of learning games, and options. Inflexible learning environments with many rules can cause these students to become oppositional and defiant.

However, they also can be disorganized because they often do not listen fully to directions and, as a result, can be confused about what is expected of them. They test rules and have a dislike for routine. These youngsters are often stressed by having to focus on sequential details that are required in many learning environments. These are the students whose desks and backpacks are a jumble.

Applying Information About Personality Preferences[5]

Knowing our students through their personality preferences (along with the self-knowledge that comes for students when they understand the potential impact of personality styles) can help us personalize education. Suppose that the students in a botany class have been studying plants, including the concepts of photosynthesis and phototropism. To help them grapple with the concepts and assess what they have learned, a teacher might offer the following series of performance tasks tailored to address style preferences and entice the different kinds of learners in the class.

---

5   Material in this section has been adapted from "Building on What Is Right About Our Students" by S. Baum, 2016, *2e Newsletter, 79,* pp. 16–17. Copyright 2016 by S. Baum. Adapted with permission.

Table 6.6 is a performance task for Practical Managers. Notice the specificity of the directions. The focus is on completing a concrete model from which these students will explain cell structure and its relation to the concepts of the unit.

Table 6.7 is a performance task for Learned Experts. Notice that this task is more complex and requires students to synthesize their findings into a coherent article with an authentic audience. Providing criteria for excellence reminds students of the quality desired.

Table 6.8 is a performance task for People Persons. This assignment is especially appropriate for People Persons because it uses the arts to build understanding of concepts through metaphor. Collaboration among students to create and perform is appealing to these learners.

Table 6.9 is a performance task for Creative Problem Solvers. These choices allow Creative Problem Solvers to use their creative ideas to design and invent products that show their understanding of the concepts. It's important to provide enough directions to these learners to remind them of what they need to show in their creations.

Let's return to the four students we visited in Chapter 2. Each student showed multiple intelligence strengths, as well as personality preferences. See Table 6.10 to look at their multiple intelligences (shown in italics) and their personality preferences (shown in bold).

When we take into consideration the different ways learners can present, we can then value the rich diversity of 2e students and what they can contribute. Their lives will work better if they can spend the majority of time in situations that align to and respect their strengths. But it is important to acknowledge that there will always be times when the demands of a task or situation require them to use alternative intelligences and skills from less-preferred styles. At those times we need to help them recognize the problem at hand and support them in developing or adapting useful strategies.

Table 6.6

Performance Task for Practical Managers

What to Do	Directions
Make and present a 3-dimensional model of a plant cell to show understanding of the cell structure and the use of the cell parts.	• Design a model of the plant cell following the diagram distributed in class. • Collect the materials that you wish to use for your model from the project table. • Complete all work at your own desk. • Label the parts and be able to explain what happens to these parts during photosynthesis. • Take 3 class periods to complete your model.

Note. From "Building on What Is Right About Our Students" by S. Baum, 2016, *2e Newsletter, 79,* p. 16. Copyright 2016 by S. Baum. Reprinted with permission.

Table 6.7

Performance Task for Learned Experts

What to Do	Directions

Write an educational article to be posted on the class/school website to inform others of what you have learned about the transfer of light into plant energy in class and through further research. Your article does not have to only be words, but can show information using video links and images.	1. Begin by doing some research:
	  • Find at least 3 additional pieces of information about photosynthesis that you didn't learn in class, but find interesting and think your classmates should know.
	  • Visit the following websites or search the Internet for information you can understand and can put into your own words to inform your classmates:
	    › http://www.biology4kids.com/files/plants_photosynthesis.html
	    › http://www.johnkyrk.com/photosynthesis.html
	    › http://sciencing.com/steps-photosynthesis-middle-school-science-8544590.html
	
	2. Prepare the article as you would like it to appear on the website. Be sure to proofread and edit it before uploading. Include any images and links to video resources you want to use.
	3. Take 3 days to complete your assignment.
	  • Day 1: Do your research.
	  • Day 2: Complete the first draft.
	  • Day 3: Publish it by the end of the day.

Note. From "Building on What Is Right About Our Students" by S. Baum, 2016, *2e Newsletter, 79,* p. 16. Copyright 2016 by S. Baum. Reprinted with permission.

Table 6.8
Performance Task for People Persons

What to Do	Directions
Design a performance to show the concept of photosynthesis using a personification.	1. In a small group create a personification of the process of photosynthesis. 2. Add music and dance to enhance the meaning. 3. You may also be in costume for your performance. 4. Find a place outside of the classroom to rehearse your dance. 5. The piece needs to be 3–5 minutes in length and ready for you to perform it at the end of the third day. 6. Make sure each part of your dance can be explained in terms of the process of photosynthesis.

Note. From "Building on What Is Right About Our Students" by S. Baum, 2016, *2e Newsletter, 79*, p. 17. Copyright 2016 by S. Baum. Reprinted with permission.

Table 6.9
Performance Task for Creative Problem Solvers

What to Do	Directions
Choose a project from the following options that you think can best show your understanding of the concepts covered in this unit. • Use iMovie to explain how plants get their energy from the sun. • With recyclable materials in the class, create 3D models to show the different stages of growth. • Create a flipbook to visually show the process of a plant growing, from seed to mature plant. • Design a board game that helps others understand the stages of photosynthesis. Make sure the game is ready to market—include an aesthetically pleasing board, directions, and any tokens or spinners you might need.	1. Outline the major points you will need to include your project. 2. Choose the option that will work best to convey your understanding. 3. Take three days to complete your work.

Note. From "Building on What Is Right About Our Students" by S. Baum, 2016, *2e Newsletter, 79*, p. 16. Copyright 2016 by S. Baum. Reprinted with permission.

Table 6.10
Traits of Students Including Multiple Intelligences and Personality Preferences

Student	Full Scale IQ Score on the WISC	Advanced Abilities and Interests, Multiple Intelligences Strengths, and Personality Profiles	Disability	Complexities of Coincidence
Debra	128	• Drama, human rights, history • *Inter-/intrapersonal, spatial, bodily kinesthetic* • **People Person, Learned Expert**	Dyslexia SLD	• Depressed, low self-concept, defiant, lonely • Failed to be identified as gifted until fourth grade
Jimmy	134	• Mechanical skills • *Highly spatial, bodily kinesthetic, mathematical* • **Creative Problem Solver**	ADHD, SLD	• Hyperactivity may have been due in part to high IQ • Failed to be identified as gifted until fourth grade
Bill	133	• History, science, military, engineering • *Spatial, linguistic, intrapersonal* • **Learned Expert, Practical Manager**	Asperger's Syndrome (now ASD)	• Passions seen as obsessions • No friends of his age • Not identified until middle school (eighth grade) for either disability or ability • Depressed • Anxious
Kyle	112	• Advanced abilities in technology, engineering, music, drama, writing • *Spatial, bodily kinesthetic, musical* • **Creative Problem Solver, Learned Expert**	GAD, executive functioning, and poor productivity	• Disability not identified until seventh grade • Selective mutism • Social anxiety • Lack of friends

CHAPTER 7

Factors Leading to Misidentification and the Perils of Misinterpretation

What Is the Problem?

Blaine is a quiet but friendly and hard-working young man, who is enrolled in a small, private academy. Depending on the subject, he works at a variety of different grade levels. His teachers report that he is a willing participant in every facet of school and becomes fervent—even obsessive—about activities of particular interest. Showing an excellent grasp of academic concepts in his homework, class discussions, and projects, Blaine occasionally suggests alternatives to teacher-directed assignments so he can show his particular skills. Blaine says with glee that the teachers most often agree with his proposals. As a result, his relationships with peers, older students with mutual interests, and adults continue to improve.

This description is taken from Blaine's psychoeducational assessment during middle school and portrays a student whom most teachers would love having in class: intelligent, interested, engaged, and socially involved. But he had a very difficult time getting to this point.

By 8 years old, Blaine was on home instruction. The resulting neuropsychologist's report when he was being evaluated so he could return to school included a confusing array of disorders. Here is an excerpt from that document:

> an eight-year-old boy being seen for neurological examination as part of a comprehensive child study team evaluation. Information provided by mother and observations in the office setting indicate that difficulties displayed by Blaine have a multifactorial basis, including: 1. Attention Deficit Hyperactivity Disorder; 2. Mild Oppositional Defiant Disorder; 3. Generalized Anxiety Disorder; and 4. Mild unevenness in skill development.
>
> Recommendations
> 1. Ongoing individual counseling and family therapy
> 2. Ritalin and Clonidine
> 3. Social skills intervention to facilitate development of appropriate skills
> 4. Consistent behavior management at home and in school
> 5. No OT (occupational therapy) or PT (physical therapy) necessary
> 6. Return to school in cooperation with special services

Note that this summary makes no mention of Blaine's high intellectual ability nor offers any indication that he might have specific interests or strengths (see Table 7.1).

The neurologist appeared focused on problems. His emphasis added weight to the following report from the public school psychologist. Although she acknowledged Blaine's superior intelligence in the body of her report and mentioned his history from kindergarten to this point, she neglected to consider a possible interaction between his cognitive abilities and his behaviors:

> There is a side of Blaine that appears anxious and depressed, the origin of which may be directly related to his diagnosed ADHD disorder. Impulsivity is noted and in keeping with the situations in the past that have suggestions of endangerment to self, he needs to be monitored in school and at home. It is hypothesized that when Blaine's stressors have been reduced, he will improve in his outlook and his problematic and worrisome behaviors will diminish.

This incomplete, and possibly erroneous, diagnosis is a path more common than one would hope. Although the co-occurrence of learning and behavioral difficulties

Table 7.1
Blaine's WISC III Profile

Verbal IQ	142	Information	19	Picture Completion	14
Performance IQ	119	Similarities	19	Coding	8
Full Scale IQ	134	Arithmetic	10	Picture Arrangement	15
Verbal Comprehension	150	Vocabulary	19	Block Design	18
Perceptual Organization	124	Comprehension	19	Object Assembly	9
Freedom from Distraction	98	Digit span	9	Symbol Search	15
Processing Speed	109			Mazes	8

with high abilities is being noticed more openly, professionals and parents still seem uncomfortable accepting that it is possible. When there are difficulties, the usual interventions are designed to address the deficits, frequently ignoring abilities and interests. It is not unusual for parents to want their child "fixed," or a teacher to want a "regular" student. But by not recognizing and addressing talents, we deny the student hope of being seen for what he or she can contribute. Ironically, an emphasis on eliminating deficits can magnify problematic behaviors, possibly resulting in additional diagnoses with even more labels, as we are beginning to see in Blaine's example.

Although it is clear that multiple syndromes can exist simultaneously, confusion caused by overlapping characteristics and the cross-pollination of high abilities with disabilities may result in under-identification, misidentification, or overidentification of multiple syndromes. The more labels, the more daunting it is to design suitable programs for these students, especially because many disorders have crossover characteristics (Baum & Olenchak, 2002; Cramond, 1994; Neihart, 2000).

The purpose of this chapter is to identify some basic pitfalls in recognizing twice-exceptional students. High-ability students who are struggling in school manifest behaviors that could result from many different causes that point to many different syndromes. Without an understanding of gifted behaviors or the characteristics of twice-exceptionality, professionals are simply not aware of alternate hypotheses that could point to what is really going on with these students. It is our hope that everyone reading this book can help spread awareness of this dilemma.

A beginning question is to wonder if Blaine really suffered from the mix of all of these disorders—ADHD, mild oppositional defiant disorder, generalized anxiety disorder, mild unevenness in skill development—as indicated in the report. How should the school and educational recommendations be handled? Examining the events that led to Blaine's diagnosis and recommendations will illustrate how the lack of understanding about twice-exceptionality obscured the professionals' vision, snowballed into more difficulties for Blaine, and resulted in inappropriate programming and treatment.

Blaine's Story

Preschool Years

An alert little boy who seemed to need little sleep, Blaine loved being read to and spent hours playing with his piles of LEGO bricks. Behavior problems first surfaced when Blaine entered nursery school. Although he had begun talking and walking later than expected, he caught up so quickly that his developmental levels in motor and verbal areas surpassed those of his age-mates. Impressed with his advanced vocabulary, wealth of knowledge, artwork, and ability to build structures, his teacher considered whether or not to adapt the program to fit his unique learning needs. Ultimately, she chose to do nothing, saying that he needed to learn to listen, follow directions, and accomplish assigned tasks. Because Blaine was becoming increasingly unhappy, his parents placed him in another nursery school where there was less emphasis on structured learning and more opportunity for exploration and play. He did well and came home with smiles.

Kindergarten

When Blaine entered kindergarten at 5, he performed quite well for the first month. But, by the end of October, his teacher expressed concern about his tendency to blurt out answers and his difficulty in reliably recognizing letters. His motor skill development slowed and lagged behind his exceptional verbal ability. Described as impulsive, Blaine was becoming a disciplinary problem, especially when he was expected to tackle tasks he found difficult. As a result, the school asked Blaine's parents to complete the Conners Parent Rating Scales (Conners, 1997), which includes items related to conduct disorders. Next, Blaine was referred to a pediatric neurologist, who diagnosed him with ADHD. He began a regimen of Ritalin, the most commonly prescribed methylphenidate for addressing attention problems in children. That summer, Blaine attended a "catch up" summer school program where he learned his letters in 2 short weeks.

First Grade

By first grade, Blaine's behavior was under control, but he was showing difficulty learning to read and was placed in the lowest reading group. To encourage him to read, Blaine's parents began to take him to the public library on a regular basis. In only a month, Blaine was reading fluently. Using books he chose—most of which were nonfiction—his literacy skills improved rapidly to the point that his teacher acknowledged he now belonged in the top reading group. For unknown reasons, however, she never moved him. By midyear, Blaine once again had drifted into a pattern of inappropriate behaviors and had become the classroom scapegoat. Classmates teased him unmercifully, chanting "Blaine the Pain," tossing things at him during recess. In the absence of any significant adult intervention, this sensitive 6-year-old defended himself by lashing out physically.

All who knew Blaine outside of school commented on how smart he was. They marveled at his talent in building. His parents had heard of a summer program for gifted students where Blaine could take a mini-course in architecture and design, and an intelligence test was necessary to qualify for this program (his results were in the 99th percentile). Blaine's parents were pleasantly surprised at the success he had in that program. His work was stellar, and he experienced no social or academic difficulties while working with intellectual and interest peer groups.

He read voraciously at home that summer—plowing through four Boxcar Children novels by Gertrude Chandler Warner in 3 days. There was reason to expect that Blaine would have a much improved school experience ahead.

Second Grade

But as second grade began, hopes were dashed for Blaine's educational improvement. He complained constantly about the writing assignments, and he refused to finish spelling and math assignments. The playground situation worsened, with incidents of cruel teasing that escalated into fisticuffs. His parents requested the support of a playground assistant—their right under Section 504 of the Rehabilitation Act of 1973 provisions—but were denied. In desperation, they sought psychiatric support. Blaine's diagnosis was expanded to include anxiety, and Clonidine was added to his existing medication regimen of Ritalin.

At school, the child study team chose not to classify Blaine for special education. Rather, to address the cognitive abilities identified when he entered the summer program for gifted students, the team initiated behavioral interventions that included 4.5 hours a day of individual instruction. Unfortunately, most of the work was worksheet-based, and Blaine continued to display low tolerance for frustration, sometimes even ripping out pages after being asked to complete repetitious or dull work during his "gifted" instruction time. Blaine did not enjoy being separated from other students because it gave them even more reasons to tease him, and, yes, they continued to harass him on the playground. Consequently, Blaine "developed" a troubling pattern of stomachaches and other maladies so he could stay home. His parents struggled to keep him in school, but after several particularly aggressive recess episodes and with noncompliant behaviors increasing, they decided it would be best to take him out of the second-grade classroom. He was placed on homebound instruction. At this point, Blaine asked his mother, "Why did God give me ADHD? I wish I would die so other kids would feel sorry for me." Remember that this child was only 7 years old.

Third Grade

Continuing the homebound programming into third grade, Blaine grew increasingly withdrawn as he expressed missing the other students. His psychiatrist diagnosed him with major depressive disorder and suggested he return to regular school. With this new diagnosis, educators wanted Blaine classified for special education services associated with emotional disturbances. At this point, Blaine's parents hired a professional special education advocate to help with this classification. All the while, however, Blaine's teacher refused to provide advanced instruction or curriculum, and his depression grew worse. During the process of classifying Blaine for special education, his advocate, along with an expert consultant, managed to convince the school district to fund Blaine's alternative enrollment at a nearby private school. The school, although not intended for students with special needs, admitted Blaine as a favor to his parents. It was thought that personalizing a program for Blaine—given his cognitive talent coupled with his need for more individual attention—might be possible in the private setting.

Fourth Grade and On

Immediately, Blaine was sent to sixth grade for math (advancing two grade levels) and fifth grade for humanities (advancing one grade level). An outstanding art program encouraged his spatial talents in the visual arts. Within their lessons, teachers offered projects as a learning outcome option, which was particularly appropriate for Blaine's love of building and creating. Small class sizes, dependably less than 15, helped him focus attention. His homeroom teacher worked to help him improve his social relationships, find acceptable responses to frustrating situations, and organize his work. Blaine's problems with written language and attention were substantially reduced by allowing him to use a computer for all written assignments. The teacher also had a quiet office set apart in the classroom where any student could go if they wanted fewer distractions. The office had an incandescent reading lamp, a headset to tune out classroom noise or listen to music, and a laptop to help with production.

Blaine graduated from eighth grade as valedictorian and attended a magnet high school for gifted and talented students. He spent his high school summers as a teaching assistant in the same special enrichment program where his own gifts were first acknowledged.

Looking at the Issues

There are several important and complex issues that come from Blaine's story: the lack of appropriate programming, the incorrect diagnosis, the role of the environment, and the misunderstanding of the underlying issues or the services offered. Were any of the labels assigned to Blaine justified? Did the original diagnosis of ADHD take into account the behaviors that might have been attributed to his high cognitive abilities? Did the problems cease when he was put on medication? Which of the behavioral manifestations were symptomatic of the stressful and mismatched learning environments in which he was placed? Did his developmental lags and difficulty with spelling and handwriting indicate the presence of a subtle learning disability? Did the behavioral manifestations present clues to correct diagnoses? Was he ultimately a "gifted" student with an undiagnosed learning disability? Did he have ADHD, or was he "gifted" along with learning and attention difficulties? Or all of the above? These questions point to the dilemma of trying to see the forest through the trees of twice-exceptional students.

Blaine's story seems like an unhappy movie script, but, unfortunately, it is true. Well-intentioned school personnel, as well as medical professionals, believed they were acting in Blaine's best interests. Their perspectives, based on their earlier training, blinded them from considering hypotheses coming from contemporary research in other areas. With their discipline-based myopia, the various adults involved in Blaine's case trapped themselves in the deficit model of diagnosing and remediating problems, which remain dominant in both medicine and education. No other course of action came to mind, and there was no drive to consider using a wide-angle lens to view Blaine's circumstances.

The school psychologist's report from when Blaine returned to school in the third grade illustrates such outdated and narrow thinking. Her conclusions articulated concerns about Blaine's social-emotional adjustment, especially about his growing depression and anxiety. The behaviors she described reinforced her opinion that ADHD was responsible for Blaine's problems. However, putting the various clues together from his documented history in his school records, one might come to an entirely different conclusion:

- he was enthusiastic in library and art class and had no behavior problems there;
- when he did blurt out answers, they were always correct; and
- problems arose in physical education class, playground behavior, and classroom written work.

In truth, Blaine behaved well in classes when his strengths were able to surface. He was an excellent artist and had superior verbal skills. Problems cropped up in situations that demanded proficient motor skills, and his assessments showed his deficiencies in those areas. In fact, within his WISC subtest scatter, there were dramatic discrepancies between his strengths and weaknesses. Blaine's WISC profile suggested the presence of a possible learning disability and might have explained his growing anxiety about the wide contrasts between what he could do well and the areas in which he was frustrated. He also had difficulties with peer relations when he was perceived as different in a negative way. The school psychologist was stymied because she focused strictly on his diagnosis of ADHD. Blaine was on medication and still showed impulsive behaviors and depression.

The school psychologist did not perceive—or at least did not report—that Blaine's learning environment had a negative impact, although she noted that he had to skip recess to finish work he missed while being tested. Even for the brief period in second grade during which attempts were made to serve Blaine with an individual pull-out program to address his cognitive strengths, the spirit of gifted education was ignored or misunderstood. Instead of creating opportunities for Blaine to be with his intellectual peers, he was separated from fellow students for most of the school day and was force-fed repetitious, drill work assignments. In contrast, the summer program in which Blaine excelled after first grade placed him with intellectual peers who had similar interests and abilities to work on challenging, real-world problems. In that program, Blaine had experienced *no* problems of *any* kind. Almost certainly, the professionals working on Blaine's case would have profited from a multidisciplinary perspective. Specialists skilled in creativity, giftedness, and contemporary theories of intelligence could have assisted the child study team in developing a deeper understanding of the complexity of Blaine's situation. A cursory examination of Table 7.2's matrix suggests numerous interpretations that could legitimately account for the behaviors Blaine displayed. For example, when Blaine lashed out against peers for teasing him and calling him names, it could be interpreted as impulsivity from an ADHD perspective, or it might be viewed as extreme sensitivity coupled with weak judgment, which is often seen in the developing gifted child.

Contemplating Problems From Diverse Perspectives

In order to be able to look at a student's presenting behaviors from diverse perspectives, professionals need to be aware that there is a wide range. Better consideration of the possibilities can help team members ask the right questions, observe students more holistically, and entertain possible causes of behaviors before settling on a particular diagnosis. These include understanding:

- the emotional development of gifted students, including the concept of overexcitabilities;
- whether a student is creative or disruptive;
- IQ testing and the use of subtests indices and scores;

Table 7.2
Synopsis of Behaviors From the Literature by Category of Human Condition

Trait	ADHD (DSM-IV-TR, APA, 2000)	LD (Baum et al., 1991)	Creativity (Cramond, 1994; Renzulli et al, 1976)	Gifted (Piechowski, 1991; Renzulli et al., 1976; Silverman, 1998)	Contemporary Theories of Intelligence (Gardner, 1993, 1999; Sternberg, 1995, 1997)
Sustaining Attention	Difficulty with sustained attention; daydreaming	Often poor memory unless in interest areas	Heightened imagination may obscure attention	Poor attention often due to boredom; daydreaming	Weak attention in situations unmatched to intelligence pattern
Listening Skills	Diminished ability to listen attentively	Auditory skills can be weak	Hypomanic to the point of not listening	Preoccupation with own ideas and concepts; appears bored	Nonauditory intelligences restrict ability to listen
Task Completion	Problems with independent task completion	Erratic task completion based on interests	Broad range of interests often prohibits task completion	Completion of tasks directly related to personal interests	Tasks often remain incomplete when unrelated to strengths
Motivation	Avoids and dislikes sustained mental activity unless interested	Motivation governed by areas of interest and strength	Concentration favors self-selected work	Lack of persistence on tasks that seem irrelevant	Tenacity linked to thinking preference patterns
Organization	Messy and may misplace items needed for work; disorganized	Poor, sometimes nonexistent organizational skills	Finds order amidst chaos	Organization may be seen as unnecessary depending on the task	Organization in the eye of the beholder
Following Directions	Difficulty following directions	Difficulty with oral or written directions, or both	Willing to take risks to satisfy creative plans and pursuits	Questions rules and directions	Directions not accounting for intelligences may be overlooked

Table 7.2, continued.

Trait	ADHD (DSM-IV-TR, APA, 2000)	LD (Baum et al., 1991)	Creativity (Cramond, 1994; Renzulli et al., 1976)	Gifted (Piechowski, 1991; Renzulli et al., 1976; Silverman, 1998)	Contemporary Theories of Intelligence (Gardner, 1993, 1999; Sternberg, 1995, 1997)
Energy Level	Heightened activity level	Hyperactive	High energy; sometimes erratic	Frequent high activity level	High energy level on work in strengths
Impulsivity	Impulsive; poor judgment in interactions (not waiting turn, interrupting)	Poor self-concept triggering poor social judgment; may act impulsively	Impulsive in actions and often disinterested in relationships; risk-taking	Highly sensitive but judgment lags well behind intellectual development	Impetuous when trying to cope with tasks in nonstrength ability patterns
Verbal Manifestations	Excessive talking	Verbal vs. ability to put ideas in writing	Asks questions about anything and everything	Magnified curiosity and need to probe yields much talking	Verbalization increased when working in preferred intelligences
Reactions to Authority	Problems adhering to rules for behavior regulation	Poor self-regulation skills	Freedom of spirit that rejects external parameters; uninhibited	Intensity that leads to struggles with authority	Self-regulation reliant on nature of tasks and relation to strengths

Note. Adapted from "The Alphabet Children: GT, ADHD, and More" by S. M. Baum and F. R. Olenchak, 2002, *Exceptionality, 10,* 77–91.

- causes and effects of attention issues in gifted students;
- the distinction between passions and obsessions; and
- the social context and emotional issues.

Emotional Development of Gifted Students

If professionals are not aware of theories about the emotional development of students with high and extremely high abilities, they will not be able to discern the difference between a behavior that results from intensities and a behavior the comes from a pathology. Consider that the high energy radiating from full engagement in a project might be seen as hyperactivity, or that a vivid, active imagination could be viewed as distractibility. Evolving ideas about the sensitivities, emotional development, and excitabilities of gifted students (e.g., Olenchak, 1994; Piechowski, 1991; Piechowski & Colangelo, 1984; Silverman, 1993) offer useful lenses through which we can examine growing diagnoses of hyperactivity, attention issues, difficulties with transitions, anxieties, and environmental sensitivities.

Dabrowski's theory of positive disintegration provides an explanation for qualitative differences of human development. He proposed that gifted persons have areas of "increased psychic excitability" that predict extraordinary achievement, or overexcitabilities (as cited in Nelson, 1989, p. 9). Piechowski and Colangelo (1984) described the concept of overexcitabilities as

> an expanded and intensified way of experiencing in psychomotor, sensual, intellectual, imaginational, and emotional areas. . . . As personal traits, the overexcitabilities are often not valued socially and are viewed instead as nervousness, hyperactivity, neurotic temperament, excessive emotionality, and emotional intensity that most people find uncomfortable at close range. (p. 81)

Piechowski and Colangelo (1984) went on to describe psychomotor overexcitability as an

> organic excess of energy or excitability of the neuromuscular system. It may manifest itself as a love of movement for its own sake, rapid speech, pursuit of intense physical activities, impulsiveness, restlessness, and pressure for action, driving the capacity for being active and energetic. (p. 81)

In informal interviews, adolescents talking about feeling jittery illustrated Piechowski and Colangelo's point:

> When I'm around my friends, I usually come up with so much energy that I don't know where it came from. . . . When I am bored, I get sudden urges and lots of energy [in school]. I use this energy to goof off.

Another student described his need to get out and do something physical after completing a long assignment: "I suddenly get the urge to shoot baskets or ride my bike." Confusingly, it seems that the high energy can result from a lack of interest or boredom as much as from the excitement of new ideas or the thrill of completing something challenging. Some students report difficulty dissipating energy in preparation for doing their work. For example, one young woman explained that when she has to sit down to write, "I have to talk out the idea (aloud) or put on music and dance before I am ready to begin."

Cruickshank (1966, 1967, 1977), known for his classic work with hyperactive youngsters, came to consider hyperactivity and extreme sensitivity to the environment as a *positive* trait in bright students rather than an irritant. He claimed that their tendencies to notice everything, take in all sorts of wide-ranging stimuli, and ask questions actually contribute to advancing their abilities. Piechowski (1991) explained that when gifted students act impulsively, blurt out, or flail, they may simply be responding to the urge to explore their world. Their curiosity and their hunger for knowledge can take precedence over a prescribed curriculum fixed in time, sequence, and space. In this sense, the regular classroom can be too inhibiting— even disastrous for such youngsters. Jonathan Mooney (Mooney & Cole, 2000), a gifted hyperactive student, observed that if he is asked to be still and sit quietly he *loses his ability to think*! For Cramond (1994), an appraisal of whether hyperactivity enhances or distracts from learning and performance is essential to a diagnosis.

Creative or Disruptive? That Is the Question

Many high-ability students are also highly creative. Cramond (1994) compared "crossover traits" between creativity and ADHD (see Table 7.3).

Definitions of creativity and ADHD are oddly similar: risk-taking, impulsivity, spontaneity, active learners, and rich imaginations. Students who are seen as cleverly avoiding tasks, providing many involved reasons for not doing their homework, or telling elaborate untruths may be viewed as oppositional defiant or nonproductive as opposed to excellent divergent thinkers. Declaring a trait positive if it drives creative production or negative because it inhibits an individual's productivity should help identify appropriate interventions. But ignoring the creative strength while "curing" the student of original thought would be unfortunate. Cramond (1994) cautioned parents and teachers "to look carefully at behaviors exhibited by children for what may be potentialities instead of deficiencies" (p. 11). But no matter which

Table 7.3
Creative or ADHD Indicative Traits

Trait	Creativity	ADHD
Inattention	Broad range of interest resulting in playing with ideas, visualizations; ease of making connections from what is said to other links; capable of multitasking	Not paying attention; unfinished products
Hyperactivity	High energy for interesting tasks	Excessive movement; restlessness
Impulsivity	Risk-taking and sensation seeking	Acting without thinking; thrill-seeking behavior
Difficult Temperament	Unconventional behavior; daring to challenge the system	Deficient social skills
Underachievement	Focusing on own projects instead of those dictated by school	Difficulty with achieving school goals

diagnosis is decided, interventions should include nurturing students' creative traits so that they will be aimed toward achievement and success.

IQ Testing and the Use of Subtest Indices and Scores

Too often, students are identified for services contingent upon test scores. If there is a lack of understanding about the meaning of these scores or an unwillingness to consider significant discrepancies between scores within tests, 2e students may be underdiagnosed for services for both special education and gifted education.

Since the last edition of the book, there have been two additional versions of the Wechsler Intelligence Scale for Children, the WISC-IV (Wechsler, 2003) and the WISC-V (Wechsler, 2014), which are used to identify high abilities as well as areas where learning breaks down. For our purposes, the major differences among the versions are changes in the subscales or indices and the subtests that comprise them. For a detailed comparison of indices and subtests of the WISC-III, IV, and V see Appendix B.

For both the WISC-IV and the WISC-V, the test's authors suggest not using Full Scale IQ scores; rather they encourage looking at the intellectual patterns of the index scores (Wechsler, 2003, 2014). Yet, specialized programs for the education of the gifted and talented have traditionally required Full Scale IQ scores to qualify students. This does not bode well for 2e students whose Full Scale IQ scores often misrepresent and/or underestimate their abilities. In our experience, 2e students tend to display identifiable patterns of strengths and weaknesses. Often their strengths are found in abstract thinking (either verbal or nonverbal areas or both). Most of these students, however, score significantly lower in subtests that measure working memory and processing speed. As discussed in Chapter 5, these are areas where learning breaks down for many of the 2e community.

Here are profiles of three 2e students that illustrate the problem with relying on Full Scale IQ scores.

Elizabeth. Elizabeth is a 10-year-old who has great difficulties in reading, writing, and spelling. She is a great thinker, however, and worries about world hunger and environmental issues. Quite knowledgeable in these areas, she is willing to argue with anyone who is willing to "take her on." Her WISC-IV scores (see Table 7.4) show her patterns of intellectual strengths and weaknesses.

Elizabeth has a Full Scale IQ score of 117, which is considered high average. This score would not allow her to gain admission to the school's gifted program, where the cut-off score for entrance is 130. But Elizabeth's score of 144 on the Verbal Comprehension index gives strong evidence of superior intellectual ability, as her performance exceeds that of 99.9% of her age-mates. Her scores on the other indices, however, are significantly lower. This profile is not uncommon for students diagnosed with a specific learning ability. Like them, Elizabeth struggles in areas that rely on working memory, attention, and processing speed. It is also easy to see that Elizabeth may not be able to produce at the same high level as her ability to conceptualize and grapple with challenging verbal material. This pattern hints at the need for intellectual challenge as well as learning support. Additional information will be required to confirm both her potential giftedness and specific learning disabilities.

Edward. Edward, a bright sixth grader, is an avid reader and is well-informed about many topics. His WISC-IV scores (see Table 7.5) present a different pattern from Elizabeth's. He tends to be nonproductive in school. Although he has fine ideas, they rarely translate into something tangible. He is often angry and can storm out of the room when he is frustrated by an assignment.

His profile shows advanced abilities in both verbal and perceptual areas. Consider, however, that his average scores in working memory and processing speed may mean that Edward's productivity is impeded in ways that might look similar to Elizabeth's but for different reasons. Even though his full scores might gain him entrance into a gifted program, his lack of productivity and his disruptive behavior will probably prevent his identification. His jagged profile—with scores ranging from 99th percentile to 34th percentile—may be a clue to his problems in school. More information is needed to document potential for gifted behavior or presence of a specific learning disability or attention deficit disorder.

Steve. Steve's profile (see Table 7.6) shows yet a different set of strengths and challenges. Steve is a 15-year-old high school sophomore. His favorite school subject is history, and he enjoys finding historical trends that he can support with facts. He enjoys anything mechanical and loves puzzles. His teachers complain that he has trouble with abstract ideas and can't see the big picture.

Table 7.4
Elizabeth's WISC-IV Index Scores

Full Scale IQ	117	87th percentile
Verbal Comprehension Index (VCI)	144	99th percentile
Perceptual Reasoning Index (PRI)	98	45th percentile
Working Memory Index (VMI)	99	25th percentile
Processing Speed Index (PSI)	88	21st percentile

Table 7.5
Edward's WISC-IV Scores

Full Scale IQ	125	95th percentile
Perceptual Reasoning Index	129	97th percentile
Block Design	13	
Picture Concepts	12	
Matrix Reasoning	19	
Picture Completion	11	
Working Memory Index	104	61st percentile
Digit Span	13	
Letter Number Sequencing	9	
Arithmetic	14	
Processing Speed Index	94	34th percentile
Coding	7	
Symbol Search	11	
Cancellation	12	

Steve's patterns of strength and weaknesses also show wide discrepancies, with scores ranging from verbal subtest abilities of 99% and 97% and an index score in the 93th percentile (VSI), to lows of the fifth percentile for subtests and indices scores of the 16th percentile (WMI) and the 9th percentile (PSI). He shows significant strengths in nonverbal areas; however, there are definite problems with processing speed and working memory. But more telling is the score variance within the Verbal Comprehension index. His advanced abilities in Information and Vocabulary and average scores in Similarities and Comprehension signify that he may have ASD, which warrants further inquiry.

Although there are no definitive patterns that identify those within the 2e population, the scores do offer clues about the mix of abilities and disabilities. In conclusion, analyzing intelligence test subtest and indices scores to better understand a student's abilities and disabilities is critical when identifying 2e learners. This infor-

Table 7.6

Steve's WISC-V Scores

Verbal Comprehension Index	113	81st percentile
Vocabulary	10	50th percentile
Similarities	15	97th percentile
Information	19	99th percentile
Comprehension	9	37th percentile
Visual Spatial Index	122	93rd percentile
Block design	13	84th percentile
Visual puzzles	17	99th percentile
Fluid Reasoning Index	118	88th percentile
Matrix reasoning	14	91st percentile
Figure weights	12 (17 untimed)	75th percentile (99th percentile)
Processing Speed Index	80	9th percentile
Coding	7	16th percentile
Symbol Search	6	5th percentile
Working Memory Index	85	16th percentile
Digit span	6	9th percentile
Forward	9	37th percentile
Backward	7	16th percentile
Letter number sequencing	5	5th percentile
Picture span	5	37th percentile

mation combined with observations, checklists, and other data collection tools will help pinpoint students' learning patterns so the resulting diagnoses are accurate.

Attention Issues and High-Ability Students: Cause or Effect?

Lack of ability to attend does not necessarily mean that students have ADHD. There are many ways that attention can be compromised for bright students. For example, the curriculum may not be advanced enough. It could be paced too slowly. Sometimes students are asked to work in areas where their intelligences are at risk (Baum, Viens, & Slatin, 2005) or where their learning suffers from undiagnosed learning disabilities, anxiety disorders, or other issues.

Curriculum and pacing. The emergence of ADHD-like behaviors can involve aspects of curriculum and instruction. Inattentiveness, hyperactivity, and impulsivity are natural responses to a lack of novelty in the curriculum or one that is not intellectually engaging. We know that many bright students are being taught well below their instructional level and that they need less practice to master a skill (Gallagher & Gallagher, 1994; Reis et al., 1993). In a dramatic example of a curricular "diet," Reis and her colleagues (1993) discovered that when up to 60% of the regular curriculum was eliminated, gifted students exceeded or equaled the achievement levels of matched students who were required to digest the entire curriculum. Although these findings bode ill for all bright learners, those with attention deficits can be doubly affected, as their symptoms become more extreme when they are understimulated.

Strength alignment. Another variable affecting attention is the extent to which students' intellectual strengths are considered. Gardner's (1983) MI theory is very useful in understanding the paradoxical behaviors of many students with ADHD under certain circumstances. We have found that many youngsters with ADHD are particularly talented in visual and performing arts, engineering, and science (Baum et al., 2001). These disciplines rely on nonverbal intelligence, especially spatial and kinesthetic intelligences. But because school transactions are primarily linguistic, these students seem inattentive and disruptive in traditional classrooms. Yet they perform well in classes where teachers reduce the amount of time they spend lecturing, allow for movement, and emphasize active engagement in learning through experiences, projects, or the arts. In fact, they can attend for long periods and complete complex projects. In a longitudinal study, Sternberg (1997) showed that 199 high school students achieved better than even their brightest peers when instruction and curricula were purposefully matched with their particular areas of ability and interests. School behaviors that had been viewed negatively were "magically" transformed to high levels of goal orientation and motivation.

Could it be that students with attention-related disorders are best served in an environment that values and incorporates alternate modes of thinking and communication? Perhaps attention deficits are connected to specific intelligences, an idea that has not yet been investigated.

Undiagnosed learning disability. Sometimes inattention could be due to a student's inability to complete a task. Perhaps a writing disability is causing the problem, or there are auditory processing issues, so the student has limited capacity to focus on the task. It is important to decide if the attention issue is behind the behavior or if there is a hidden learning challenge that is interfering with attention.

Excessive Engagement: Passions or Obsessions?

The debate intensifies over the idea that students with ADHD or those with ASD tend to *hyperfocus*, which is defined as excessive engagement in tasks that are interesting and have intrinsic value. For some of these students, the excessive engagement with a topic is seen as cognitive rigidity, indicating the inability to engage in topics outside of their interest area. Their focus on specific topics can be all-consuming and cause them to have difficulty switching tasks.

Neurotypical individuals are able to modulate, switching at will from one task to the next, but students with ADHD cannot sustain attention unless arousal is intense. Lacking that extra-strong "stimulus fuel," their focus fades, but once it is found, they are also prone to overengage (Berg, 2003). Students with ASD can use their intense focus to sustain attention for vast amounts of time to accomplish a goal in their passion area.

Hyperfocus can be confused with the idea of "flow," as Csikszentmihalyi (1990) described in his theory of happiness. Great personal satisfaction stems from engaging in difficult or complex experiences that demand sustained physical or mental effort. The particular form of experience is unbounded; it might be mountain climbing, reading, solving a math problem, or playing a piano piece before a large audience. He argued that these kinds of activities create a state of total absorption—flow—that people feel when they are so completely involved in an activity that they lose track of time, are unaware of fatigue, hunger distractions, or anything but the activity itself. In a sense, they are lost in the present. The joy they get from the experience is totally intrinsic, worries disappear, anxiety evaporates, and they are truly "in the moment." In many ways, Csikszentmihalyi (1997) observed, "the secret to a happy life is to learn to get flow from as many of the things we have to do as possible" (p. 113).

The determining factor between hyperfocus and flow is to what degree students can engage in areas of interest but still be able to redirect as necessary to more mundane tasks. From this perspective, being highly focused through intrinsic motivation is a desired state, not one to be cured. Temple Grandin (personal communication, February 2016) argued that the passions of students with ASD need to be nurtured. She does not see these passions as obsessions but rather as clues to what these students can be in the future. We think it is vitally important to view intense engagement as a positive trait, without which one is unlikely to accomplish extraordinary feats. In the school environment, students who have in-depth interests can focus and learn in ways that are aligned to their strengths. It behooves us to create learning environments that aim to meet individual needs rather than insist that individuals stretch or shrink themselves to fit the mold of the school. Finally, we need to be careful not to label the love of a topic as an obsession (fearing that it will lead to hyperfocus and cognitive rigidity) but rather call it a passion that can be developed into a talent.

Understanding Social Context and Emotional Issues

The social-emotional issues faced by 2e students often have their genesis in both categories of their exceptionalities. To diagnose the student as having an emotional behavioral disorder because he or she lacks social skills, is lonely, and is perhaps antisocial might be inappropriate. Forging friendships can be difficult if students do not have age-mates with similar interests and intensities (Lovecky, 2004). The more children feel different from their peers, the more difficult it becomes to relate. For young, verbally precocious children, even talking to their age-mates can be difficult. They prefer to socialize with those older or younger. Coupled with the differences due to their abilities, these children can lack relationship skills as their precocity may have put them at "stage center," where they became accustomed to "hogging" all of the attention. Being in the audience or even sharing the stage with others is foreign territory for them.

If these highly able students also have attention deficits or ASD, they may have difficulty reading social cues and knowing how to relate to others. Slow processing speed increases the potential number of pitfalls. By the time these students process the social context, the group has moved onto another topic or activity. It is important to understand what the actual issues are for each 2e learner.

Another area of possible misdiagnosis is the diagnosis of oppositional defiant disorder. Some 2e students use defiance to survive a system that feels antagonistic to them. When the environment is hostile, they jump into survival mode—they fight or flee (Medina, 2008). It would be helpful to allow these children to reset and learn in a psychologically safe environment where they are welcomed and included on the basis of what they can do.

Finally, anxiety plays a key role in obstructing learning and behavior. Living with the knowledge that they are not meeting the expectations of others, can't perform simple tasks like many of their peers, and disappoint those they wish to please, as well as the fear that there is no bright future if they cannot be "fixed," can create high levels of anxiety. And anxiety impacts students' abilities to attend to tasks, contribute to relationships, and approach life with a sense of confidence.

As we noted at the beginning of the chapter, recognizing a student as twice-exceptional is complex. The lack of a comprehensive understanding of their traits and the comingling of positive and negative attributes blur the issues and require us to challenge assumptions. In the next chapter, we provide practical guidelines, strategies, and tools to assist in formally identifying the twice-exceptional student.

Part III

Comprehensive Programming

CHAPTER 8

Identifying 2e Students in Educational Settings

As described in Chapter 3, students who are 2e can be found in three different populations. In the first group are students who already are identified as gifted and talented but are having difficulty achieving in school, especially as the curriculum becomes more complex. One reason for their lack of school success may be undiagnosed learning disabilities. For these students, identification will be aimed at finding evidence of why they are struggling so that they can receive learning support. The second group of students is made up of those already identified as having special needs, but their areas of strength, gifts, and talents have not been noted or addressed. Many of them are increasingly anxious and/or depressed because they are being seen as special ed—not as the highly able students they can be. For them, the issue is to find ways to identify their potential and put strategies in place to nurture their abilities. The third group of students appear to be of average ability, as their abilities and gifts mask each other. Identifying them as twice-exceptional may be difficult until signs of giftedness or challenges begin to emerge.

This chapter will address how to identify twice-exceptionality within the first two groups of students. First, we will outline the challenges that prevent identifying learning disabilities in gifted students (searching for "blue"). We offer practical guidelines and suggest alternate strategies that will help these students receive the services they need. The second part of the chapter (searching for "yellow") provides ways to see and identify the hidden gifts and talents in students already receiving special education services, noting that traditional approaches to identifying gifted students are not valid for these students.

Searching for Blue: Challenges and Practices for the Identification of Learning Disabilities and Other Special Education Needs in Gifted Students

In a perfect world, identification of 2e students should follow the guidelines set forth by Reis, Baum, and Burke (2014) in "An Operational Definition of Twice-Exceptional Learners: Implications and Applications":

> To be identified as twice-exceptional requires comprehensive assessment in both the areas of giftedness and disabilities, as one does not preclude the other. Identification, when possible, should be conducted by professionals from both disciplines and, when at all possible, by those with knowledge about twice exceptionality in order to address the impact of co-incidence/comorbidity of both areas on diagnostic assessments and eligibility requirements for services. (pp. 222–223)

Over the past decade, schools have used a process called Response to Intervention (RtI) to provide early attention to students who are showing atypical development or do not seem to be thriving in school academically, behaviorally, or socially. RtI is a problem-solving approach for school-based teams to help students who are not meeting grade-level expectations by collecting both schoolwide assessment tools and observations of their learning. From this information, educators select and implement research-based strategies targeted at helping students catch up and continue meeting targets. This proactive approach has been growing since the last edition of this book, where we hinted at this new way of helping students before they fail or fall so far behind that special education services are warranted. RtI can be an effective way to identify and intervene with 2e students, as discussed below, along with strategies for identification under IDEA (2004) when RtI is not meeting a student's needs appropriately.

RtI and Identifying the Disabilities of Twice-Exceptional Students

According to the National Center on Response to Intervention (2010), the RtI approach was designed to integrate assessment and intervention within a multilevel prevention system to maximize student achievement and to reduce behavioral problems. With RtI, schools use data to identify students at risk for poor learning outcomes, monitor student progress, provide evidence-based interventions, and adjust the intensity and nature of those interventions depending on a student's responsiveness, and identify students with learning disabilities or other disabilities. The key components are:

1. universal screening for students' performance in reading, writing, and mathematics (some schools also use a behavioral assessment as well);
2. a problem-solving team approach with evidence and observations of students used to draw hypotheses of what is needed and set goals for implementation;
3. three levels of services that support learning and behavior needs (the three tiers increase in intensity as students require additional interventions);
4. evidence-based interventions that are used when students are not responding satisfactorily to typical classroom activities and are in the need of targeted instruction; and
5. ongoing monitoring that allows teachers to document students as they respond to instruction and meet expectations.

As a multilevel prevention system, RtI opens the door for services at increasing levels of intensity when classroom modifications are not helping to alleviate problems. The first level or tier involves high-quality core instruction for all students. The second level or tier comes into play when the student is not making satisfactory progress and requires different and/or additional evidence-based strategies to effect positive changes in the areas targeted. This instruction can also happen in the classroom, often using small-group instruction. Finally, lack of progress at the second level signals the need for an individualized approach with increased intensity, often under the auspices of special education services. During this process, the school or parents can recommend that the student be given a comprehensive evaluation, according to the Child Find components of IDEA (2004).

The RtI process is not just for students who are falling behind, but it has also been applied to students whose advanced abilities make the regular classroom curriculum not appropriate. In theory, the RtI approach should allow (and encourage) educators to put on both "yellow" and "blue" lenses to see students who may be twice-exceptional. Practically speaking, this happens only when teachers are aware of the signs that indicate high abilities (yellow) and learning challenges (blue) among 2e students and are able to find evidenced-based practices that pertain to the uniqueness of these students' social, emotional, and cognitive needs (green).

Over the past decade, we have developed a process to help create appropriate responses for 2e students, *Reflective RTI* (Baum, Schader, Dismuke, & Sly, 2012; see Appendix C). The booklet guides teams through the problem-solving process that begins with a unique screener, Presenting Behaviors Checklist (see Appendix D). This checklist taps both the positive and negative traits often exhibited by 2e youngsters (interestingly, it include characteristics that can even be seen as both positive and negative, depending on the situation and the viewpoint of the rater). It is to be completed by a variety of people who see the student within the school, as well as outside, so that the ratings will reflect times when interests are at the forefront and other times when learning difficulties surface. The steps outlined in the booklet help teams identify areas of strengths, interests, and talents, along with areas that may need support.

A group of professionals within the 2e community believes that RtI can be an effective and practical way to respond to the disparate needs of twice-exceptional students (Coleman & Hughes, 2009; Pereles, Omdal, & Baldwin, 2009). They argue that, with sufficient professional development, teachers will become aware of 2e students and be able to offer both targeted academic support along with advanced curriculum. But because RtI appears to focus primarily on students who are not meeting grade-level expectations, it is important to understand that untrained or unaware teachers might miss seeing 2e learners within their classroom. For this reason, professional development must include information about presenting behaviors for students whose high abilities may allow them to survive in spite of their academic challenges. Frequently, these students are able to compensate, but at great personal cost. Students' complaints about going to school because they are bored, their stubbornness during class participation, or their acting-out behaviors at home and in school, are red flags that school is becoming a stressful environment for them. Unfortunately, educators may attribute these signs as laziness, emotional problems, or defiance. With appropriate training and awareness of strategies that address the intellectual, environmental, social, and emotional needs of these students, RtI can be a helpful tool that reframes school and learning into positive experiences for these students.

Why RtI Might Not Be the Best Solution

Although there are professionals and researchers in the field who believe in the RtI approach, there are others who argue that RtI ignores the benefits of early identification for both high abilities and disabilities. They feel that these students will be best served when they have been identified and served prior to experiencing the failures that would bring them to a teacher's attention (and thus the RtI approach is called for). As the Gifted Development Center (n.d.), known for its work with gifted and twice-exceptional students, explained on its website:

> Many twice-exceptional students will not qualify for either RTI or an IEP if they perform at grade level. If they do, services are discontinued as soon as they reach a designated grade-level per-

formance criterion, instead of continuing services to ensure skills more commensurate with their ability. (para. 4)

It is possible for gifted students with disabilities to perform at grade level and, in some instances, earn high grades if the curriculum they encounter is too easy (Assouline & Whiteman, 2011). And, some 2e students may actually exceed grade-level expectations if they consistently put forth more time and effort or have more support than should be required for others without the challenges but at their intellectual level.

For this reason, identification remains tricky. Because of their extreme behaviors, twice-exceptional students with ADHD, ASD, and GAD may come to school (or be identified more quickly) with medical diagnoses that confer special services. More problematic are those 2e students who suffer from SLD, for they can blend into the regular classroom more easily.

The good news is that the reauthorization of IDEA in 2004 and 2008 allows students with advanced abilities to also be classified as learning disabled (National Center on Response to Intervention, 2010; Yell, Shriner, & Katsiyannis, 2006; Zirkel & Krohn, 2008). The new wording had major implications for 2e students. Before the advent of IDEA, school teams were required to present documentation of a discrepancy between a student's ability level and his or her achievement level to establish the presence of specific learning disabilities. Sometimes psychologists even looked for large differences between and among subtest scores of the WISC to document discrepancies.

Today, however, discrepancies are not a necessary piece of identifying students for services. Instead, policy indicates that informal identification and support should happen efficiently through the RtI process, as described earlier, using below grade- or age-level performance as the primary indicator of learning difficulties. This IDEA (2004) regulation is most often used by districts to identify an SLD:

> SLD refers to disorders in one or more of the basic psychological processes involved in understanding or using language, spoken or written, that may manifest itself in the imperfect ability to listen, think, speak, read, write, spell, or do mathematical calculations.

The regulation further elaborates on the criteria for establishing the presence of a learning disability:

> The child does not achieve adequately for the child's age or to meet State approved grade-level standards in one or more of the following areas, when provided with learning experiences and instruction appropriate for the child's age or state-approved grade-level

standards: oral expression, listening comprehension, written expression, basic reading skills, reading fluency skills, reading comprehension mathematics calculation, and mathematics problem solving.

Although this practice is helpful in identifying some students with learning disabilities, it can be problematic for students with both advanced cognitive abilities and learning disabilities. Focusing on age- and grade-level benchmarks for high-ability students will obstruct and delay appropriate identification and recommendations for services because they may be able to use their advanced abilities to achieve at grade level for years, by which time there will be much damage done and time lost.

To avoid this danger, we prefer to cite the regulation below as a more effective way to identify SLD among high-ability learners. This section of the regulation (IDEA, 2004) clearly states that a specific learning disability can be identified when:

> The child does not make **sufficient progress** to meet age or State-approved grade-level standards in one or more of the areas identified in 34 CFR 300.309(a)(1) when using a process that is based on the child's response to scientific, research-based intervention; or the child exhibits a pattern of strengths and weaknesses in performance, achievement, or both, **relative to** age, State-approved grade-level standards, or **intellectual development**, that is determined by the group to be relevant to the identification of a specific learning disability, using appropriate assessments, consistent with 34 CFR 300.304 and 300.305; and the group determines that its findings under 34 CFR 300.309(a)(1).

The law also states that students do not have to be failing or achieving below grade level to qualify for special education services. According to IDEA (2004), states must make a free appropriate public education (FAPE) available to any individual child with a disability who needs special education and related services, even if the child has not failed or been retained in a course or grade and is advancing from grade to grade. For this to happen, there needs to be a comprehensive psycho-educational evaluation from a qualified psychologist with a background in twice-exceptionality to make sure a student's needs are understood and addressed (Assouline & Whiteman, 2011; Gifted Development Center, n.d.). Such evaluations should include a test of intelligence, tests looking at cognitive processes and academic achievement levels, behavior scales, and social and emotional indices. A variety of assessments and observations of students in a variety of settings will help to pinpoint the salient issues, identify special education needs, and provide necessary data that meets the criteria stated in the law for services. The results from these assessments will also provide a composite of strengths and weaknesses that can help to formulate appropriate curriculum, instruction, accommodations, and remediation.

Collecting Evidence: Understanding the Problem

It is important to understand the particulars of why and where a gifted student is having learning or behavioral difficulties prior to putting interventions in place. Without full awareness of the student's neurological and emotional makeup, using a particular strategy may not have the desired effect.

Appropriate identification relies on a body of information that confirms initial hypotheses with data and observations. For example, looking at an intelligence test does not offer a useful snapshot unless we are sure there are no social or emotional issues depressing the scores. Some diagnoses require input from the medical community, while others rely on evaluations completed by certified psychologists. A survey of the most popular instruments currently used to identify 2e students is shown in Table 8.1—with results offering specific kinds of information that must be integrated into a final diagnosis. But, more importantly, these tests reveal patterns of strengths, weaknesses, and issues that are helpful in recommending special services. As explained in Part II of this book, considering information about where learning is breaking down, issues of anxiety, motivation, and executive functioning is critically important.

Once data are collected, it is critical to corroborate initial hypotheses with observations of the student in a variety of contexts. Using the guidebook for *Reflective RTI* (Appendix C) is one way to augment test data with qualitative support that can lead to appropriate diagnosis and recommendations.

Searching for Yellow: Challenges and Practices for the Identification of Gifts and Talents in Special Education Populations

How we recognize advanced potential in students whose abilities, gifts, and talents may be obscured because of an attention deficit, a specific learning ability, or social and behavioral issues can depend on the kind of giftedness or talent sought. There are distinct differences in how to look for schoolhouse giftedness, advanced abilities within a domain, and/or creative-productive giftedness. In all cases, however, it is imperative that flexible procedures are used to see the best in students. Finding traits indicative of high ability, giftedness, or creativity requires that we look for academic-based evidence, as well as evidence in activities outside of school. It is also vital to remember that signs of gifted potential may manifest in negative ways. For instance, clever excuses, preoccupation with a consuming interest, or incessant

Table 8.1
Instruments Helpful in Identification of ADHD, SPD, ASD, and More

Academic Achievement	Tests of Social and Emotional and Behavioral Functioning	Attention and Executive Functioning	Tests of Memory and Attention, and Learning	Psychological Processing: Auditory and Visual Motor
Woodcock-Johnson Test of Achievement IV	Conners Comprehensive Behavior Rating Scales (CBRS)	Conners Comprehensive Behavior Rating Scales (CBRS)	Behavior Rating Inventory of Executive Function (BRIEF)	Bender Visual-Motor Gestalt Test (2nd ed., Bender-Gestalt II)
Wechsler Individual Achievement Tests	Behavior Assessment System for Children (2nd ed., BASC-2): Parent Rating Scales (PRS) and Self-Report of Personality (SRP)	Behavior Rating Inventory of Executive Function (BRIEF)	Children's Auditory Verbal Learning Test-2 (CAVLT-2)	Beery-Buktenica Developmental Test of Visual Motor Integration (6th ed., BEERY VMI)
	Devereux Assessment Scales of Mental Disorders, Child Form	Children's Auditory Verbal Learning Test-2 (CAVLT-2)	Wechsler Intelligence Scale for Children (5th ed., WISC-V)	Rey Complex Figure Test and Recognition Trial (RCFT)
	Thematic Apperception Test (TAT)	Wechsler Intelligence Scale for Children (5th ed., WISC-V)		Children's Auditory Verbal Learning Test-2 (CAVLT-2)
	Three Wishes Inventory	Stroop Color and Word Test		
	Draw-a Person Test	Rey Complex Figure Test and Recognition Trial (RCFT)		

Table 8.1, continued.

Academic Achievement	Tests of Social and Emotional and Behavioral Functioning	Attention and Executive Functioning	Tests of Memory and Attention, and Learning	Psychological Processing: Auditory and Visual Motor
	Social Language Development Test	Delis Rating of Executive Function (D-Ref)		
	Adaptive Behavior Assessment System (3rd ed., ABAS-3)			
	Childhood Autism Rating Scales (2nd ed., CARS2), High Functioning Version Rating Booklet			
	Revised Children's Manifest Anxiety Scale (2nd ed., RCMAS-2)			
	Reynolds Children's Scale (2nd ed., RCDS-2)			
	Social Responsiveness Scale (2nd ed., SRS-2)			
	Vineland Adaptive Behavior Scales (2nd ed., Vineland-II)			

arguing might be viewed as irresponsible or avoidant behaviors rather than signs of creativity, high motivation, or debating prowess unless teachers are trained in how to look for and correctly interpret these behaviors.

We approach the process of identifying giftedness in two ways. The first, which we call *a priori identification*, entails collecting and analyzing test data and information from behavioral checklists and interviews about and with students. The second, which we refer to as *dynamic identification*, involves using activities purposely designed to elicit creative responses that signal possible areas of student interests and high abilities. Dynamic identification is akin to the authentic audition process used in athletics and the performing arts. The purpose of both approaches is to obtain convincing evidence of well-above-average aptitude, ability, and creativity.

A Priori Identification

Using IQ test scores. As we explained in Chapter 2, the work of Lewis Terman (1959; Terman & Oden, 1947) has guided the field of gifted education for many years. One of Terman's legacies has been a strong emphasis on intelligence testing as the basis for determining which students are gifted and which are not. Although this is still a dominant feature of many gifted education programs, the approach has come under considerable criticism in recent years because intelligence tests are fairly weak predictors of adult accomplishments. In other words, having a score in the superior range on an IQ test may forecast the *possibility* of significant accomplishment, but there is no real link with significant accomplishment. There are so many intellectually capable people who do little with their abilities and others with lower scores who, through sheer effort, overcome deficiencies that there is only a modest correlation between measured intelligence and accomplishment (Gardner, 1999; Kaufman, 2013; Sternberg, 1988). Nonetheless, performance results on an IQ test offer a carefully controlled sampling of a child's intellectual performance and can be a valuable starting point for predicting what a child might do in challenging situations.

Using a Full Scale IQ score, however, may underestimate the intellectual potential of some twice-exceptional students. For example, high scores in abstract tasks can be counterbalanced by low scores in other areas, such as processing speed or working memory. Because wide discrepancies between and among subtest and/or scale scores negatively impact the Full Scale IQ, it can be difficult for students to meet IQ cut-off criteria for gifted programs (often set at 125–130). Rather, analyzing index scores and subtest patterns can provide a far more accurate picture of a student's conceptual abilities.

For these reasons, we believe that IQ tests should not be the sole determinant of giftedness in children—the IQ cut point should not be set so high that other information becomes irrelevant, nor should the diagnostician become fixated on IQ information just because it might be the first or easiest information collected. We are concerned when we see state and district policies that require 2e students to qualify with the same scores as those without any special learning needs. Such guidelines will result in wasteful underdiagnosis of potential in students who show their aptitude in ways not measured on a traditional IQ test.

Interpreting the WISC. When putting together the clues found within WISC profile scores, it is most important to look for areas of distinct strengths that are logically connected, such as the indices scores on the WISC-IV and -V shown in the previous chapter. For example, Steve's scores on the Visual Spatial and Fluid Reasoning indices are as high as the 99th percentile, with three other subtests above the 90th percentile (see Table 7.6). All of them involved nonverbal information, possibly indicative of the abilities required for engineering and design. These scores would encourage a team to investigate Steve's abilities by looking at other performances where these abilities manifest—like complex building projects or contributions in robotics class. Or, perhaps, these abilities support high performance in math or visual arts. Looking at the kinds of in-depth interests the students have or their patterns of strength on a multiple intelligence assessment tool, for instance, can uncover the abilities hinted at through subtest analysis.

Let's be careful not to assume a student should be identified as gifted just because he or she is able to obtain superior scores on certain indices or subtests on an intelligence test. It is essential to use those scores as a starting point and to find other sources of evidence to support the presence of specific abilities or potential.

On the other hand, areas of weakness on subtests should not be used to negate the possibility of high potential in other areas. It is not unusual for twice-exceptional students to have subtest scores that are one or more standard deviations below the mean.

In our experience, typical patterns for the 2e child will include higher scores on the WISC indices of Verbal Comprehension, Visual Spatial, or Fluid Reasoning, all of which are indicative of reasoning and abstract thinking. The weaknesses will most likely show up in Working Memory or Processing Speed. Consider Steve's test pattern (Table 7.6). How high do test scores need to be to support evidence of high abilities? Within the indices revealing abstract thinking and reasoning, at least three scaled scores of 14 or above, with at least one score of 16 or above, provide reason to look further for evidence of aptitudes. This range meets Renzulli's (1978) criterion of showing distinctly above-average ability, while not putting the standard so high that students with strong motivation and unusual creative potential are automatically eliminated.

Checklists of gifted behaviors. Checklists can be very helpful in identifying specific abilities and in-depth interests. The *Scales for Rating the Behavioral Characteristics of Superior Students* (Renzulli et al., 2010) is an outstanding instrument. Supported by research, these scales are area specific and offer a way to isolate talent areas in students who show potential for advanced performance. The scales include the following areas and are completed by adults who would have knowledge about a student's potential strengths:

- learning characteristics,
- creativity characteristics,
- motivation characteristics,
- leadership characteristics,
- artistic characteristics,
- musical characteristics,
- dramatics characteristics,
- communication characteristics (precision),
- communication characteristics (expressiveness),
- planning characteristics,
- mathematics characteristics,
- reading characteristics,
- technology characteristics, and
- science characteristics.

Using a structured interview. Once above-average intellectual ability has been documented, you can collect information about task commitment, interests, and creativity.

A structured interview with adults who are well acquainted with the student is one way to get at the information. The interview format presented in Table 8.2 was adapted from items on *Scales for Rating the Behavioral Characteristics of Superior Students* (see Appendix E for a blank interview form). Questions are open-ended and can uncover ways in which students might use their abilities to survive in school.

This sample form is for Brad, a fifth-grade student whose WISC profile indicates high verbal abilities (95th percentile), slightly lower strengths in spatial areas (88th percentile), and other areas all below average. Brad had been identified as having a specific learning disability and was nominated to participate in an enrichment program designed for students with learning disabilities. The identification procedure included a structured interview with Brad's learning disability resource room teacher. It is apparent from the interview that Brad had learned a lot on his own, liked talking to adults, showed his creativity through the ways he avoided tasks, and had a fine sense of humor. Combining this information with his profile on the WISC does show a potential for developing gifted behaviors (see Table 8.3).

Once again, it is important to remember that characteristics can be interpreted as either positive or negative (promise or problem), depending on the experience and perspective of the viewpoint of the rater. For example, he argued with the teacher, showing great amounts of righteous indignation, as he defended why he hadn't completed his work. His dramatic flair along with his copious ridiculous reasons tended

Table 8.2
Sample Structured Interview

1.	Describe this child's interests. *History (Civil War and other wars)—does not read well, but learned a great deal of history. Sports.*
2.	Have you observed situations in which this child:
• becomes totally absorbed in a particular subject area? *History. He reads all books on history, biography and on various periods and eras. He spends time absorbed in these books. No school subject interests him as much. Science is another strong interest. Any verbal discussion absorbs him as long as he does not have to write anything down.*	**Yes** / No *(If yes, please explain.)*
• has discussed adult topics such as politics, religion, or current events? *Yes, all of them. Everything was a topic of discussion for him (for example, his father's college reunion). He is interested in all adult topics, enjoys discussing them with adults, and even asks adults about their own lives.*	**Yes** / No *(If yes, please explain.)*
• becomes self-assertive, stubborn, or aggressive. *Stubborn when he had to turn in a hard assignment. He had a lot of excuses and a lot of righteous-wounded indignation if you did not accept his excuses.*	**Yes** / No *(If yes, please explain.)*
• avoided tasks? *Ditto as above. Everything involved with his LD he would avoid. He had all sorts of excuses: his dog died, his mother took him out, etc. Very clever avoider (for things he found hard to do).*	**Yes** / No *(If yes, please explain.)*
• was particularly curious? *He has an inquisitive mind, questioned everything, and asked many times, "Why do you think such and such is so?"*	**Yes** / No *(If yes, please explain.)*
• was highly imaginative? *Yes. His written (or dictated to LD teacher) stories revealed his imagination. He would take these stories, then shorten them and put them on paper. They had complicated plots and many characters. He also wrote a play.*	**Yes** / No *(If yes, please explain.)*
• was humorous or seemed to be aware of nuances of humor? *A crooked smile. When you saw that smile, you knew he was getting the humor of the situation. Even his excuses were funny, and he said them with humor.*	**Yes** / No *(If yes, please explain.)*

Note. Adapted from *Scales for Rating the Behavioral Characteristics of Superior Students* (3rd ed., pp. 37–51), by J. S. Renzulli et al., 2010, Waco, TX: Prufrock Press. Copyright 2010 by Prufrock Press. Adapted with permission.

Table 8.3
Brad's Evidence of Gifted Behaviors

Well-above-average ability
- WISC profile—strengths in verbal areas 95th percentile; nonverbal 88th percentile
- Interest in adult topics
- Knowledge of history
- Inquisitive mind, incessant questioning
- Author of plays with complicated plots and many characters

Creativity
- Fluency of ideas—generated lots of excuses
- Clever task avoider indicating originality
- Inquisitive mind—incessant questioning
- Imaginative stories as shown in playwriting
- Sees humor in situations

Task commitment or motivation
- Passion for history—learned a great deal of history on his own
- Reads many books on history (notice that this student does not read well in a traditional sense but studies print materials of interest)
- Spends much time absorbed in books in interest area

to defuse the situation. This student had abilities in drama, problem solving, and people skills that could be developed as well as integrated into different units.

Dynamic Identification: Using Authentic Activities to Tap Potential

Dynamic identification involves engaging students in activities through which observers can notice potential, creativity, and high levels of motivation in students. Typically, we first define the kinds of abilities and talents being sought and then develop corresponding activities that will elicit particular behaviors. The students' responses to these open-ended, creative activities are excellent indicators of high abilities. Whole-group lessons, interest center activities, visitations, guest speakers, and exploratory activities present fine opportunities to recognize student enthusiasm, a passion for a topic, strengths, and possible talents. Critical, however, is the teacher's ability to notice the potential. Teachers must observe student behaviors during and after these experiences, noting problem-solving abilities, leadership, original ideas, in-depth questions, elaborate products, and a desire to do more, to go further, or to continue with the activity or specific topic even when others are done. Checklists to document behaviors as they occur can be far more dependable than trying to recall events at the end of a long day.

Using dynamic assessment to identify students for talent development programs within specific domains has proved to be highly effective (Baum, Cooper, Neu, & Owen, 1997; Baum, Owen, & Oreck, 1996; Delcourt, 1998). One example is the identification process used in Project High Hopes, the 3-year project designed to recognize and nurture talent in students with disabilities (described in Appendix A). The targeted students were from all over the diagnostic alphabet: LD, ADHD, ODD, severe emotional disorder (SED), pervasive development disorder (PDD), and hearing impaired (HI). To implement the grant, we developed the Talent Discovery Assessment Process (TDAP), a reliable and valid assessment tool to identify talent potential in the domains of visual and performing arts, physical and biological science, and engineering (Baum, Cooper, Neu, & Owen, 1995). We based this audition-oriented tool on evidence that the most accurate predictors of potential talent are observations of student behavior over time when they are engaged in authentic, domain-specific activities. Once identified, these students would participate in advanced activities within their talent domains.

We invited all fifth graders from the participating schools who were classified as having special needs according to federal guidelines to participate in the audition activities, which took place over the course of 3 months. A professional or content expert within each domain designed and administered the activities, and two observers tracked specific behaviors associated with the domain on corresponding observation sheets. We also encouraged observers to take notes on their observations (see Figure 8.1).

At the end of each session, the observers and specialist discussed their observations and rated the students with a simple 3-point scale. The scale indicated a student's readiness for more advanced development in that particular talent area. Figure 8.2 displays a student summary sheet with a list of the behaviors for each domain.

The identification activities are included in Appendix F. These dynamic identification activities described are examples of the creative options that open doors for these students. There can be activities created for any specific domain. For example, we have seen experimentation and inquiry activities to identify talent in math or the social sciences. It's essential to offer a variety of hands-on activities so any difficulties in reading or writing will not interfere with the child's performance.

In conclusion, identification should ideally include both a priori (WISC profile and structured interview) and ongoing, dynamic identification. *A priori identification* is frequently sufficient to document entry into a gifted program. However, when trying to understand specific abilities and areas in which these students are most comfortable, dynamic identification is especially useful. Dynamic identification is also well suited for identifying students who may not test well, along with students whose gifts are not easily measured by existing tests.

High Hopes: Talent Discovery Student Summary Sheet

Student: School: Site Code: Special Ed Setting:

Free/Reduced Lunch: Child ID: Disabling Condition: Ethnic Group:

Performing Arts

- Uses facial expressions
- Uses expressive voice.
- Uses body language
- Shows clear communication of intent.
- Creates elaborate movements, characters, or skits.
- Accepts and incorporates others feedback.

Visual Arts (2-D / 3-D Observer 1 2 1 2)

- Achieves balance in artwork.
- Uses form (dimensionally and design to produce the desired effect.
- Communicates intent clearly.
- Creates a unified design which relates parts to the whole and uses appropriate inclusion/exclusion ratio.
- Experiments with different ideas, materials, or techniques.
- Combines disparate parts to create a unique solution.
- Uses details to show complexity of ideas.
- Uses tools and materials effectively
- Accepts and incorporates others' feedback.
- Is able to talk about work.

Science (Bot Zoo Phy Observer 1 2 1 2 1 2)

- Displays curiosity by asking relevant questions.
- Shows a lot of knowledge related to today's topic.
- Actively manipulates materials.
- Communicates clearly the results of the project.
- Systemically tests hypothesis.
- Tries to predict outcomes.
- Represents ideas in the form of a model.
- Finds means of overcoming obstacles in problem-solving.

Engineering

- Actively manipulates materials.
- Tries to predict outcomes.
- Understands the main concepts of each lesson's topic.
- Creates a product which shows clarity of thought and focused plan of action.
- Puts materials together in a unique way.
- Explains the logic of alternative solutions.
- Shows problem-solving skill by pursuing an unprompted investigation.
- Observes patterns in experimentation.
- Finds means of overcoming obstacles in problem solving.

Holistic Ratings

Performing Arts			Visual Arts / 2-D			Visual Arts / 3-D			Science / Botany			Science / Zoology			Science / Physics			Engineering		
OB1	OB2	CS	OB1	OB2	CS	OB1	OB2	CS	OB1	OB2	CS	OB1	OB2	CS	OB1	OB2	CS	OB1	OB2	CS

Figure 8.1. Sample talent discovery summary sheet. *Note.* Project High Hopes is a Javits Act Program #R206R00001.

Notes on Talent Discovery

Directions: To further understand the individual student ratings recorded on the "Talent Discovery Checklist," please provide anecdotal information (comments, descriptions, examples) for each student. Comments regarding each student should be clearly identified by placing the student's name in the space provided to be followed by specific comments related to that student's ratings.

Student's Name: Darren • Very interested in specimens. Knows about caring for reptiles (friend has a snake). • Is not afraid of handling specimens. • Is very interested in the details of each specimen. • Does incredible drawings of specimens. • Has asked good questions but seems more interested in drawing. Keep an eye on him in 2-D and 3-D art.	**Student's Name:** Nathan • Has had very good questions about the Anolis. Wants to know where to buy them. Has detailed questions about the care and keeping of reptiles. • Is very careful when handling specimens. Turns specimens in containers and in his hands to get a desired angle for observation. • Clearly describes differences in skin between reptiles and amphibians. Then checked other specimens to make sure skin differences were the same. • Designs details habitat for maintaining specimens in the classroom. Very concerned about the moisture problem.

High Hopes

Student's Name: Sean • Asks questions about where the specimens are from and what they eat. • Does like to hold the animals and will hold specimens for other students to observe. Started to lose interest in other parts of the session.	**Student's Name:** Allison • Knows about local frogs. Has some confusion over the difference between lizards and salamanders. Asks how they are different, then checks it out by examining specimens. Knows what reptiles and amphibians are, just seems confused over salamanders having tails. • Knows that toads have poison glands. Asks if salamanders can be poisonous like poison arrow frogs. (Very good point.) • Devises way of folding notebook paper to keep salamander from walking off the edge of the desk while she is observing. Predicts why salamanders should not be handled for long periods.

Figure 8.2. Sample talent discovery note sheet. *Note.* Project High Hopes is a Javits Act Program #R206R00001.

CHAPTER 9

Elements of Strength-Based Plans for 2e Students

Programming for Green

Students who have a dual diagnosis—advanced abilities on the one hand and troubling learning challenges on the other—have unique needs made even more complex by the coincidence factor. Although such plans may vary in kind and intensity, they all must include opportunities that address the advanced abilities, interests, and talents while simultaneously offering support and strategies designed to address academic, behavioral, and social challenges.

Developing plans for 2e students requires a team of informed professionals and parents who identify the learning needs of the students and then begin the process of creating educational opportunities that will help students find success. Preferably, the team should have representatives from gifted education, special education, counseling, the classroom, and the family. When multiple perspectives are brought to the table, plans will have a higher probability of being effective. "Effectiveness" is not just how well the plan addresses specific learning objectives, but also how well it results in a student who wants to go to school, fits into the learning environment, and feels like a smart, contributing member of the community, with hope for the future.

The potential success of a student's plan can be estimated through how well it fulfills the five research-based factors outlined in Chapter 4 (psychologically safe environment, time, tolerance for asynchronous behaviors, positive relationships, and a strength-based, talent-focused environment). The five-factor basis for individual plans extends to school-based programs, as well. In fact, any educational environment can benefit from this approach.

Critical Factors Grounding Successful Program Development

When envisioning or agreeing on a plan of action for these students, the team members, including the family, should ask the following questions.

Does It Provide a Psychologically Safe Environment?

Many times these students are bullied, laughed at, and not included in the social milieu of the school. As we know from the work of Maslow and his hierarchy of needs (1958), learning begins when an environment is both physically and psychologically safe. Students need to experience feeling valued along with a sense of belonging before they are able to engage fully in the learning process.

We have found addressing these needs by finding and respecting what students *can* do, as well as engaging them in learning through their strengths, interests, and ability area, results in having them feel that they are contributing members of the learning community. "Green" students may feel like second-class citizens in school because what is asked for, admired, and rewarded most are the very tasks they find difficult. They view whatever successes they achieve as minimal because either they are taking advantage of accommodations or the teacher has watered down the curriculum in an attempt to meet the level of their disability. However, if teachers applaud, value, and make use of the many strengths students bring to the community (such as their abilities to troubleshoot computer software, create a winning science fair project, or build a three-dimensional model of working gears, etc.), these bright but challenged students will gain a sense of agency and pride. What opportunities like this are possible within the classroom or school environment? Will the student have access to them?

Does It Respect the Need for More Time?

Time in this context is considered in two ways: long-term growth and time to process, transition, and produce. First, because executive functioning and social-emotional awareness can lag up to 2 years or more when compared to their age-mates, time must be variable and relative to students' profiles of strengths and weaknesses. Why adhere to traditional timelines for course completion or even the number of years it might require for some students to complete elementary, middle, high school, or college? For many, completing high school in 5 years instead of the traditional 4 years could not only allow them to mature over that timespan, but also would reduce their course load to be more manageable by distributing the number of course requirements over more time. Likewise, taking a gap year between high school and post secondary is highly beneficial, especially if the experiences during that gap year help these students gain independence and develop confidence. Another way to look at time is more immediate. Time can relate to how long it takes these students to transition between classes (or from activity to activity), and to adjust to anything new, such as a different teacher or a new experience (even if it's going to be fun). In addition, it frequently takes 2e students extra time to process information and produce work, as described in Chapter 5. In these cases, students might need extended time to complete assignments or take tests. Are there conversations about time embedded in the plan, both for accommodations and productivity? Have the team and family looked at ideas such as a 5-year plan for high school or a gap year?

Does It Take into Account the Asynchronous Development of 2e Students?

Tolerance for asynchrony requires adults to put aside their assumptions that students can act in ways that correspond to their advanced intellectual abilities or even their age. Just because they speak like an adult does not mean they are socially or emotionally mature. The uneven development of these students across their cognitive, social, emotional, and physical domains affects how performance should be measured. Students should not be evaluated on the degree to which their performance is commensurate with grade-level benchmarks, but rather if their work shows growth. Suppose a student is developmentally advanced or delayed in a particular area. It is important to ask, then, how will this student's work be measured and is their asynchrony considered? Adopting a growth model to track development, comparing students to themselves—how much change occurs within the student in particular areas within specific time frames—is more indicative of progress. Again, for some students, the development of reading prowess or organizational skills may simply take more time. Are educators familiar with the concept of asynchronous development? How do curricular demands and expectations take into account uneven development?

Does It Foster Opportunities to Forge Positive Relationships?

Does the plan include meaningful ways for students to work and play together? This relates to a previous point, for positive relationships help in building a psychologically safe environment. Interest groups, both within and outside of the curriculum, are powerful, authentic opportunities for youngsters to identify and bond with each other. Encourage multiage groupings and opportunities where students collaborate around common interests, goals, or intellectual abilities. Working together around these commonalities builds relationships and social awareness.

Caring, attuned adults within the school environment also make a positive difference in the lives of 2e students. These teachers, mentors, advisors, gardeners, secretaries, custodians, and bus drivers forge positive relationships with 2e students by understanding them, believing in their abilities, and, not only holding high expectations for these students' future success, but also noticing and greeting them with joy. Such adults connect to these students by conversing about their favorite teams, sharing information about a favorite recipe, recommending a movie or recent book that they believe a student would enjoy, or even quickly showing a photo they took of something that reminded them of a student's interest area. These little connections aren't involved or time-consuming, but remind the student that he or she is not invisible.

Does the plan incorporate opportunities to foster such relationships between a caring adult at school, such as a counselor, mentor, or teacher, especially in an area of talent or shared interest?

Does It Incorporate a Strength-Based, Talent-Focused Philosophy?

As we explained earlier, focusing on students' strengths, interests, and talents not only helps them to succeed in their academics but also contributes to their positive sense of self. Opportunities for all students to develop in strength and interest areas promote a positive learning environment where students are intrinsically motivated and often engage in problem solving and creative productivity (Renzulli & Reis, 2014). Commitment to this approach led to our development of a model for 2e students where talent recognition and development is the center component. We believe that students deserve to have their strengths, interests, and talents developed in their own right. Understanding the basis for these strengths and interests can inform educators of creative and enticing ways to engage students in better understandings, production, and skill development. Does the plan include opportunities to collect information about students' strengths, interest, and talents? To what degree does this knowledge inform strategies for learning? Finally, is there a plan for developing a student's talents and interests?

Necessary Components for Comprehensive Plans

Programming for 2e students requires much flexibility, a philosophy based on the tenets of positive psychology, and learning environments that recognize the intellectual, physical, social, and emotional needs of these highly asynchronous youngsters. As described in earlier editions of this book, such plans included:

- talent development—attention to students' gifts and talents;
- challenging curriculum;
- differentiated instruction and compensation strategies including accommodations;
- social-emotional support; and
- targeted remediation where warranted.

The importance of these components were confirmed by Reis et al. (2014) in their article operationalizing the definition of twice-exceptionality:

> Educational services must identify and serve both the high achievement potential and the academic and social-emotional deficits of this population of students. Twice-exceptional students require differentiated instruction, curricular and instructional accommodations and/or modifications, direct services, specialized instruction, acceleration options, and opportunities for talent development that incorporate the effects of their dual diagnosis.
>
> Twice-exceptional students require an individual education plan (IEP) or a 504 accommodation plan with goals and strategies that enable them to achieve at a level and rate commensurate with their abilities. This comprehensive education plan must include talent development goals, as well as compensation skills and strategies to address their disabilities and their social and emotional needs. (p. 223)

Baldwin, Baum, Perles, and Hughes (2015) added that plans for twice-exceptional learners should include "enriched/advanced educational opportunities that develop the child's interests, gifts, and talents meeting the child's learning needs" and "simultaneous supports, accommodations, therapeutic interventions, and specialized instruction" (p. 213).

Researchers and practitioners in the fields of gifted education and special education—all of whom worked with and supported 2e students—endorsed both of these definitions.

In 2009, it became obvious that these components were not just a list of discrete, unrelated components, but rather their success was dependent upon an interaction beginning with recognizing and developing students' strengths, interests, and talents. Understanding how students learn when engaged meaningfully in their talent or interest areas could influence how to design and implement the other components. In fact, we feel that talent recognition and development is a non-negotiable for 2e students. Because even a mere mention of developing talent is not included anywhere in the IEP or 504 plan process, we created the Talent Centered Model for Twice-Exceptional Learners. It has become a practical and thoughtful way to structure plans for 2e youngsters.

The Talent Centered Model for Twice-Exceptional Students

This model is best described through metaphor. It is an integrated system with its elements interacting with each other much like the solar system. As shown in

Figure 9.1, the model's center sun is talent recognition and development, which fuels the system.

The other five elements in the model spin from and revolve around talent development. Talent development keeps the other elements linked to the light within these students. Because they are bright and have specific interests and abilities, they require talent development and intellectual engagement much like their gifted peers. But because their abilities are compromised by deficits in learning and attention, these students also require differentiated instruction including modifications of the physical environment, accommodations, and targeted remediation in order to achieve. Finally, because of the discrepancy between their strengths and weaknesses, 2e students profit from social-emotional support. Over the years, we have watched students evolve and even flourish when IEPs or other plans address the full range of these needs (the six components).

The Talent Centered Model places talent development and recognition at its center with all other elements circling around it. Without the sun, the solar system would not function at all. Likewise for the role talent development plays within this model. Talent recognition and development opportunities are responsible for energizing the students. All of the elements of the model are working together when students are engaged in areas of interest and talent (such as drama, building, robotics, drawing, music, debate, working with animals, etc.). In those environments, students are stimulated with intellectually engaging curriculum and working in an appropriate physical environment with opportunities for socialization and self-discovery. Differentiation and accommodations are naturally in place because students are in their element. In these times and places, students can feel authentic "giftedness"—showing initiative, striving for high-quality work, and sensing how learning should be. Talent development sets the stage for students to work hard in spite of their weaknesses . . . because they want to. Observing students while they are involved in an area of interest offers clues to working with them in other settings, including the regular classroom.

Several years ago, Susan had the good fortune of meeting the teenager, Melanie, whose story illustrates how the model's elements work together to provide a culture of achievement.

Melanie

The art room was filled with a collection of student displays, all interesting and indicative of budding talent. As I glanced, about I was suddenly drawn to a very unusual piece of art—an old door that had been used as an inviting canvas for creative artistic expression. The art teacher said that many students had taken their turn at transforming this door into a powerful piece of art, but none were so accomplished as this piece. Asking more about the artist, Melanie, I learned

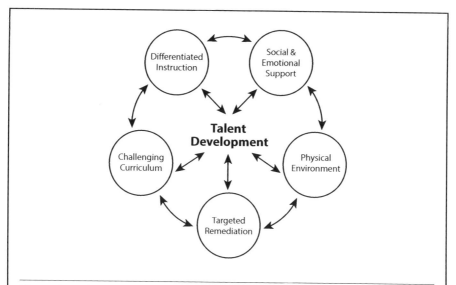

Figure 9.1. Talent Centered Model for twice-exceptional students. From "Talent Centered Model for Twice-Exceptional Students" by S. M. Baum, in *Systems and Models for Developing Programs for the Gifted* (2nd ed., p. 24), by J. S. Renzulli, E. J. Gubbins, K. S. McMillen, R. D. Eckert, and C. A. Little (Eds.), 2009, Waco, TX: Prufrock Press. Copyright 2009 by Prufrock Press. Reprinted with permission.

that she was severely dyslexic. But, the art teacher revealed, Melanie was doing well in school because of the support she received from her mother, friends, and teachers. My interest was now sparked, so I took the time to interview some of her teachers, the learning specialist, and Melanie herself. Interestingly, all of their stories combined turned out to paint a picture of the model at work. The account of Melanie's academic journey captures the essence of what can be accomplished when professionals collaborate to educate the whole child through talent development, classroom modifications, and differentiated instruction—all influenced by a talent development approach.

Melanie had entered this school in the third grade. Prior to this, she had attended a school where no one seemed to see her problems, talents, or unique academic needs even though she had been diagnosed with dyslexia and was having extreme difficulty learning. Melanie described a particular incident:

> I had been absent the previous day when the other second graders wrote their poems. The teacher said I was to write mine that day about spring. I had no idea what to do. The only thing I could think of was to copy the first line of everyone else's poem and turn it in. My teacher loved the poem. I got an A, and she never realized what I had done. I could not even read the words I had copied. The A only made me unhappier about school. No one knew I couldn't read, and I was too ashamed to confess.

Her parents, sensitive to her anguish and lack of genuine accomplishment, enrolled Melanie in her current school. Two things happened—the school emphasized art and students took art classes several times each week, which is how she discovered her interest in and talent for art. In her other classes, she received help from the learning support team. Because of this, she felt valued in the school setting for the first time. Melanie's mother read to her and became her scribe so she didn't fall too far behind in her school assignments. Reading came slowly and writing was painful. But, little by little, she began to read and write, although still with difficulty. By the time she entered high school, she knew how to work hard and could advocate for what she needed from the environment in order to be successful.

Her lack of reading and writing skills had not kept her from being successful within the curriculum because the teachers in the school frequently integrated art projects into their classrooms. For example, the language arts teachers offered art activities to all students in every literature unit. On one occasion, after reading Joseph Conrad's *Heart of Darkness*, the students chose from a variety of projects, including creating a mural that illustrated the characters' attributes. The students were required to justify their visual depictions of the characters—including color and facial expression—with relevant text from the book. Melanie opted to work with the mural group. She told me that her group's lively discussions during the planning process gave her much deeper insight into what she had read. As she explained, "I knew there would be a question on this novel [on the final exam]. When I read the question, I just closed my eyes and visualized the mural, and the words just came!"

Melanie, her teachers, and her learning specialist collaborated to develop modifications for assignments that required writing. One such modification allowed Melanie to use her artistic abilities to express her understandings of targeted concepts. For example, instead of the required English class essay, Melanie was able to produce intricate mind maps showing abstract and mature insights about characters and plot development. An illustration of her drafts and final piece appear in Figure 9.2.

On some occasions, however, Melanie decided to write the regularly assigned essay and declined the offered accommodations. During those times, she worked with the learning specialist, who would help her to organize her ideas into a thoughtful written piece. Using the computer program Inspiration, which uses mapping as a prewriting exercise, Melanie was able to transfer her visual ideas to the computer. Spelling and grammar checks on her computer helped her turn in well-written assignments.

Melanie was not always as confident as she is today. Looking back, she attributed her ever-increasing sense of efficacy to her art experiences:

> Art is more than a talent. It is my therapy. I know my friends respect me and admire my talents. But I often turn to my art when I am stressed. Through my art I can explain who I am and how I feel. Art is where I

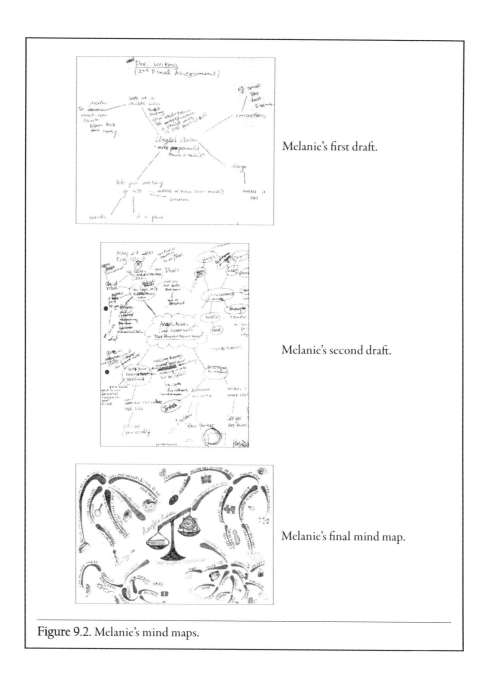

Melanie's first draft.

Melanie's second draft.

Melanie's final mind map.

Figure 9.2. Melanie's mind maps.

am most likely to reveal and represent, often metaphorically, the pain, anguish, and isolation I often feel. My painting of the green chair in the red room, displayed in the art room, reveals my anguish at not fitting in. The green chair almost clashes in this setting. That's how I can feel at times. That's what being different is all about. (personal communication, January 23, 2003)

Melanie hid the fact that she had difficulty reading from her peers until she was in ninth grade. The accepting atmosphere at this school made her feel safe enough to tell her friends that she was dyslexic. Since explaining her problem, her friends have become another set of supporters. They take notes for her and help talk through difficult reading material. It is not a one-way street, however. Melanie remarked,

I could not accept help from them if I could not reciprocate. I help my friends see the bigger picture. They often count on me to give them a structure for their writing. We bounce ideas off each other, and they know I will give them different points of view.

The Model in Action

Melanie's story brings the elements of the model to life and shows how they work in concert. Once Melanie's talent in art was engaged, it positively influenced her school success academically, emotionally, and respectfully. Art class provided her with an identity, a "therapy," and an opportunity to be herself (social-emotional needs). Frequent art classes nurtured her art skills, leading to an award-winning piece (talent development). Melanie was enrolled in the school's International Baccalaureate program, offering her the intellectual engagement commensurate with her abilities (intellectual engagement). Because the teachers used student strengths to differentiate instruction, Melanie was able to be overcome her learning difficulties and achieve success (strength-based differentiation plus accommodation). Furthermore, learning support helped Melanie understand how to compensate for weaknesses and provided appropriate remediation, as necessary (targeted remediation).

Using the model as a guide can foster collaboration among professionals as they design plans for their 2e students. In Melanie's case, her classroom teachers and special educators were not only informed of her potential by the art specialist, but they also then helped the art specialist understand Melanie's angst. As a team, they could teach the "whole child." This story points out a need to deliver curriculum to students in ways that honor their intelligence and, in doing that, offer other windows of opportunities for success. Melanie's teachers found ways to optimize her strengths in delivering the curriculum while also supporting her in areas of weakness. Again, Melanie's story is not unique.

Least Restrictive Environment, Individual Educational Plans, and 504 Plans

The special education law is very explicit about making sure the student is in the least restrictive environment—usually meaning one most like his or her age-mates' that can allow him or her to find success. The RtI model encourages serving students within the regular classroom as promoted by an inclusion model. Twice-exceptional students *can* succeed in the regular classroom when the teacher offers differentiated strategies for all students and provides a range of options for accessing information and communicating learning. They will fare even better if there are opportunities for talent development along with resource room support. Many of these students benefit from time with others with similar learning characteristics. The talent development environment (including advanced classes) will provide the challenge and peer group needed to engage the mind of the 2e student if the program addresses individual students' interests and ability areas, rather than adding additional content through "enrichment units." Likewise the resource room can be a safe haven where the 2e learner can explore dealing with deficits and learning challenges with other students who have similar issues. The resource room teacher can offer both emotional and academic support. In the best of all worlds, the school can offer a special program for 2e students that provides both talent development and academic support. We will describe these in greater depth later.

As explained in Chapter 8's RtI section, there may be circumstances in which 2e students require a different setting with more intensive services. For example, when students are reading considerably below grade level, cannot put ideas in writing, are highly anxious, or require settings with fewer students, it is doubtful that there can be success in the regular classroom. The need for a specialized setting becomes more likely as students get older and/or reading and writing dominate the academic setting. Particularly troublesome is the sensitivity and shame 2e students feel about their learning disabilities, which prompts them to hide or try to deny their differences when in a mainstream classroom. In addition, they may be unwilling to accept an accommodation if they feel that accepting it makes them look stupid, disabled, or just different in the eyes of their peers. One bright high school student explained,

> I dread walking into the classroom to get my test so that I can complete it in the resource room. I wish the teacher would just give the test to my resource room teacher so no attention would be drawn to me.

If these high-ability youngsters are intellectually more capable than most of their classmates, they will have even more difficulties fitting in and finding success. Under these conditions, behavior problems can arise, as in the case of Blaine (Chapter 7), where more time in a program for highly able students would have made a difference.

Some students simply need a smaller class size so they feel comfortable asking questions and actively engaging in the curriculum. Others may elect to take online courses where the challenge, pace, and environment can be more easily controlled. Several districts have self-contained programs for those gifted students with severe learning challenges—where students don't feel different. The need for school environments that are sensitive to 2e students is increasing, as noted by the growing numbers of private schools that welcome 2e students. These independent schools offer unique programs that pay attention to students' abilities and interests, as well as offer specialized instruction and necessary compensation techniques.

For a twice-exceptional student, finding successful learning options often requires either an Individual Education Plan (IEP; IDEA, 2004) or a 504 plan (Rehabilitation Act, 1973). The major difference between the two is that the IEP comes along with a special education label or diagnosis. The 504 plan is a more flexible and less complex process that pertains to students who have special needs that hinder their progress in the classroom, but who do not meet the stringent requirements of special education. Modifications under the 504 plan can include any number of strategies to help the student succeed, including extra time for classwork or tests, having test questions read aloud, and being given shorter assignments than other students. Typically, students with ADHD are served with a 504 plan.

Both of these plans focus on weaknesses, as they are designed to bring a student up to grade level. Rarely is there any recommendation for integrating enrichment or talent development opportunities. Even though IDEA does say that gifted students can have learning disabilities, there is no federal mandate to provide services for gifted students and no place on the forms to include enrichment or advanced services in obvious ways. Some districts may allow wording or recommendations as found in Column 3 of Table 9.1.

The educational therapist at Bridges Academy, a school for 2e students, designed a format for planning that aligns to the types of information we describe as necessary. Teachers refer to this plan as they create learning environments that address a student's ability areas *and* challenges—both within the regular curriculum—as well as enrichment and talent development opportunities, along with outside support for social-emotional or learning needs. Note that this plan is very specific about including the strengths, interests, and high abilities, *and* the learning difficulties. Going back to the metaphor with which we opened this book, there are examples in this plan to show how the "yellow" and "blue" inform programming for "green."

Table 9.1
Completing an IEP to Address the Needs of a 2e Learner

The IEP Contains . . .	Completing an IEP With Special Education Language	Including Necessary Language for 2e Learners
A statement of the student's present levels of academic achievement and functional performance.	The academic levels are listed only in terms of grade-level performance and level of independence. These are usually skill oriented. For example, what are a child's reading or math skills?	Also include areas of advanced abilities and how they can impact learning and focus in the regular classroom (i.e., skills already mastered can result in poor attention). Include a summary of the student's strengths and challenges so both will be integrated into the plan.
Specific goals for weak areas along with suggested strategies and timelines for growth.	What strategies are needed to bring the skills to grade level, and what is the projected time?	Expand goals to address the student's advanced areas. Choose research-based strategies from gifted education, such as acceleration and/or curriculum compacting.
Accommodations[1] and modifications[2] to help students succeed in the regular curriculum.	Examples of accommodations may include additional time to complete assignments, notes or outlines being provided, untimed tests, and reduced numbers of test questions. Examples of modifications include use of alternate books, pass/no pass option, reworded questions in simpler language, daily feedback to student.	IEP accommodations are listed as stated because they deal with the student's areas of weakness; however, they should be designed around issues unique to the 2e learner. Accommodations must be allowed in any advanced program for which the student qualifies. The student is entitled to use accommodations in advanced classes (Reis et al., 2014). Modifications for advanced abilities can include additional options, such as independent study or using advanced resources. It is important to introduce the idea of dual differentiation so that any specialized instruction simultaneously considers the student's high abilities with the challenges.

Table 9.1, continued.

The IEP Contains . . .	Completing an IEP With Special Education Language	Including Necessary Language for 2e Learners
When alternate assessments are used or aligned to alternate achievement standards, a description of the benchmarks or short-term objectives must be listed.	List the type of learning benchmarks. For example, having a test read out loud to a student with dyslexia to measure comprehension and understanding in a content area.	Make sure the benchmarks and standards are suitably advanced and include alternate achievement options such as less emphasis on writing (yet with intellectually engaging content).
A description of how annual growth will be measured as required by 34 CFR 300.320(a)(2).	Must include description of progress reports and timeline.	In addition to progress towards grade-level standards, growth should also be described in terms of progress in areas of strength and interest—not just areas of challenge. Also include qualitative information of circumstances in which the student is at his or her best.
A statement of the special education and related services, supplementary aids and services, based on peer-reviewed research to the extent practicable, to be provided to the student, or on behalf of the student (such as an advocate).	List all services, like speech and language therapy or social skills classes.	The statement should include talent development opportunities and dual differentiation to modify the curriculum and outside support for academic, behavioral, or emotional issues. The law requires that scheduling cannot present conflicts that require that a student choose between remedial services and advanced academic programs. Qualified 2e students must be given the same opportunities to compete for and benefit from accelerated programs and classes as are given to students without learning disabilities.

1 Kessler and Schneider (n.d.) defined accommodations as allowing students to "complete the same tasks as their typical peers but with some variation in time, format, setting, and/or presentation" (para. 2). These can be categorized into four variations: (1) time (e.g., allowing more time for tests/assignments); (2) input (e.g., changing instruction methods); (3) output (e.g., how a student can complete an assignment); and (4) size (e.g., how much a student needs to complete).

2 Modifications are alterations to "instructional level, content or performance criteria" on "any given assignment," or "changes in what students are expected to learn, based on their individual abilities" (Kessler & Schneider, n.d., para. 5). It might be that 2e students need modifications in assignments as opposed to accommodations. It is important to note the difference. Modifications would allow for acceleration, alternative levels of resources (higher, not simpler). As stated in Column 2, the modifications make the assignments less complex and perhaps at lower levels. There is no reason that the modification can't be tiered upward along with the accommodations. Using these two possibilities together can allow dual differentiation.

Table 9.2 is a fine example of how recognizing abilities and interests informs the elements of the plan—intellectually engaging curriculum, differentiation, physical environment, targeted remediation, accommodations and modifications, and social-emotional considerations. It is just one way to design a strength-based environment where the elements of the model can be included. Throughout the next several chapters, we will introduce strategies and provide additional tools that should be helpful in planning, implementing, and monitoring personalized plan for these students.

Table 9.2

Educational Plan for Mike

Student	Grade	Advisor
Michael	9	Mary

Areas of Interest	Possibilities for Talent Development
Reading—varied genres AYSO Soccer Weights Baseball Football Stock market **Product Choices:** Stories, discussion, building, business, painting, computer, performing, role playing **Multiple Intelligences Strengths:** Linguistic Logical/Mathematical Bodily Kinesthetic Intrapersonal	Debating team Drama electives and auditions for performances Scouts Stock Market Club Entrepreneur Enrichment Cluster Robotics Club and Robotics competition Sport teams

Social-Emotional Needs—meeting with parents, psychologists, teacher and administrator: Goal: Issues and recommendations for next 2 months

Mike is starting to leave the classroom at will, which has been observed in the past. It was less of an issue in classes in which he was comfortable and engaged but now this pattern is returning. When he is out of class, he is missing necessary teaching and work, which then seems to add to his resistance about being in class.
 	
    Now that he is transitioning from Middle School to High School, he is again having a hard time adjusting to the workload. He will meet with the educational therapist and learning support teacher to receive more support considering his developmental lags in executive functioning and emotional self-regulation.
 	
    Mike has a rule-based approach, yet the rules he has made seem arbitrary. When he discusses his observations of what he needs to be flexible at school, it doesn't mean that his 'demands' can always be met. He has yet to develop his ability to flexibly problem solve an approach.

Actions to Take: It is recommended that Mike resume sessions with his therapist, about what it means to be a high school student and how his rules and the school's rules can be interwoven. Engage in areas of high interest, creativity, and motivation. During these opportunities there will be a focus on executive functioning skills and social skills.

Table 9.2, continued.

Dual Differentiation/Instructional Strategies	
Critical Variables to be Addressed	**Critical Responses to be Considered**
Areas Of Strength, Interest, And Ability • Advanced verbal abilities • Knowledgeable in politics, humanities, economics-high interest in many real world topics • Debating talent • High interest in entrepreneurial activities • Creative thinker	**Talent Development** • Participation in one or more of the enrichment and talent development opportunities described above. **Dual Differentiated** • Instruction aligned with strengths, interests, and abilities **Content:** At the level of cognitive ability • Oral discussions, opinion groups, informal debates within the classroom content • Oral analysis and synthesis **Process:** • Thoughtful questioning of guest speakers at school and offsite on field trips. **Product:** • Debates, editorials **Physical Environment:** • Opportunity to walk around, independent study options
Learning Issues • Lack of productivity, especially when asked to write • Short attention span • Cognitive rigidity • Lack of pragmatic social skills	**Dual Differentiated For Areas In Need Of Support** **Content:** Give choice for topic and resources to gain more information. **Process** *Attention:* • Make sure content is novel and complex • Given his high verbal abilities, ask Mike to verbalize his plan for next steps and how he'll know it's working. • Provide items to discuss in advance of the discussion so he is prepared

Table 9.2, continued.

Dual Differentiation/Instructional Strategies	
Critical Variables to be Addressed	**Critical Responses to be Considered**
Learning Issues, *continued.*	*Cognitive Rigidity (use abilities in logical, analytic thinking)* • During classroom discussions have students defend the opposite positions. • Use moral dilemma activities. • Use film clip analysis to talk about characters who are stubborn and how that trait compromised their goals and development *Dysgraphia:* • Dictation • Use of voice to text technology • Use apps to encourage writing such as Live Stream, Animoto, and Voki *Social:* • Support success in his enrichment cluster in Entrepreneurial Adventures. • Provide structure for small group work • Set firm expectations for pragmatic skills • Support Mike to disengage from arguments that have previously ended **Product—Time Management** • Allow choice. • Provide a management plan and backward planning for time management skills. • His ADHD profile would respond well to chunking parts of project and setting short term deadlines. • Provide for daily check-ins. **Environment** • Use his love of reading to give him time to refocus and have down time. Find a quiet place for him to read—preferably bean bag chair or rocking chair. • Provide a place to rest in class and outside of class, as needed • Allow one short break • Allow snacks

Note. Developed by Marcy Dann, M.A., BCET, 2011. Reprinted with permission of the author.

CHAPTER 10

Talent Recognition and Development

> Neglected or suppressed strengths are like infections
> under the skin; eventually they cause serious damage.
> (Levine, 2002, p. 300)

Particularly poignant for gifted students with learning, attention, or behavior difficulties, Levine's comment strongly reminds us of how essential it is to provide ways for 2e students to develop their abilities, for too often the ways they shine are unrecognized, seen but ignored, put on hold, or irksome because they are in the wrong content areas for conventional school achievement. Such negative reactions from others compromise students' motivation, academic self-efficacy, and self-esteem, and thereby inhibit their growth and chances for success.

We continue to argue that the key to 2e students' success is found in their strengths, interests, and talents. Indeed, the Talent Centered Model (Baum, 2009) calls first for the recognition of talent along with a deliberate plan for its development. In order to accomplish this, plans and programs for these students must collect information about strengths, curiosities, interests, and talents. We have discussed intellectual strengths as indicated by intelligence tests such as the WISC, learning strengths as they come to light on other instruments, and academic achievement through grades, products, and other measures. Although this information is useful, it paints only a partial picture in helping us really open up a discussion of interests, passions, abilities, and talents. Any program for these students must include information about the types of activities they like, how they like to spend their time, their hobbies, and what they feel they are good at doing. We began to explore these traits in Chapter 6 with information about student profiles of multiple intelligences and personality preferences. Many tools are available to gather this information. Some of our favorites are listed in Table 10.1.

As shown in Chapters 8 and 9, this information is vital in creating useful RtI and IEP plans. We have learned that allowing time and space for students to grow in preferred areas promotes growth across all domains.

A Rationale for Talent Development

Bryan's story, below, illustrates how developing something he was interested in offered a window into where he was having difficulties. Importantly, without focused attention on his abilities, Bryan probably would have been placed in a highly restrictive environment for students with social-emotional disorders.

Bryan

Bryan had done well during his elementary school years. He showed particular ability and interest in the areas of language arts and music, but only managed to squeak by in the areas of math and science. When he entered sixth grade (middle school), Bryan's performance, even in language and music, deteriorated. He seemed to lose all ability to focus on tasks. He became disorganized, failed to complete most assignments, and showed a variety of attention-seeking behaviors. His grades dropped from A's and B's to B's and C's. His teachers were concerned with his downward trajectory and finally referred him for testing, suspecting that he had some sort of learning disability or attention deficit.

In the fall of seventh grade, a comprehensive psychoeducational evaluation revealed that Bryan was highly intelligent, but there were also areas of concern. His scores on the WISC hit the 99th percentile on the verbal scale, but only the 40th percentile on the performance scale. On the Woodcock Johnson Cognitive and Ability Test, Bryan was at the 99th percentile for overall cognitive ability. His weaknesses were in motor and perceptual speed (74th percentile) and math (26th percentile). Despite these discrepancies and his behavior problems, the pupil personnel team did not feel that Bryan had a learning disability or attention deficit. They also felt that his profile did not indicate a need for direct services. Deciding that his behaviors were more symptomatic of behavioral problems, they classified him as having emotional or behavioral disorder (EBD). Bryan and his teachers were to establish behavior contracts with weekly monitoring by his parents.

Table 10.1

Tools for Collecting Information on Strengths, Interests, Learning Styles, and More

Tool	Purpose	Publisher
Starring Me A. Cuthbert	Interests and learning preferences for primary-aged students.	Center for Talent Development (https://drive.google.com/file/d/0B6rNasUAfT1dd1Rqb05FaGhOQkE/view)
My Learning Print™ R. Schader and W. Zhou	Information about students' strengths, interests, talents, learning styles, and experiences.	The 2e Center for Research and Professional Development Bridges Academy, 3921 Laurel Canyon, Studio City, CA 91604
My Way K. E. Kettle, J. S. Renzulli, and M. G. Rizza	Information about expression styles—preferences for products and projects.	The Renzulli Center for Creativity, Gifted Education, and Talent Development University of Connecticut, Storrs, CT (http://gifted.uconn.edu/wp-content/uploads/sites/961/2015/10/myway.pdf)
The Quick Personality Inventory™ (QPI) S. Baum and H. Nicols	Personality preferences (adult and student versions).	The 2e Center for Research and Professional Development Bridges Academy, 3921 Laurel Canyon, Studio City, CA 91604
Multiple Intelligences Self-Assessment Edutopia	An online tool to look at students' profiles of strengths and weaknesses in terms of multiple intelligences (Gardner, 2000).	Edutopia (https://www.edutopia.org/multiple-intelligences-assessment)
Things My Child Likes to Do J. Renzulli and S. Reis	Parent survey about activities children pursue at home that includes hobbies, clubs, and pastimes.	The Renzulli Center for Creativity, Gifted Education, and Talent Development University of Connecticut, Storrs, CT (http://gifted.uconn.edu/wp-content/uploads/sites/961/2015/02/things_like_to_do.pdf)

Throughout that year, Bryan continued to show attention problems and immaturity. His teachers reported that he was "inattentive, restless, impulsive, lacked perseverance and had trouble following directions." They complained that he did not "exert sufficient effort" in his studies and often handed in work late, if at all. He was frequently in trouble, especially on the school playground. His academic performance slid into the C/C- range in most subjects. Although his parents reported that their weekly monitoring efforts might have had some effect, they voiced a growing concern that Bryan seemed unmotivated and had little self-control. They feared that his underachievement would restrict possibilities for future academic possibilities.

Talent development opportunity. Serendipitously, during Bryan's eighth-grade year, the teacher of the gifted happened to be participating in a study measuring underachievement in high-ability students. She asked her colleagues to nominate students who were achieving below their potential as measured by scores on tests of intelligence or cognitive ability (IQ in the superior range or above). Bryan's profile met the criteria perfectly, and he was invited to participate in the program. The goal of the research study was for the teacher to collect information about the student's strengths, interests, and talents, and then work with that student to design and implement an investigation he was excited to undertake.

The intervention was based on Type III Enrichment[6] from the Enrichment Triad Model (Renzulli, 1976).

The process. Bryan initially met with the enrichment specialist two periods a week to work on his project. At their first meeting, Bryan complained about his social studies curriculum. His eighth-grade class was pursuing a mock trial that Bryan found "hokey and frustrating." He argued that he could write a better court case for the eighth-grade courtroom simulation:

> I don't like the old one. It's got some stupid character named Candy Cane in it, and I think I could do a better job. My friend and I already have some ideas for the case. Can we work together?

Although his friend soon lost interest, Bryan stayed committed to the task and decided to continue the project on his own even though it seemed overwhelming.

Bryan and the enrichment teacher brokered a management plan that both agreed would serve as the organizational framework for the project. First, they defined the problem at hand (the inappropriate law simulation), the projected solution (a new, original simulation), and the anticipated audience (eighth-grade students in civics class). Next, they identified the necessary information, the available resources, the

---

6   Type III enrichment opportunities are individual or small-group investigations of real-world problems. This type of project is not an independent study, but an inquiry conducted with the assistance of an adult facilitator or mentor. In Type III projects, students engage as "practicing professionals" while engaging in solving genuine problems and using authentic means of inquiry. Ultimately, they report their results to an actual audience (Renzulli, 1976).

steps needed to complete the project, and a projected timeline. He then was ready to begin his inquiry. When Bryan began to see the enormous amount of work that was required, he convinced his social studies teacher to compact his curriculum[7] so he could spend more time in the enrichment center to work on the project. Bryan chose to test out of the unit on "How a Bill Becomes a Law" and then was able to use this time with the enrichment specialist to complete his project. Figure 10.1 is a copy of the management plan, which also served as a contract between Bryan and the enrichment specialist. The plan helped Bryan see the bigger picture, pointed him in the right direction, and offered targeted, authentic strategies to gather information about the subject.

Following the management plan, Bryan worked on the court trial script over the course of the entire academic year. The enrichment specialist offered suggestions, shared in Bryan's excitement as the plot began to take form, and acted out the parts so Bryan could critique the clarity of what he had written. In addition, he asked two civics teachers to take a look at his work, and then willingly returned to the drawing board for edits.

Overcoming obstacles. During the course of the project, the enrichment specialist became more aware of Bryan's strengths and weaknesses. His lack of organizational skills was apparent from the start. The enrichment specialist described him as "totally disorganized at all times," even though he had the management plan to use as a guide! Together, they invented simple strategies to help keep the materials organized. There was a box next to the computer labeled "Bryan's Stuff" and a file folder on the bookcase where he kept all draft copies of the printed script. Because Bryan did his writing directly on the computer, he taught himself to make back-ups in case his file was erased, and used the cloud so he could also work on the draft at home. Bryan began to think about how these strategies might help him organize assignments and materials for all of his other courses.

At first, Bryan was put off by all of the feedback he received on his work, which required him to rewrite many sections—saying it wasn't all that hard, it was just "plain monotonous." However, he observed that his attention span, focus, and attention to details greatly improved when he worked on the computer, especially when he listened to music through a headset. He even amazed himself with his level of concentration one night when he got "in the flow" and spent more than 3 hours editing his draft. Bryan used this discovery to convince his language arts teacher that he could leave the classroom during writing process time because he found the classroom environment too noisy and distracting. With a spirit of inquiry, the teacher agreed to see what would happen if Bryan completed his writing assignments in the computer lab, plugged into his favorite music.

---

7   Curriculum compacting consists of pretesting a student on concepts or skills to be mastered during a unit of study and then excusing the student from assignments on material already mastered (Reis, Renzulli, & Burns, 2016).

Management Plan for Individual and Small-Group Investigations

Name(s) *Bryan*	Beginning Date *10-6-89*
School *MJH*　　　 Grade *8*	Estimated Ending Date *2-89*

What idea do you plan to investigate? Why?
Jury Trials. Because we want to write a better one for the 8th grade.

What form(s) will the final product take? *Role play for class use.*	List some possible intended audiences: *8th grade classes* *Social Studies Publisher*
How will you communicate the results of your investigation to an appropriate audience? *Devise role play situations and rules that simulate a jury trial.*	

Getting Started: What types of information or data will be needed to begin your project?
Packet of information on court room procedures from Civics teacher.
Court room procedures.

Where can you find that information?
Media Center, Attorneys, Court observations

How-to-do-it books/written materials: Use bibliography format.

Check the boxes below to complete your project and list the specific sources:
☐ Viewing TV, videos, films, etc. (which?) _____
☑ Interviewing people (who?) *Jo Marie Alexander/attorney, Mrs. Rosenbaum,*
　　Court room: Hampton Court
☑ Observing/collecting data (what?) *Court justices interviews* _____
☐ Surveying (who?) _____
☐ Taking a class or working with a mentor (specify) _____
☐ Attending a performance (specify) _____
☐ Other (specify) _____

List all materials and equipment needed:
Computer

Figure 10.1. Management plan developed for Bryan. Adapted from *The Schoolwide Enrichment Model: A How-to Guide for Talent Development* (3rd ed., p. 169), by J. S. Renzulli and S. M. Reis, 2014, Waco, TX: Prufrock Press. Copyright 2014 by Prufrock Press. Adapted with permission.

TASKS: List in the order necessary to complete your project	Complete by:
1. Get info, talk with people about how it works.	Oct.
2. Examine other role play simulations.	Oct.
3. Decide how we want to design the format for our role play.	Nov.
4. Decide on plot and characters.	Dec.
5. Skeleton of drama.	Dec.
6. Divide responsibilities for roles and directors.	Jan.-Feb.
7. Write.	Jan.-Feb.
8. Conference with teacher and attorney.	April
9. Edit/Copy/Put together.	May
10. Evaluate performance.	May
11. Revise and submit for publication.	May

Figure 10.1. Continued.

Reflection and metacognition. The final phase of the intervention was to reflect on what was learned over the course of the project. The close interactive relationship between Bryan and the enrichment specialist led to a new appreciation of the ingredients crucial to Bryan's success.

Bryan was elated that the sixth-grade social studies teacher had agreed to try out the court case simulation with her class to get their reaction before actually using it with the eighth grade. Bryan's hope was that the students would better understand courtroom procedure after using the new simulation, and perhaps even become interested in studying law or the court system. When the enrichment specialist asked him what he thought he had learned about himself during the process, Bryan mulled over various aspects and commented that he learned how disorganized he was and that the box and file folders helped him stay organized, as did the management plan (even though he didn't always stick to the deadlines). He realized that he loved planning the simulation and developing creative ideas, but following through on it and adding all of the details were difficult for him. In the past he would have given up, but not this time, probably because he was determined to finish the project and because he was given school time to work on it.

As Bryan explained,

> I think it would have helped me more if I paid attention to deadlines. I would have been done a lot sooner. I know that. I guess I would recommend using a schedule more than just keep going. I get bored easily and want to quit and switch to something else. The schedule helps you break the project down into manageable pieces so you don't have to do it all at once. Probably the best thing

I learned from writing this trial is just to keep going and no matter if it bogs down, you've just got to stick with it. Eventually it will be done, and then you can go on to something else. You just keep looking forward, not like "Thank God it's over," but to see the project put to use is just overwhelming.

The enrichment specialist, too, analyzed her own growth in understanding how Bryan learned, what had motivated him, and what hurdles had plagued his progress. She was regularly astonished by his level of productivity, his task commitment, and his courage to try activities that demanded skill in areas that had previously been identified as severe weaknesses. She recalled one moment as pivotal:

Bryan was finishing up doggedly on his court simulation because it was going to be piloted in a sixth-grade classroom as a preview before the eighth graders used it. In the midst of the last stages, he started writing a novel—actually he began two novels simultaneously. He had written about 40 pages, came into my room, threw it on my desk, and said, "Here's a new novel and it's on Norad." Enclosed within was an intricate diagram of an underwater installation, visually a perfect graphic, and this was done by a student whose test scores indicated poor spatial abilities? He said it came to him as a visual image after a 14-hour stint at the computer working on his novel.

It appears that productivity begets more productivity. I hadn't seen Bryan as excited and eager to work in all the years he'd been at this school. I guess he wondered if he needed multiple projects to keep him focused. And, it seemed that when he feels motivated, he finally can finish them all.

Turning point. Bryan completed his project in June. His report card, still erratic, began to move upward to A's and B's, especially if he was interested in the subject. His year-end testing revealed a gain of 2 years in math, which had been an earlier area of weakness. More importantly, he began to take charge of his own learning. At the end of the year, he initiated a discussion with members of the pupil personnel team and requested support for the following year from the special education teacher in math and science—subjects he dodged previously because he found them so difficult. No longer was Bryan depressed and unmotivated, nor did he lack self-discipline. For the first time in years, he expressed a desire to improve academically, and he was now confident that he could actually accomplish his goals.

Lessons Learned From Bryan's Story

Why was the focus on Bryan's interests and abilities more effective than the behavior modification techniques employed initially? To understand the complex dynamics involved, let us review what happened with Bryan and try to identify what might have contributed to both his problems and his success.

Factors contributing to the problem. When we first met him in middle school, Bryan's performance had been spiraling downward. He had become a behavior problem and seemed uninterested in reversing the pattern. Ultimately, he was labeled as EBD. This label directed the intervention to eliminating poor and inappropriate behaviors with a behavior modification program. Bryan was expected "to shape up and be rewarded."

The classification of EBD and its subsequent treatment plan factored into Bryan's continuing underachievement. There is no doubt that the team misdiagnosed Bryan.

Problems. The results of his psychoeducational testing, coupled with multiple and varied observations of his behavior, provided strong evidence that Bryan had subtle learning disabilities in the areas of math, spatial abilities, organization, and time management. This profile is common for many 2e students. Because elementary grade-level work doesn't put high demands on these particular skills, these students with subtle disabilities can usually use their strengths to compensate sufficiently for their weaknesses in organization.

As assignments in middle school became more rigorous, however, Bryan was no longer able to keep up the charade. First, he was frustrated, and then it turned into depression, aggression, and discouragement. Because he lacked the skills necessary to perform well at this level, both his achievement and behavior worsened. Strong extrinsic rewards may have reduced acting-out behaviors, but they did little for the fundamental problem, which was a mismatch between his abilities/disabilities and classroom requirements. A behavior contract simply couldn't provide him with the skills or strategies needed to overcome his learning difficulties.

The second problem, layered on top of the first, was the team's decision not to give Bryan direct services. In truth, with every poor mark he received, Bryan became less confident in his abilities and his behavior deteriorated. A more careful look at how Bryan's motivation, confidence, and achievement levels were heading downhill might have steered the team in a different direction.

There are several mediating precursors to achievement (Bandura, 1989; Zimmerman, 2002). Consider confidence, self-efficacy, or a person's belief that he can organize and carry out some behavior (Bandura, 1997). Compared to those with weak self-efficacy, people with a robust sense of efficacy spend more energy at a task, pay more careful attention to the task, work harder at planning how to go about the task, persevere longer, set more challenging goals, and persist in the face of barriers and occasional failure. Success becomes more likely for them, which in turn boosts self-efficacy. This, in turn, translates into a can-do attitude, as opposed to resistance, avoidance, or anxiety about performing some task.

We also know that competent learners have a collection of effective learning strategies stored in memory and they know how to select particular strategies for particular purposes. A learner's knowledge about, use of, and confidence in his or her available skills and strategies allow him or her to seize control of his or her learning (Dweck, 2012; Levine, 2002; Mooney & Cole, 2000; Zimmerman, 2002). Bryan, like so many underachieving students with learning disabilities, lacked these essential prerequisites for achievement.

Without a sense of self-efficacy, a repertoire of successful learning strategies, and some self-regulation skills, students feel powerless in their efforts to learn. Kaufman (1991) argued that such students are severely discouraged, and what they need is encouragement and understanding, not punishment or remediation. When an intervention finally focused on Bryan as a capable student with interests and capacity, a very different learner emerged (Dweck, Mangels, & Good, 2004). Motivated to write a law simulation, Bryan was willing to work through his weaknesses to reach the goal. Thus, the journey provided a context for change—an opportunity to achieve success by engaging in an enriching and meaningful experience where the end (his goal) justified the means (learning and applying strategies).

Factors contributing to success. Bryan's talent development experience suggests a set of factors that align well with those discussed in Chapter 8. These factors include a relationship with a caring adult, an emphasis on pursuing abilities and interests authentically, and the integration of self-regulation strategies in a strength-based environment.

Relationship with a caring adult. Bryan developed a relationship with a caring teacher who respected him for what he could do. The enrichment specialist played a vital role in helping Bryan gain confidence. She offered emotional and cognitive support as he pursued his self-determined goal. Her feedback was constructive, and she continuously conveyed confidence in his ability to write the court case. Students who reverse their pattern of underachievement often attribute their turnaround to a special teacher or mentor. These adults possess specific qualities: They show respect for the student; hold explicit, attainable expectations; and demonstrate a belief that the student is capable and can succeed (Baum, Renzulli, & Hébert, 1995; Baum, Schader, & Hébert, 2014; Emerick, 1992).

Many kinds of talent development experiences—such as internships, mentor programs, and small-group interactions with a teacher-facilitator—offer opportunities to develop these special collegial relationships.

An emphasis on pursuing students' abilities and interests in an authentic manner. The enrichment specialist encouraged Bryan to pursue an area of interest in the way a professional would go about it. He became emotionally committed to solving the problem of writing a legitimate court simulation to substitute for the existing "goofy and immature" case. The project had real purpose; it was not just one more school assignment to be graded. In other words, Bryan was caught up in learning for intrinsic reasons rather than for reasons imposed on him by others. Previously, the school had focused only on helping Bryan overcome his learning deficits. Contracts, meetings with teachers, and parental monitoring, all well intentioned, were aimed at helping Bryan complete school tasks. Methods that are based on extrinsic rewards often have limited success with high-ability students (Clinkenbeard, 1994; Duckworth, 2016).

Integration of self-regulation strategies. Another contributor to Bryan's success was the addition of specific self-regulation strategies, as they were needed in the process—organizational boxes and folders, a computer for writing and editing, background music, and a management plan and deadlines. Bryan learned how to use these strategies when he needed them.

Twice-exceptional students learn within meaningful contexts, especially when they are interested in the topic. And, when students are committed to a project, a remarkable assortment of study behaviors step forward. Students seek more information, set about organizing the information, and strive to create a meaningful product. Experiencing success and then reflecting on the strategies used to get there build self-efficacy about what they could possibly accomplish next (Bandura, 1997; Duckworth, 2016; Zimmerman, 2002). Our work has shown that students can then transfer and adapt the learning strategies to other curricular areas and to other areas of their lives (Baum, Renzulli, & Hébert, 1995; Oreck, Baum, & McCartney, 2000).

Finding Talent Development Opportunities

Identifying the pertinent opportunities for 2e students to develop their strengths, talents, and interests may be complicated and/or require out-of-the-box thinking. Generally gifted education programs provide complex, stimulating situations that do just that. However, simply dropping "green" students into a traditional program for gifted ("yellow") students may be inappropriate and lead to negative results. Again, these students may not fit well into existing programs for several reasons:

1. The programs may be content-centered with little regard for individual strengths or interests. These programs are likely organized by topic and themes rather than interest areas. For example, the gifted program for a specific grade level might focus on ancient Egypt or Greek and Roman mythology. This would not be a good match for a 2e student with a strong interest in robotics and engineering, no matter how high his or her aptitude.

2. The program orientation may place heavy emphasis on reading and writing.

3. If the gifted curriculum is built around enrichment units, it adds to, instead of replaces, existing curriculum requirements—making a heavier workload, no matter how enjoyable.

4. Some programs lack sufficient structure and guidance because it is assumed that students can work and produce independently.

Programs for 2e students should serve to validate individual abilities. As we saw in Bryan's case, the enrichment specialist created an environment where students felt appreciated and where what they could do was recognized and valued. Such programs:

1. encourage students to seek information, as well as communicate their ideas in creative ways based on their interests and abilities;

2. convey sophisticated content through guest speakers, demonstrations, active inquiry, visitation, films, or mentorships;

3. use experts, equipment, and the modes of inquiry of practicing professionals;

4. acknowledge and appreciate students' individual differences by offering options that align with their strengths and interests; and

5. include a metacognitive approach where students reflect on the compensation strategies that enable them to succeed, in spite of their learning differences.

In short, successful programs for 2e students should include personnel who welcome individual differences, feel comfortable highlighting student strengths, and communicate their belief in a student's ability to create or accomplish great things. They must also help students find and develop strategies that will help them in compensating for weaknesses as they pursue their goals. Such teachers agree that advanced reading and writing skills are not a necessary prerequisite for learning and creative productivity.

Placement in Existing Programs

There are many documented cases of 2e students doing well in existing school programs. These are typically students who were first recognized for their gifted abilities—and their disabilities are more subtle and/or do not involve extensive problems with reading or writing. Below are common alternatives that can already be found in most school districts.

Acceleration. Accelerated programs in a particular area of strength help the 2e student cultivate specific abilities and participate in a content area at a more sophisticated level, and often at a faster pace. Advanced courses could challenge a student with a strong aptitude in specific disciplines, such as math, music, computer programming, etc. This same student can remain in regular or remedial classes for content areas requiring more support or slower pacing. In Montgomery County, MD, gifted students with learning disabilities—students whose high abilities are in math or science—participate in Advanced Placement (AP) or honors classes. After AP classes, they attend a special class for 2e students. According to the program director, these students are competitive and achieve at a level similar to their "regularly" gifted peers.

Established enrichment program. Students are pulled out several times a week from the regular classroom for enrichment classes. Sometimes these programs provide innovative curriculum, critical and creative thinking skills, or opportunities for students to pursue specific areas of interest. The opportunity to interact with peers of similar intellectual abilities and interests promotes a positive self-image for 2e students. Focused attention is given to an area of strength, which can help balance the disproportionate amount of time and energy expended on overcoming weaknesses.

Schoolwide Enrichment Model. Programs based on the Schoolwide Enrichment Model (SEM; Renzulli & Reis, 2014) have been found to be particularly 2e-friendly for several reasons. SEM is the most widely used model in the world for gifted education, so we will not go into detail here, other than to explain why this is such a good fit. First, flexible identification allows 2e students to qualify for advanced programming. Second, the Enrichment Triad Model organizes learning experiences into three types of activities designed to expose students to a wide variety of purposely-selected activities that will ignite their interest and encourage creative productivity. These activities offer general exploratory experiences, group training, and individual and small-group investigation. General exploratory activities (Type I Enrichment) offer exposure to potential areas of interest not necessarily found in the regular curriculum. Students with learning deficits may be introduced to ideas through lectures, demonstrations, movies, interest centers, or other approaches that bypass their weaknesses in reading. These are no-fail activities meant to expose students to new ideas in a nonthreatening atmosphere where they are given free rein to explore.

Type II Enrichment activities provide training in areas such as critical thinking, creativity, and problem solving, using authentic skills of a discipline. For example, students who are interested in history will learn how historians conduct inquiry—use primary sources, triangulate their data, and report their findings using timelines and documentary films.

During Type III activities, students become investigators of relevant, real-world problems. Students are mentored in the development of a product that should have an impact on an intentional audience, preferably outside the school setting. Students focus on original solutions to "problems" and proceed as "practicing professionals" to solve the chosen problems. Within the pursuit of the real-world problem, the student is learning *how* to address problems and *how* to self-regulate learning behaviors. And, thanks to self-evaluation during the process, the student comes to understand that he or she is capable of focusing, persisting, and coming to some closure on a worthwhile problem.

Finally, the Schoolwide Enrichment Model brings creative productivity to the total school population through enrichment clusters. Enrichment clusters are multi-age interest groups where youngsters meet together once a week for 6–10 weeks to create a product or service in particular areas of interest. The teacher is a facilitator as students look at real-world problems and issues. They decide how to address them and proceed to use authentic methods to address the problem similar to those used by the practicing professional. The teacher/facilitator helps students decide what they will produce and how they can organize for success. The students consider their areas of strength and then discuss in what ways they might contribute to help the group meet its goal.

Special Opportunities

As mentioned previously, sometimes a school's traditional gifted program is not a match for 2e students, especially if the program has a prescribed curriculum and requires large amounts of reading and writing. It is then important to find opportunities in particular disciplines, which can be a better match between the student's particular ability area and the way they learn best. For instance, 2e students who are technically advanced and have interests in building, electronics, and physics are served well in programs like FIRST Robotics, Invention Convention, and Odyssey of the Mind competitions. Or, students who like to write might do well in working with other student writers in preparing pieces for publication. A teacher/facilitator can arrange a variety of learning experiences and help them ready their work for submissions. School drama programs offer talent development for actors, technical engineers, set designers, costumers, etc. Other opportunities for stimulating interests and developing emerging talents include participation in storytelling festivals, debate teams, mock trials, National History Day, science fair competitions, MATHCOUNTS, and, of course, arts and athletic programs.

It is a big mistake when districts try to find time for extra remedial support and take these students out of enrichment activities, not letting them enjoy what they do best (or feel best doing) until they "catch up" academically. When this is a school's practice, we wonder if it does not constitute "educational abuse."

Mentorships

Another program option offered in many schools is the opportunity to use mentorships in areas of talent. The benefits accruing from the special relationship between mentor and mentee are well documented, as noted by the Institute for Educational Advancement (Williams, 2013). Many 2e students perform better in one-to-one settings, partly because such an environment maximizes the students' observational learning and, additionally, the student builds a sense of satisfaction and self-worth when working side-by-side with an expert or professional in an area of mutual interest.

UConn Mentor Connection was an innovative summer opportunity for gifted high school students at the University of Connecticut attended by a 2e high school junior. Lara had been suffering with severe depression. She sacrificed any social life in high school because it took all her "free" time just to maintain the high grades she wanted in her academic program. Lara's parents had been thinking about sending her to a summer program for study skills sponsored by a university interested in students with learning disabilities. However, concerned about her depression, they agreed that she needed a positive educational experience and enrolled her in the UConn Mentor Connection, where Lara was assigned to a female biologist. She and two other gifted young women worked together as research assistants with the biologist, helping her study communication among mice. Lara found the experience very positive, especially because it enabled her to form meaningful relationships with her mentor and peer researchers.

Another talented high schooler, Welles, explained how this program raised his feelings of self-efficacy:

> I was told in sixth grade that I was smart and had a learning disability. I had a lot of trouble organizing myself. Since that time, I doubted myself until I attended UConn Mentor Connection. When I went to Mentor Connection, I worked in one of my favorite subjects: medieval literature. A special mentorship site was created for me, and I loved working with my mentor, Mr. John Sexton. John was a doctoral student in the medieval studies department. He was so enthusiastic about his work, and he took a very personal interest in me.
>
> I worked one-on-one with John, and we translated parts of *Sir Gawain and the Green Knight* and *Beowulf*. I never thought I could do this, but I did, and I know that I did a great job. John told me that I was doing work that graduate students complete. I was truly motivated because I loved what I was doing.
>
> Throughout my 3 weeks in the program, I was pretty much on my own. I learned that I could do anything I put my mind to. I can recall saying to myself, "Oh yes, I did all that, and I can be really proud."
>
> John really influenced my life, and I have kept in touch with him. He made me believe in myself. I helped him to create parts of

the mentorship site the year after I attended the program. We still e-mail each other once in a while.

Other mentorship programs have enjoyed similar successes over the years. Some of the earliest programs for these students were sponsored by the Westchester County Bureau of Cooperative Education Services (BOCES). Both Northern and Southern BOCES involved high school 2e students in programs through which students were matched with professionals. At times, the student served as a research assistant to the mentor and, in some circumstances, the students conducted their own inquiry under the aegis of the mentor.

The Montgomery County, Maryland Public Schools, offers the Wings Mentor Program, among their other offerings for 2e students. Wings is designed for elementary-aged students whose mentors guide them in projects such as whales, math components, and horses. After one third grader presented her project on horses on sharing day, her father confided, with tears in his eyes, that this mentorship experience in horses was the most wonderful thing in the world for his 2e daughter.

Special Programs and Schools

Because of learned behavior patterns, repeated failures, learning and attention deficits, or the nature of the existing gifted program, no matter how intelligent or capable, some 2e students may not fit. Sometimes it is necessary to find or design special programs and opportunities for them.

There are programs in both public and independent school settings. We will describe one from each. First, Prince George's County, in Maryland, has a comprehensive, flexible model. Second, Bridges Academy, in California, is an independent school whose student body is entirely twice-exceptional.

Prince George's County Public School Program for Gifted Students with Learning Needs (GSLN). For more than 20 years, Prince George's Public Schools in Maryland have implemented a continuum of services for their 2e students whom they call Gifted Students with Learning Needs (GSLN). The program is a collaboration between the gifted and special education departments. A specialist designated to oversee the program collaborates with and supports teachers as they implement services for students from elementary through high school. Teachers are trained in dual differentiation, talent development, and strength-based learning strategies. Students identified as GSLN receive both advanced curriculum either in a designated "site" school (a gifted and talented magnet school) or in a regular school that has advanced opportunities along with specialized support services available.

At schools with identified GSLN students, the collaborative or academic resource support team identifies a student's strengths, instructional needs, and ancillary support needs that can allow performance at an optimal level. This determination allows the student to access advanced classes, coursework, and enrichment/talent opportunities, while ensuring that appropriate specialized services and strategies are in place (Blucher & Wayland, 2015). Table 10.2 outlines the service model.

Bill, mentioned in Chapter 3, was a student in Prince George's County and received the services described above. During elementary and middle school, he attended a magnet school for gifted students. In high school, he took advanced placement courses and honors courses. He also attended forum sessions where strength-based skills were embedded into enrichment opportunities and students had the opportunity to discuss their issues, identity, strengths, challenges, and set goals. Most important, students learned to self-advocate.

Bill chose to finish high school in 5 years. Taking fewer courses was less taxing on his working memory and processing speed issues. In addition, the team of his teacher, the GSLN coordinator, his guidance counselor, and his parents developed a plan that included talent development and advanced opportunities aligned to his strengths and learning preferences. These are some of the modifications that were made:

1. Bill was able to take English courses online so he could control the complexity of content and pace. Online courses also helped him to sustain his attention.
2. Bill became a lab assistant for his chemistry teacher during his senior year and earned science credits for the work.
3. Bill participated in the ROTC program where he was in charge of equipment—a perfect opportunity, as it was structured and the responsibilities were sequential and detailed. This experience helped him strengthen his self-efficacy.
4. The teachers also adapted the point system for grades in his history class—giving more points for projects and tests than those for completed homework assignments.

Programs like these exemplify the components of the Talent Centered Model because student needs are met by also considering their social-emotional world, not just their academic challenges. Other programs exist around the country. Indeed, states are publishing guidebooks to help districts identify and serve 2e students. Currently, there are online guides for the following states: Colorado, Idaho, Maryland, Montana, and Virginia. Additionally, the National Parent Teacher Association (PTA) has published its own handbook as a means to advocate for twice-exceptional students.

Bridges Academy, an independent school for twice-exceptional students. Bridges is an accredited independent school in California for grades 4–12 with curricular and instructional approaches designed with the 2e student in mind. As noted in a forthcoming book chapter (Sabatino & Wiebe, in press),

Table 10.2
Prince George's County Program for Gifted Students With Learning Needs

How Services Are Implemented		
At Elementary-level Site Schools	At Elementary-level Site Schools	At Elementary-level Site Schools

• GSLN Biweekly Forum—pullout sessions that:
  > Teach students about their unique needs as 2e learners
  > Emphasize the importance of developing their talents while also addressing areas of deficit
 	
• Classroom teachers incorporate GSLN strategies into their accelerated instruction
• Special educators incorporate GSLN strategies into their specialized instruction. The GSLN Resource Guide (PGCPS, 1994; 1996; 2006), provides guidance to the team as they conduct collaborative team lessons
	• A full-day program of advanced or accelerated coursework
	• Daily Honors Academic Resource Support class, which:
	  > Provides a highly supportive environment where students develop compensatory strategies based on strengths to ensure high academic achievement and consistent social-emotional development.
	  > Depends on coordination between the Academic Resource Support Class instructor and general education teachers to be successful.
	  > Provides cyclical instructional modules that embed teaching of self-regulating strategies and explicit skill instruction within the context of the student's advanced coursework (PGCPS, 2008a, 2008b)
		• Biweekly Forums and the Honors Academic Resource Support classes when there are enough identified GSLN students to form and schedule groups
		• Direct teacher support and training in how to incorporate appropriate GSLN strategies within the classroom setting

Note. From "Supporting 2e Students in Prince George's County" by R. Blucher and S. Wayland, 2015, *2e Newsletter, 71*, p. 3. Copyright 2015 by R. Blucher and S. Wayland. Reprinted with permission.

We have learned that strength-based education invariably involves getting to know students well personally, developing comprehensive student profiles, and creating an educational culture that values time spent on strength and talent development. It is a culture that prides itself on providing opportunities, resources, and encouragement for students to wonder, explore, and produce....

We make choices all the time that can dramatically impact our students and their school experiences. Sometimes, those educational decisions center on whether to accelerate or compact curriculum, whether to emphasize social-emotional growth over academic goals, whether to assign less or different better-aligned course and homework, or whether to refer a student for therapeutic support.

Teachers at Bridges recognize that difficulties in one or more areas do not in any way preclude the existence or the enormity of their gifts and talents in other areas. The school offers an advanced college prep program that includes many opportunities for developing expertise in interest and talent areas both within and outside of the defined curriculum. For example, at the high school level, students can participate in differing types of music ensembles, as well as music composition—taking classes taught by professional musicians. Students perform at annual festivals including Jam Fest, a jazz extravaganza for independent schools in the area, and appear right alongside the professionals in various venues in the Los Angeles area. Technology-minded students can participate in FIRST Robotics, where they combine their talents to compete in the annual national competition—again working with professional engineers. Drama productions throughout the year are forums for actors, stage designers, lighting experts, and future directors. Verbally advanced youngsters participate in Model UN or the debating club.

At the middle and elementary school levels, talent development occurs through enrichment clusters (described earlier in this chapter) and weeks set aside for problem-based learning projects. At the elementary level, one day per week is dedicated to a semester-long enrichment cluster. Past projects have included developing their own businesses, creating sustainable gardens, and becoming young experts in game theory. The middle school devotes two afternoons a week to similar but more sophisticated clusters in publications, Japanese anime, School of Rock, and stock market simulations, for example. Each semester, new offerings appear based on students' interests and faculty talents. Several times a year, both the elementary and middle schools abandon traditional classroom subjects to work on a project- or problem-based learning unit. Students are grouped by their interests, styles, and talents, as each project needs particular groups to fulfill certain roles in the 2- to 3-week curriculum. For example, in one project-based learning unit, students worked on creating a Pyramid Museum to celebrate ancient Egypt. The students were grouped into four talent groups—builders, mathematicians, scientists, and artists. The builders were tasked with creating an 8-foot-tall pyramid, which would house the museum. The mathematicians established the budget, provided supplies for each group, and calculated the area within the museum for different exhibits. The scientists, among many tasks, mummified a fish and created papyrus. The artists created artifacts, such as a model of the Sphinx. Each group spent as much time researching as actually creating. As one student exclaimed, "This did not feel like research. We really needed the information or we could not complete our tasks!"

Key to the talent development process were the opportunities for students to connect with adults who are successful and who share the passion of their particular areas of interest (Sabatino & Wiebe, in press):

> Our faculty members often come to us from a rich, successful career before moving into teaching. For them, teaching is not so much job as it is a vocation that they evolved into over the course of their lives. Most, if not all, of our teachers are deeply committed to their own personal growth and engage in entrepreneurial activities outside of their teaching careers. They are not only subject-specific teachers, but working artists, actors, writers, musicians, martial artists, equestrians, computer programmers, political organizers, research scientists, and environmental advocates. Some teachers are involved with nonprofit and affinity-based organizations. They live their lives taking initiative, setting goals that are personally meaningful, persevering through challenges and setbacks, and accomplishing creative and entrepreneurial objectives—and the students notice. Our students are learning in an environment where their teachers are also visibly active learners, providing a model of what it means to truly be a lifelong learner. It is not uncommon for a student who is gifted in a certain area to take on a quasi-apprenticeship related to the teachers' own projects. We also look for similar opportunities with parents and friends of the community.

Importantly, the enrichment opportunities at all levels are not seen as outside of the curriculum, but as an essential part of the curriculum that includes social-emotional objectives. Friendships are forged, identities established, and goal setting and other executive function skills taught. These intentional opportunities are written into their educational plans, as shown in Chapter 9's plan for Mike.

As we detailed in this chapter, there are many ways to involve students in advanced opportunities through which they can develop their strengths, interests, and talent areas both within and outside of the school environment. It is essential that we carefully plan how this will happen for 2e youngsters. To that end, we suggest developing a talent agenda to accompany students' comprehensive program plan (IEP or 504 plan). We encourage parents and school personnel to develop this plan with the students themselves based on the information gathered from interviews, instruments, and knowledge of the students' abilities. For us, having such a plan is non-negotiable.

Tables 10.3 and 10.4 are two completed talent plans. The first is for Bill (the Science Competition winner and Civil War expert introduced in Chapter 2). The next plan is for Debra (the young historian introduced in Chapter 2).

Table 10.3
Talent Plan for Bill

Personalized Talent Development Plan

Beginning/Ending Dates: *January–April*   **Student:** *Bill*   **Grade:** *Senior*   **Date:** *December 15*

Classroom Teacher or Advisor: *Justin Clark*   **Mentor:** *Dr. Rodriguez, biologist*   **Updates:** *N/A*

Current Interests and Talents: *Civil War, science fair competition, Science Fiction books and video games on conquering worlds*

Talent Development Activities	Frequency and Location	Guiding Adult	Proposed Outcomes and Dates
Science fair projects	*Saturday and Sunday: Dr. Rodriguez's laboratory*	*Dr. Rodriguez*	*January–February: Submit project to Intel Competition*
Attend Battle: 155th Commemoration of the Battle of Shiloh	*One time Corinth, MS*	*Billy's Dad*	*April 6–9: Document with photographs and commentary using iPhone video and audio*
World Domination Game club	*Weekly after school club*	*George Thomas*	*Competition: January–March*
ROTC	*Weekly elective*	*Captain Milligan*	*As assigned*

Student's Signature: Parent's Signature:

Advisor of Other School Personnel: Other:

Table 10.4
Talent Plan for Debra

Personalized Talent Development Plan

Beginning/Ending Dates: *September–November* **Student:** *Debra* **Grade:** *5* **Date:** *September 10*

Classroom Teacher or Advisor: *Lila Jones* **Mentor:** *Janice Brown, curator* **Updates:** *Monthly*

Current Interests and Talents: *History and historical sites, drama, ecology*

Talent Development Activities	Frequency and Location	Guiding Adult	Proposed Outcomes and Dates
Noah Webster House Junior curator program	*Weekly:* *Noah Webster House*	*Janice Brown*	*September–November:* *Give guided tours*
Improvisation lessons for children	*Downtown Theater:* *Thursday evenings 5–7 p.m.*	*Mom* *Improv group*	*December public performance*
Book club in school for historical fiction	*Lunch and Learn program*	*School librarian, Angela Farkas*	*Weekly discussions*

Student's Signature: Parent's Signature:

Advisor of Other School Personnel: Other:

Part IV

Strategies That Work

CHAPTER 11

Creating a Strength-Based, Dually Differentiated Classroom

Dual differentiation and strength-based learning are foundational concepts for creating and selecting strategies that can excite, engage, and include even the most reluctant 2e students.

What Is Dual Differentiation?

In Chapter 3, we introduced the notion of "green dichotomies"—the paradoxical learning behaviors demonstrated by bright, but challenged students. Each dichotomy can lead to a dual diagnosis (the "blues" and the "yellows"), which then must be recognized and addressed through the practice of dual differentiation. Baum et al. (2001) defined dual differentiation as

> the fulcrum that maintains the delicate balance between students' strengths and limitations. It must be challenging enough to engage these students in their learning, provide alternate ways of accessing information, and offer options for communication that tap into their unique talents. (pp. 485–486)

The fundamentals of dual differentiation are shown in Table 11.1. Two examples below provide clarity about this concept. Consider the dichotomy of high-level comprehension (which needs sophisti-

Table 11.1
Fundamentals of the Dually-Differentiated Curriculum

Problems Associated With Special-Needs Students	Characteristics of Gifted Students	Curricular Accommodations
<ul><li>Limited skills in reading and math</li><li>Difficulty with spelling and handwriting</li><li>Language deficits in verbal communication and conceptualization</li><li>Poor organization</li><li>Problems with sustaining attention and focus</li><li>Inappropriate social interaction</li><li>Low self-efficacy and esteem</li></ul>	<ul><li>Propensity for advanced-level content to accommodate the gift or talent</li><li>Need to communicate creative ideas and knowledge</li><li>Facility with and enjoyment of abstract concepts</li><li>Often demonstrate nonlinear styles of thinking and learning</li><li>Need for intellectual challenges based on individual talents and interests</li><li>Need to identify with others of similar talents and interests</li><li>Heightened sensitivity to failure</li></ul>	<ul><li>Alternate means to access information</li><li>Alternate ways to express ideas and create products</li><li>Visual and kinesthetic experiences to convey abstract ideas concretely</li><li>Visual organization schemes, e.g., time lines flow charts, webbing</li><li>Interest-based authentic curriculum</li><li>Group identity based on talent or ability</li><li>Recognition for accomplishment</li></ul>

Note. From "Dual Differentiation: An Approach for Meeting the Curricular Needs of Gifted Students With Learning Disabilities" by S. Baum, C. R. Cooper, and T. W. Neu, 2001, *Psychology in the Schools, 38,* p. 482. Copyright 2001 by Wiley. Adapted with permission.

cated content) *but* with reading limitations. A bright fourth-grade student might be struggling with reading fluency and decoding automaticity; however, with a comprehension level equal to that of a sixth grader. Poetry would be an entry point for him or her to enjoy reading, because many well-known poets use simple language to convey complex ideas. Here is a poem by Emily Dickinson:

> A word is dead
> When it is said,
> Some say.
> I say it just
> Begins to live
> That day.

The verse is perceptually pleasing (there are few words on a page so it's not over-whelming) and the individual words themselves are at an easy reading level. The idea behind the verse, however, leaves much to be explored and discussed—these prima-ry-level words convey an intellectually engaging idea that can be discussed within an honors English class, as well as enjoyed by a group of advanced third graders.

Another example of how a dually differentiated approach could be used within a whole class would be to teach research skills through historical photographs like Figure 11.1.

For this lesson, divide students into small teams of three or four for a research "competition." Ask each group to hypothesize about what year the picture was taken and the direction the couple is facing. In a class discussion, identify the variables that will help the answer the questions (i.e., clothing, kind of vehicle, and the White House facade). From those clues, students will then build ideas of what they might explore within their individual research group. All groups are given two class periods to confirm their hypotheses supported by at least three different online reputable sources. And, each group will choose its own creative way to report their findings. This activity not only involves students through critical thinking, but the assign-ment's specific tasks also appeal to (or are appropriate for) different kinds of minds:

- competition is often motivating for learners with ADHD,
- historical research primarily through photographs as primary sources allows engagement for poor readers, and
- paying attention to details appeals to students with ASD.

In short, designing activities like these will engage 2e students through their "yellow" abilities, while simultaneously avoiding their areas of "blue" difficulties.

What Is a Strength-Based Approach?

The term *strength-based* has become a popular term in both education and psy-chology, and it has a variety of meanings depending on the context and persons using the term. In Chapter 4, we provided our definition for the term *strength-based* and repeat it below. Strength-based (Baum, Schader, & Hebert, 2014) is defined as

> curricular and instructional approaches that are differentiated to align with students' cognitive styles, learning preferences, and pro-files of intelligence. (p. 312)

Providing choice is also an important part of strength-based learning, for it encourages the student to participate more comfortably and with less anxiety while learning the concepts and skills of the core disciplines.

Figure 11.1. Couple on a bicycle.

In strength-based learning, we use strengths in two ways: to support skill development in challenged areas and to use students' strengths to bring them into the curriculum, as well as offer opportunities for communicating what they have learned.

Leveraging Strengths to Support Skill Development

This is particularly critical when we want students to overcome learning challenges. The story of Michael illustrates how leveraging strengths can work.

> Michael sat in class staring into space. He was supposed to be writing the introduction to his essay, but he could not get himself to begin even the hint of a first draft. His teacher was concerned. Michael had become anxious about writing recently and hadn't produced much of anything for several weeks. Finally, his teacher, the curriculum director, and the learning support specialist met together to discuss strategies they could use to help Michael get back on track. They began their meeting by reviewing his strengths and interests, and also analyzed the times when writing did not appear to be a problem. In the past, much of Michael's writing was about topics that could be considered "fringe," or on the edge of acceptable—such as reviewing the irreverent musical, *The Book of*

Mormon, or addressing the pariah status of Holden Caulfield in the novel, *The Catcher in the Rye*. Michael had also completed a research paper on the controversial Westboro Baptist Church a few years before. Michael's teachers had a copy of his learning profile, including multiple intelligences, which indicated considerable strengths in spatial areas (visual representations of ideas and space) and intrapersonal intelligences (self-awareness). With this information, his teachers decided to create a unit in which Michael would study the art of the graffiti painter and political activist, Banksy, about whom there is much debate as to whether he is an artist or a criminal defacer of public property. After learning about Banksy, Michael would need to develop a thesis and a well-developed argument to support his opinion.

The teachers also invited Michael to talk to them about the kinds of environments in which he worked best when generating ideas and writing his assignments. He told them that when he does write, he preferred to be alone in his room. He also said that when he found the topic interesting, he felt fluent and was productive; otherwise writing was really a struggle. It seemed that Michael could benefit from a quiet spot within the school to do his writing. They proposed finding a "writing cave." The learning specialist said he could monitor Michael's writing from anywhere if Michael used Google Docs while working.

So, Michael agreed to the assignment and chose to work in an empty office that was available during his English class period. The learning specialist monitored his work and could always tell (even from afar) when Michael seemed frustrated or when there was a break in the writing. At those times, the learning specialist would make suggestions through Google Docs, and offer prompts to help Michael get back on track. They conversed through the Internet, and, in this way, Michael could also ask for support. Not only did the strength-based assignment result in an excellent writing piece, it also seemed to ease Michael out of his writer's block. He was able to return to English class for the rest of the year. (M. Singer, personal communication, April 15, 2014)

Using Strengths to Encourage Active Participation in Learning and Productivity

This aspect of a strength-based approach may be more obvious. When we entice students to learn by offering an exciting menu of opportunities to engage in the curriculum, students are then able to learn through choices that circumvent or compensate for their weaknesses or areas in which they feel uncomfortable. Having many resources available and offering grouping opportunities based on abilities and interests not only builds self-efficacy, but also offers ways to build deep understanding of concepts and principles. For example, when studying biodiversity in particular regions of the world, students might form interest groups by region. Members of each group could have choices about how to research the biodiversity of their region (by watching a documentary, finding an online source, reading an essay by a biologist, or interviewing a local expert, etc.). When finished, the group then can decide how best to share their findings (through an essay, short film, or podcast, etc.). At each stage of learning, students have options for how they access information and accomplish the learning outcomes.

Offering product choices that align to students' areas of proficiency and pleasure gives students appealing ways to communicate what they know, and isn't that the goal? But, even more important, working in an area of strength and interest permits these students to display or show off what they *can* do and what they have produced. Too often, others know 2e students for how they're failing, not for how and what they can contribute.

Revisiting Olivia, Blaine, and Melanie

Throughout this book, we have described students who were able to reverse their pattern of underachievement when there were people who understood them and arranged learning environments that could flexibly align to the students as individuals. Let's revisit the stories of Olivia (Chapter 3), Blaine (Chapter 7), and Melanie (Chapter 9) to see how various strategies that were successful with them can be used as guides for creating inviting and successful learning environments for other 2e learners. We have organized the strategies in Table 11.2. Notice that the first step is to have knowledge of students' strengths, abilities, interests, and talents (yellow) along with an understanding of where their learning breaks down (blue). This information informs decisions about how to begin creating an optimal learning environment for a student's particular shade of "green." Ideas about engaging students in learning using dual differentiation will then flow naturally—along with ways to use strength-based strategies to address deficit areas. The last row of the table includes suggestions for accommodations and additional support for each student's learning profile.

Notice that the ideas pertain to all students. When we teach with the students in mind, all students benefit from the same choices. Furthermore, when choices are available for all, the 2e students are just like everyone else. They are not the "weird ones." The next two chapters detail ways to find the best strength-based strategies for use in the curriculum and ideas for modifications and accommodations for 2e students.

Table 11.2
Developing Appropriate Strength-Based Strategies

	Olivia	Blaine	Melanie
Strengths, Interests, Abilities, Talents, and Styles	Art; drama; metaphorical thinking; stating her opinion; high verbal skills Learned Expert and Creative Problem Solver	Advanced verbal and spatial skills; avid reader; talent in engineering (great LEGO builder); strengths in math and drama Learned Expert and Creative Problem Solver	Visual arts; politics & human rights; inter- and intrapersonal intelligences People Person
Where Learning Breaks Down	Writing; note-taking; focusing attention; understanding math concepts	Focusing attention; putting ideas in writing; hyperactive and easily distracted; sensory issues	Reading; writing; memorization; slow processing speed
Engagement Ideas to Dually Differentiate Curriculum and Instruction (to Address the Dichotomies or the "Buts")	Incorporate arts and use informal debates as entry points, as well as for ways to demonstrate what she has learned (performances of understanding)	Use experiential entry points (start the unit with an activity); offer opportunities for engineering and design within the curriculum, such as building bridges or build a 3-D story set; provide accelerated math; give choices for accessing curriculum	Aesthetic and foundational entry points (starting off with looking at a work of art to introduce the topic or participating in a moral dilemma activity relating to a concept in the unit); use visual arts to create products that show understanding and learning; use graphic novels with sophisticated content, as well as picture books of poets like Emily Dickinson and Robert Frost

Table 11.2, continued.

	Olivia	Blaine	Melanie
Strength-Based Strategies to Support Skill Development in Deficit Areas	Use visual doodling for note-taking; integrate higher level thinking skills into writing assignments, like using metaphors to describe concepts in science or literature; incorporate "arguing" into writing an editorial or opinion piece	Use movement within the curriculum to assist with attention; allow exploration of advanced websites when classroom discussions are going too fast or too slowly	Integrate arts to process information; use friendship and talent groups in completing course projects
Accommodations, Modifications, and Additional Support	• Use technology for writing and math • Bring in academic support in math • Allow access to the art room on breaks and lunch to work on her own art projects or when she needs a refocusing break	• Use of technology for writing • Pretest skills before teaching a unit and eliminate assignments on concepts and skills already mastered • Adjust pacing to allow for fewer homework assignments to learn new material • Allow movement • Supply a "writing office" with reading lamp and headset to listen to music • Needs direct social skills and emotional regulation support	• Use mind maps for prewriting • Offer extended time for tests, as she processes information visually • Allow access to the art room on breaks and lunch to work on her own art projects • Wilson reading program intervention

CHAPTER 12

Classroom Strategies for Success

Intellectual, Physical, and Emotional Environments

The stories of success threaded throughout the earlier chapters accentuate the importance of explicitly addressing intellectual, physical, and social-emotional needs within a comprehensive plan for 2e students. It is clear that these intellectually advanced students are better able to stay engaged in a curriculum that respects their levels of intelligence and simultaneously offers options so they can work with and around their deficits. Rather than watering down curriculum or lowering expectations, successful teachers find creative ways to use strengths, abilities, interests, and talents so students can succeed in spite of their challenges.

Although considering intellectual needs is important, it is equally vital to review the match of physical environment, as was the case for Bill, Michael, and Blaine. For good learning to take place, room arrangements, class size, and available resources within the classroom should reflect student needs. For example, many 2e students benefit from the option of moving around; others need a quiet, uninterrupted space to work. Some learn better with music, while others simply need fidgets or a bouncy chair to focus their hyperactivity. The physical environment, then, must provide ways for students to optimize attention and production.

Finally, in understanding how the emotional state of these students can negatively impact their learning and behavior, we must find ways to tune into their emotional and social needs. We continue to see that, with a shift away from their deficits to focus on their strengths, 2e students begin to succeed academically. Their sense of self becomes more positive, and that helps them become "emotionally available" for learning. In this chapter, we talk about practical strategies for creating responsive environments in the three domains.

The Intellectual Environment

Twice-exceptional students require an intellectual environment that engages their intellect, specific interests, and talents. We have identified four strategies that are strength-based and offer opportunities for dual differentiation:

1. offering appropriate entry points,
2. performance-based assessments with differentiated exit points,
3. investigating authentic problems, and
4. integrating critical and creative thinking.

Using them has proven to be particularly successful with bright but challenged students. Most important is that these strategies are used with the whole class—where all students can engage optimally and few modifications or accommodations are necessary.

Using Appropriate Entry Points

Gaining students' attention at the start of any lesson is critical. Many of us do exactly what our own teachers did—automatically jump into a discussion or lecture without evaluating its motivational value. We learned from Project High Hopes (Chapter 4 and Appendix A) that too much "teacher talk," is rarely successful in engaging and holding students' attention, especially when their areas of ability are not linguistically oriented. In fact, for our spatial learners (engineers and visual artists), words get in the way. Their working memories simply can't process excessive verbiage. Think of typical lesson starters—classroom discussions, assessing prior knowledge verbally, vocabulary review, and reading the text. All of these can be barriers that keep 2e students from engaging. Initial activities must *invite* 2e students into the lesson or unit of study by creating meaningful contexts in which these learners can successfully connect ideas to prior understanding and form new concepts in ways that their brains may prefer. Teachers can use entry points in two ways: to develop skills or to introduce concepts within a unit (Baum et al., 2005).

Skill development. Twice-exceptional students with significant challenges in mathematics, reading, or writing often need a way to relieve their anxiety about these subjects at the start of new learning. Starting them in an area in which they feel efficacious (or have a talent for) can bridge them to learning the targeted skill. For example, using improvisational drama to develop and write about a character can be an important entry point for students with strengths in performing arts but who may also be reluctant writers. We worked in a seventh-grade classroom with students experiencing learning, attention, and emotional difficulties. Their teacher had described how it was nearly impossible to get the students to put their ideas in writing. We decided to use character interviews as an entry point. We started with some warm-up activities to set the stage for creative drama. The teacher took the role of a brilliant taxi driver, and one of us interviewed him. The students were then invited to ask the driver their own questions. (Interestingly, the students who had never said much before posed the most intriguing queries.) Next, we asked students to volunteer to play different characters, and we repeated the activity. One young man became a mad scientist, another a lazy dragon slayer with a Scottish brogue.

After these warm-ups, we brainstormed and listed questions we would want to know about any character. We then provided a list of interesting characters for the students to become (e.g., David the dangerous dentist, Lucky Lucy the hairdresser, and Clarence the exhausted clown). Asking the students to work in pairs, we explained that one would become the character and the other would assume the role of interviewer. We gave the students 5 minutes to conduct the interviews—no writing, just role-playing. At the conclusion of the "interview," we asked the students to write about themselves (if they were the character) or about the character they interviewed. We told them that they should just start writing or typing their ideas on the computer. We asked them to let the words flow without fretting about punctuation, spelling, or grammar. Over the course of a week, the students worked on polishing their drafts. Working with the draft on the computer made editing and revising a much simpler task for those who made that choice.

Using entry points for skill development is a fine example of leveraging strengths. Examples are found in Table 12.1. Note that the entry point, which should be relevant to students' strengths or interests, initiates the learning and is meant to engage the students. However, essential to the success of any entry point is the teacher's skill in guiding the students from the experience to the targeted goal. In this case, we brainstormed questions anyone would want to know about a character and presented a list of interesting characters for the students to describe. These prompts provided students with the structure that allowed them to develop and write about a character. Finally, using computers, students transformed their first drafts into credible pieces of writing.

Introduction of unit concepts. The second use of entry points provides different ways to introduce students to topics and concepts within a unit of study. Field trips, movie clips, guest speakers, demonstration, or pieces of artwork can provide information and perspectives about the content of any unit of study. Much like interactive museums that offer a variety of exhibits and activities to draw visitors into the room, teachers need to consider the kinds of teaching activities they implement to seduce the learner, especially at the early stages of a unit of study. Howard

Table 12.1

Entry Points to Skill Development

Instructional Strategy	Intelligence(s) Tapped	Example
Movement and writing	Bodily-kinesthetic	Bilingual 1st graders move to song "Monster Mash." Their monster movements generate descriptive vocabulary in English to use in writing.
Character interviews	Bodily-kinesthetic, Interpersonal, Intrapersonal	Sixth graders use improvisational techniques to develop characters for a story they are writing.
Storyboarding	Spatial	Fifth graders develop visual stories to improve their writing. They use storyboarding, filmmakers' techniques to organize and focus their ideas, and topic sentences and paragraphs.
Logic puzzles	Logical-mathematical	Third graders use a deductive reasoning puzzle to improve reading comprehension.
Music and graphing	Musical, Bodily-kinesthetic	Fourth graders practice writing music to learn and understand graphing.
Movement exercises	Bodily-kinesthetic, Spatial	Fourth graders develop their use of imagery and metaphors in writing poetry through movement exercises.

Note. From *Multiple Intelligences in the Elementary Classroom: A Teacher's Toolkit* (p. 66), by S. Baum, J. Viens, and B. Slatin, 2005, New York, NY: Teachers College Press. Copyright 2005 by Teachers College, Columbia University. Reprinted with permission.

Gardner (1999) argued that there are many windows into a room. The key is finding ones that invite different kinds of learners into the topics at hand. He argued that teachers should initiate units of study in ways that grab students' interest into a topic. For artistic students, the entry point might be using a painting or movie at the start of a unit on the French Revolution through which students are guided to notice the looks of despair of the population or the opulence of the upper class. For the block-building crew, it might be asking them to create a three-dimensional model of a building from that period to gain perspective on the times as the unit *begins.* For students strong in logical mathematical intelligence, a lesson on facts and figures about the economy that drove the French Revolution might connect them to the history unit early on. Gardner described seven possible entry points that align to the intelligences, as shown in Table 12.2.

When activities align with students' strengths and interests, teachers can entice even the most reluctant students to engage in learning in ways that interest these

Table 12.2
Howard Gardner's Entry Points

Entry Point	Description
Foundational/Existential (Aligned with the existential intelligence, for people who ask "big questions" or questions with philosophical overtones.)	Starting a unit with a big question: *Why are humans drawn to war? Why do humans allow other humans to starve? Why should we spend money on space exploration?*
Narrational (Aligned with linguistic intelligence, for people who like learning through stories.)	Presenting a story to introduce a unit.
Aesthetic (Associated with spatial and perhaps naturalist intelligences, for people who like to see a visual representation of an idea.)	Using works of art to analyze some aspect of the topic to be studied.
Quantitative/Numerical (Connected with logical/mathematical intelligence, for students who are attracted to numbers, who observe the world quantitatively.)	Describing numerical aspects or perspectives of a topic, such as the amount of money lost during the stock market crash of 1929 to introduce a unit on the Great Depression.
Experiential (Connected with bodily-kinesthetic, perhaps personal and spatial intelligences, for students who prefer hands-on experiences.)	Using hands-on activities like performances and experiments. (Introducing a unit on molecular bonding with a movement exercise or experiment.)
Social (Aligned with personal intelligences, for students most attracted to simulations, role-playing, working in groups to solve social problems.)	Beginning a unit on Westward expansion by simulating the trip. Students take on roles of the pioneers and solve problems daily concerning resources and relationships.
Musical (Aligned with musical intelligence.)	Beginning a unit with musical metaphors, such as listening to the message of the music in the Battle Hymn of the Republic to get a sense of the urgency of the Civil War, or comparing and contrasting music of a period to get a sense of the rhythm or tempo of the era.

Note. Adapted from *Intelligence Reframed: Multiple Intelligences for the 21st Century* (pp. 169–172), by H. Gardner, 1999, New York, NY: Basic Books.

bright youngsters and allow them to access information in ways that are not compromised by their individual learning issues.

We have been very successful using a multiple intelligences approach with 2e students. For example, we were introducing a unit on genetics to a group of bright seventh graders who had attention deficits along with difficulties in reading and writing. We started the unit using an experiential entry point in which we simulated the random assignment of X and Y chromosomes. One of us took the role of Mom and held sticky notes with "X" written in bold to represent the X chromosome given by females. The other assumed the role of Dad and held sticky notes of an equal number with "X" and "Y" markers to represent male contributions. The students drew a sticky note from each "parent" and affixed it to their shirts. Predictably, students found it hilarious when boys got to be girls and vice versa. But, on top of the humor, they very quickly understood the random nature of heredity. And, in the process, they absorbed new vocabulary and principles during the experience—"chromosome," "inherit," "females carry the X chromosome," and so on.

The next concept was introduced using a narrational/aesthetic entry point. Through a story and slideshow, we introduced the students to one of our families in which red hair was passed down from grandmother to daughter to grandchildren. Further into the topic, we told a story of the gene for hemophilia that also existed in that family but had remained hidden until a son was born. The students were very curious about the disease and paid close attention as the story of the young man unfolded through the slideshow. We then explained how the gene for hemophilia is carried on the X chromosome. It only remains hidden if another X chromosome is present *without* the gene for hemophilia. The students used cards with "h" on some and not on others to generate all of the possibilities of random combinations of X and Y chromosomes with some of the X chromosomes carrying the gene for hemophilia. We repeated the initial demonstration experience with the sticky notes, where, as before, they received their genetic makeup from Mom and Dad. This time, however, using a chart like Figure 12.1, they identified whether they had hemophilia, were a carrier, or did not have the gene at all.

During the second lesson, the students continued to learn new terms—*sex-linked genes, carriers, genotype, phenotype*. At the end of the sessions, they developed Punnett squares predicting the outcome of the grandchildren's children should they marry someone with no hemophilia. For homework, they read a brief summary of the concepts covered in the lessons as a review. The teacher remarked that she had never seen this group so attentive, and she noted that they could remember the language and principles 3 weeks later on a written exam.

We consistently find that when we present advanced content through alternate entry points, learners are thoroughly engaged and demonstrate that they understand the targeted concepts. Note that when using entry points to initiate learning, reading and discussion *follow* the lesson rather than precede it. Students learn vocabulary in the context of the experience and review it at the end of the session.

Genotype	X	X
X_h	XX_h Female carrier for hemophilia (phenotype)	XX_h Female carrier for hemophilia (phenotype)
Y	XY Male with no hemophilia (pheonotype)	XY Male with no hemophilia (pheonotype)

Figure 12.1. Student activity about chromosomes and hemophilia.

Performance-Based Assessments With Differentiated Exit Points

Another problem for students who have writing, organization, or attention difficulties is how teachers assess mastery of curricular objectives. Evaluating learning through conventional written tests and assignments may not be valid for some twice-exceptional students. Performance and product assessment are usually better evaluation tools. (In truth, we believe this type of assessment is better for all students.) According to Gardner (as cited in Checkley, 1997), to demonstrate whether a concept is understood, individuals should be able to represent their knowledge in more than one way using more than one symbol system:

> We have to put understanding up front in school. Once we have that goal, multiple intelligences can be a terrific handmaiden because understanding involves a mix of mental representations entailing different intelligences. (p. 11)

The group mural described in Melanie's story in Chapter 9 signaled how powerful it was in conveying meaning. Likewise, having students construct a working model of a complex machine is far more likely to tap their understanding of gears, levers, and pulleys as compared to a multiple choice test. Imagine how asking students to build a three-dimensional model of the Pythagorean theorem can lead to deeper and more authentic understanding of the meaning of the formula. Similarly, asking students to choreograph a dance sequence that would represent good versus evil in a particular novel would allow the performing artists in the class an outlet to creatively articulate the dance of conflicting forces.

The products described in the examples above parallel specific, real-life disciplines. Artists design murals, engineers build structures and models, and choreographers create movement stories. By concentrating on the real-world abilities and interests of twice-exceptional students, we can generate many choices for acceptable products. Table 12.3 offers more examples.

Table 12.3

Discipline-Related Products

Discipline	Products
Writers Communicate with words	Poetry, stories, editorials, speeches, scripts, song lyrics, letters to the editor
Artists Use visual images to communicate ideas	Paintings, sketches, photography, film, cartoons, digital art
Engineers Make models to explain or design how things work	Architectural models, working models, prototypes, three-dimensional models
Performing Artists Communicate ideas and feelings through performances	Skits, monologues, choreographed pieces including dance or music, gymnastic or other rhythmic stunts
Mathematicians and Economists Express ideas using mathematical representations	Formulas, tables, charts, graphs, timelines, equations
Social Activists Focus on bringing about awareness of social problems and creating change through action-oriented events	Public services, letter-writing campaigns, legislation, speeches, demonstrations, media events, effective use of the arts
Historians Recreate the past through documenting and analyzing primary sources and communicate their findings using appropriate products	Storytelling, photo essays, video documentaries, interviews, timelines, historical essays
Leaders Use their inter- and intrapersonal intelligences to organize others to accomplish goals	Lead an event, chair a committee, organize a trip
Scientists Design and carry out research and summarize findings	Hypothesizing, interviews or surveys, graphs, statistical summaries

These kinds of performances of understanding offered throughout a unit of study provide a foundation or schema for 2e students to help them with both writing assignments and taking traditional tests. Melanie was able to write about the characters in Conrad's *Heart of Darkness* by visualizing the mural. After using a simulation to introduce the genetics unit, the seventh graders were successful on their end of the unit test. For these students, active learning and authentic products readied them for more traditional writing assignments.

Investigating Authentic Problems

Bryan, the student who developed the court case simulation (Chapter 10), and the students in Project High Hopes (described in Appendix A) show how students can thrive when involved in problem-based learning and while investigating real-world problems. In these learning opportunities, students act as firsthand inquirers while developing authentic products (or performances) in response to real situations. They apply their strengths and abilities naturally. Solving genuine problems makes learning relevant and highly contextual— conditions of learning that make sense for many 2e students. Such experiences encourage them to become involved— addressing issues just as professionals do in their work, using methods of inquiry, materials, and strategies applicable to real-world domains. In this kind of learning, students see that their individual gifts are valued, respected, and often needed to solve the problem. They also learn that problem solving requires them to:

- think and act like a professional;
- work collaboratively, giving and receiving assistance, along with constructive criticism;
- understand how professionals go about modifying solutions to improve them;
- acknowledge that failures happen to everyone, and failures can offer good pointers about what *not* to do in the future;
- get back on their feet after failure or frustration;
- take advantage of their abilities; and
- appreciate that creative productivity is a realistic and socially useful objective.

Many of these incidental discoveries are related to aspects of self-regulation and executive function. In that sense, they do not address learning content but rather learning about learning. But, in the same regard, when these students engage in pursuing individual investigations, their executive function improves as they begin to regulate their learning. Let's revisit Debra and Bill.

Debra. Recall Debra, our young historian described in Chapter 2, who was in an enrichment program for students with learning disabilities. At the beginning of the program, the class explored several self-regulation strategies. She applied these strategies as she conducted her research study. Debra used mapping to organize her ideas, she visited the Noah Webster House several times to remember details (strategy for memorizing details = repeated oral and visual exposure), and she chose to assume the role of Jerusha Webster and to portray her life in a slide and tape presentation (strategy for communication = using her talent in dramatic expression). Finally, she asked if she could practice her narrative at home where there would be fewer distractions and where she could rehearse until she was pleased with her effort (strategy for focusing attention = finding an environment where there were fewer distractions).

Bill. Bill, who found it difficult to sustain attention, especially if the work was tedious, showed remarkable self-regulatory behaviors while involved in his science fair project, "Photorhabdus luminescens and the Inhibition of Pathogens & Its Possible Relationship to the Healing of Civil War Wounds That Glowed." Remember that Bill's primary goal in entering the science fair was to work with his friend; plus, he reasoned that the probability of winning was better through the team part of the competition. Combining his friend's interest in science with his own expertise in the Civil War—especially about the Battle of Shiloh and the mystery of the wounds that glowed in the dark—would make an unusual topic that could catch the attention of the judges.

The boys understood that their work would best be accomplished in a lab where they had the equipment needed to conduct their experiment. They also realized that they would need to find ways to be patient, as they anticipated lots of waiting time to see if Photorhabdus luminescens would produce antigens to inhibit the growth of pathogens they simulated. Another potential problem was that they would have to create grids and stencil them onto each Petri dish. This not only was tedious and boring, but labor-intensive as well. To help them stay on task, the boys decided to schedule "brain breaks" that included playing video games about conquering the world. This helped them return to the tasks with refreshed attention.

Some of the strategies they discovered could generalize to other situations, such as finding friends with common interests to collaborate, anticipating stumbling blocks of a project, and taking specific steps to plan for those blocks. And, of course, selecting projects that are intrinsically motivating and align to interest areas.

As noted earlier, an important incidental benefit of using authentic problems is that this practice allows students with different abilities to work together. Students can collaborate—mixing their interests, knowledge, and prior experiences—to bring innovative solutions to the problem and the ways they communicate results. In the best of all worlds, they learn from one another and come to value each other's unique perspectives. Compare this approach with the widely used cooperative learning arrangements in which students with challenges in reading and writing work with "experts" to reap the benefits the more advanced learners can offer. In these groupings, the challenged students often perceive that they are "less than," and are not given an equal opportunity to contribute.

In short, using an "authentic problems" approach allows students to join together through common interests and then contribute in ways that align to their abilities, strengths, and past experiences—applying basic skills within a meaningful context and engaging cooperatively in active inquiry and problem solving. Figure 12.2 provides a planning template for teachers to use when creating a problem-based

Identify (select, generate) a problem.	Problem:
Is there an issue or problem that will intrigue my students into inquiry, problem solving, and action?	Purpose:
	Audience:

Identify the professional roles students will assume and the talents needed. Assign student roles and organize groups.	Roles	Talents
What talents are needed to solve the problem? Which roles will the students assume?		

Align the problem-based experiences with curricular content and basic skills.	Curricular areas/ activities	Targeted concepts and skills
How can I cover basic skills in my yearly curriculum through problem-based learning?		

Figure 12.2. Planning template for problem-based learning. From *Multiple Intelligences in the Elementary Classroom: A Teacher's Toolkit* (p. 108), by S. Baum, J. Viens, and B. Slatin, 2005, New York, NY: Teachers College Press. Copyright 2005 by Teachers College, Columbia University. Reprinted with permission.

learning experience. Links to the regular curriculum and to students' talents are carefully identified.

Engaging Students in Critical and Creative Thinking

Simulations, debates, and role-playing are instructional strategies that encourage critical and creative thinking We know that many 2e students have considerable strengths in creative and higher order thinking. Where more unusual or creative answers are preferred, these students can excel. Such opportunities to contribute original and clever ideas should increase their self-efficacy, as well as add to their self-perception of being smart and valued. Experiences that encourage these higher level thinking opportunities will also help them develop alternate paths to reach goals and solve problems that bypass their learning problems. Strategies such as Creative Problem Solving, Synectics, and Talents Unlimited are especially suited to the learning styles of many 2e students. These strategies offer a systematic instructional approach that requires critical and creative thinking to solve problems and produce high-quality responses. Teachers can easily apply the techniques to both enrichment activities and the regular curriculum.

Creative Problem Solving (CPS; Eberle & Stanish, 1996) is a six-step procedure that guides students through idea generating (divergent thinking steps) and focusing (convergent thinking steps). CPS can be used to help solve real-world problems, personal problems, or problems embedded in the curriculum.

Synectics (Joyce, Weil, & Calhoun, 2014) is a model of teaching that helps students think about the world metaphorically. Students are introduced to three kinds of analogies—direct analogy, personal analogy, and symbolic analogy. Training activities help students make connections and see things in new ways. These skills enhance writing and also promote deep understanding of concepts.

Talents Unlimited (Schlicter, 2009) is a popular research-based strategy that develops skills in planning, forecasting, decision-making, communication, and productive thinking. These skills can be applied to any curricular area and also to real-world problem solving.

A final note: The instructional strategies included here are good for all students. But, through the use of strategies like these in the classroom, 2e students will be able to participate fully by applying their strengths and high cognitive abilities. Providing strength-based choices along with sophisticated and authentic content provides a dually differentiated intellectual environment.

Modifications to the Physical Learning Environment

Learning style theorists argue that no one learning environment suits all, for, depending on preferred styles of learning, particular physical conditions will enhance (or detract from) our ability to learn. Some of us prefer working in small groups around a table, and others prefer working independently seated at a desk with a straight back chair. Some can't concentrate with hubbub or background noises, while others prefer the blabber of a television show or music. Some of us read better by lamplight, and others prefer bright fluorescent lighting. Some of us need to move around while learning, while others need to sit quietly and reflect. The point is that in each classroom there should be options that allow students to discover (by trying different alternatives) and then choose to use their optimal setting for completing assignments, listening to a lecture or discussion, or getting themselves organized. The rest of this section will focus on strategies for

1. helping with hypersensitivity and other distractions,
2. accommodating the need for movement in learning,

3. seating and grouping arrangements, and

4. providing resources.

Strategies to Help With Hypersensitivity and Other Distractions

In what ways can teachers (and parents) help filter out extraneous stimulation so 2e students can concentrate and attend to the tasks at hand? Classrooms are often highly stimulating with lots of materials in view (i.e., books and games on open shelves and bulletin boards covered with student work or other eye-catching information). Even productive noise at tables where students are working together can permeate the room. For students with sensory issues, these distractions are not the only culprits. The glare and hum of the fluorescent lights, the feel of the plastic chair, or the sweet smell of the bouquet of flowers on the teacher's desk can be too much. Each classroom needs a quiet zone where these stimulants can be at a minimum. One or two cubicles with a small table laptop and headset could help those students who need "office" time. Some students would appreciate a reading corner with a comfortable chair and table lamp. Beanbag chairs to snuggle into during activities like circle time or class meetings can help to center or ground students with sensory issues.

For students who are distracted by random sounds, allowing them to listen to music often helps them find focus. Rhythmic, predictable, and probably familiar music has been shown to shut out extraneous noise. As we learned from Bryan's story, some students fare better when they are tuned into their music through headphones.

Accommodating the Need for Movement

We have found that hyperactive 2e students, and/or those with bodily kinesthetic strengths often benefit from environments that provide outlets for their energetic learning style and need for movement. Some students are packed with energy and have difficulty sitting still for sustained periods, so it is important to think about how much time we ask our students to sit still. Recent brain research points to the need for exercise and movement to stimulate the brain for all of us (Medina, 2008). In his book *Brain Rules*, Medina explained that the ability to pay attention is developmental. The number of minutes is directly related to the number of years, until the age of 15. For everyone, attention begins to wane after the first 10 minutes of a lesson unless there is a shift of activity. Consider the use of circle time in early childhood where sitting still can be very difficult. We have observed classrooms where young students (3–6 years old) are expected to sit in a "crisscross applesauce" position (backs straight and legs crossed) for up to 20 minutes of "circle time." Hyperactive youngsters, especially little boys, are *always* in trouble during those times, as they can be found rolling around on the floor, picking at the rug fibers, or tapping the child next to them. Yet, frequently, they can answer any question asked about the topic under discussion. Their movements enabled them to listen and attend. Jonathan Mooney, a popular speaker about neurodiversity, insisted that his brain works better when he is moving (Mooney & Cole, 2000). Making him sit still at a desk effectively turns off his brain.

Providing chairs that allow for wiggling, such as therapy balls or "wiggle seats," has shown much success in helping hyperactive youngsters stay seated and focused. There are varieties of seating available that allow gentle bouncing and rocking, some even equipped to create deep pressure to calm students. Appropriate accommodations for increased attention and focus could also include "a walking corridor" in the back of the room where students can stand up and pace or a writing desk or lectern so students can stand.

Movement can be part of learning that not only enhances attention but also helps students understand concepts. For example, teachers have used movement to illustrate molecular change from solids, liquids, and gas when students become the air molecules and move with others to show physical bonding. Some math teachers use movement to help students understand abstract concepts, such as the relationships among the concepts of distance, rate, and time. Not only do these activities engage the learner through movement, but they also enhance conceptual understanding of the lesson.

Other useful movement activities can help students attend while processing information. Instead of using the "pair-share" strategy where students stay seated to talk to their neighbor about what is being taught, for example, have them walk with their partner around the periphery of the room while responding to a prompt or just reviewing the main elements of the lesson. Even opportunities for smaller movements can help students stay focused, calm, and connected. Fidgets (objects that can be held, squeezed, rolled in their hands) include items like stress balls, play dough, objects to bend, and Squigglets. There are even fidgets for the feet. In some instances, chewing gum can provide calming, kinesthetic input.

Seating and Grouping Arrangements

Other classroom arrangements can be helpful. We have found that for large-group discussions, 2e students usually need to be seated close to the teacher and out of the way of distractions, such as windows and doors. Having a study buddy sitting nearby might prompt the student for attention and details about assignments. Whole-class teaching should be kept at a minimum, as these students fare much better in small-group learning. Grouping arrangements particularly effective for cooperative learning are those that put students together by talent or interests. Clear written directions, expectations for productivity, and a timetable help 2e students work effectively within the group. Putting a timer on the group's table can also help keep everyone on task. Under these circumstances we have found that small table arrangements work well, as students can easily watch the teacher, and the teacher can easily observe each student.

Providing Resources

Another important consideration is to make resources accessible that align with the students' strengths and interests. For example, having blocks available for the young engineer to use for product development or art supplies for the talented artists should enhance their ability to succeed across the curriculum. Also, a variety of multimedia resources, including books on tape, websites, podcasts, picture books, and film clips that all students can access to enrich the content of a unit, will allow 2e students to choose how to explore a topic in ways that do not make them feel different. Finally, many of these students need healthy snacks and proteins to help them stay regulated. Using frequent snack and water breaks for all students would enhance the learning environment for them and their classmates.

Flexibility is key to creating a nurturing physical environment for 2e students. Discuss options with your students and include them in experiments to learn which conditions help them work at their personal best. Listening to your students' suggestions will reinforce the idea that their ideas count and that you are all on the same team.

Creating a Supportive Emotional Environment

The emotional climate of a classroom can promote a sense of well-being and acceptance where each child feels like a valued member of the community, or it can be a place of anxiety and threats with fear of punishment, ridicule, and unreasonable demands for these highly sensitive students. As we discussed in Chapter 5, anxiety and stress will compromise all aspects of learning, often resulting in lower performance and negative behaviors on the part of 2e students. Twice-exceptional learners often lack skills in emotional and social regulation, organization, stress management, and conflict management. Easily overwhelmed by negativity or challenge, they can find themselves unable to cope emotionally with the demands of learning, as shown in the stories throughout the book. In this section, we offer five major guidelines to help build a supportive environment in which 2e students can become emotionally available to learn:

1. create learning communities;
2. teach executive function skills, including time management and organization;
3. teach stress management, conflict resolution, and anger management skills;
4. create contextual opportunities to create social awareness and practice social skills; and

5. provide ways for students to recover emotionally with short- and long-term breaks.

Create Learning Communities

To create a positive learning environment, it is essential to take the time to set up a learning community where all students feel valued and respected. Students are taught to honor diversity in the largest sense of the word, and opportunities are created for students to be respected for what they can do. Below are some ideas for a working learning community.

In a learning community, students create essential agreements as they formulate the rules that will help them learn. Some rules should promote positive behavior such as "our behavior keeps everyone safe" or "we are respectful of people and our environment," or "we are here to learn." Examples of each of the rules will provide students with clear boundaries. Once the rules are understood, the students sign the essential agreement, showing their willingness to abide by them. When an agreement is broken, students need to problem solve how to resolve the issue so they can participate again as active members in the community.

In a learning community, members care about each other and understand what each other needs. For example, some classes start the day off with a "meet and greet" with students gathering in a circle to acknowledge each other with prompts such as "this would be a better day if . . . ." One by one, students respond in turn by recognizing what the previous student said and then offering his or her own thought. Some of the responses we have heard 2e students make were particularly revealing:

> "It would be a better day today if I had someone to play with at lunch."
> "For me, it would be a better day if I was noted for what I did well instead of what I did not do."

"Meet and greets" serve as emotional check-ins through which teachers and students become more aware of what each other needs emotionally. Then, they understand how they can help each other get what they need. Other prompts might be "what I would like to learn today," or "if this day could have one more hour I could. . . ." We recommend that classes hold "meet and greets" several times a week.

In a vibrant learning community, all students have strength-based choices. Rather than accommodating the needs of a select few, all students are offered options for mastering the curriculum. Each option is valued and respected. Twice-exceptional students are very sensitive to being different and may refuse accommodations to avoid appearing less capable or not like the others. Offering a diversity of options to the whole class lets students know that their special abilities are important. For example, a student can feel satisfaction by producing a quality video about life in the Amazon that is as valued as well-written essay on the same topic.

Sometimes our use of language can inadvertently make students feel incompetent. Consider the differences in asking students to contribute a piece of work to the class's writing center in contrast to asking them to contribute a work to the publishing center. In a publishing center, we might find creative writing, a well-narrated podcast, or a photographic essay. This subtle change in language is powerful in helping students whose anxiety is raised as soon as the word "writing" is mentioned. (Yes, at times all students *will* need to write, but being an author or creator of a "published work" can be broadened to accommodate the many ways one communicates in the real world.)

In a learning community, students work together to help each other learn and produce. Working as teams or in small groups builds a sense of belonging among students, especially when each member can contribute to a quality body of the work. Talent groups work particularly well, as students with similar abilities often combine their talents to create impressive projects. For example, a group of young architects can design and build a prototype of a futuristic city they will use as a setting for story. During the planning stage, students hear each other's ideas and figure out how to work cooperatively with each other (even discovering the power of compromise). Another type of grouping is to place students with different interests and abilities to form a multitalented group or team. Pairing a writer with an illustrator can result in an innovative picture book reflecting the topic being studied. Project High Hopes used multitalented groups of scientists, engineers, artists, and performing artists. Each member of the group contributed to the final outcome as they worked jointly on the "pond problem" (described in Appendix A). Groups work best when teachers help the members review the rules for working together as a team and devise an action plan in which tasks are delineated and a time frame established.

In a learning community, students feel comfortable reaching out and asking for help. Designing a bulletin board where students can place "situations wanted" ads and "help wanted" ads can facilitate this process. All students can "advertise" their strengths and seek help in areas of their challenges. An ad might read, "Do you need a great cover to put on your social studies report? See Suzy, the local artist." Or, "Help Help Help! I need someone to review what is assigned for homework each afternoon before dismissal. If you have great organizational skills, please apply for the position."

Teach Executive Function Skills: Time Management and Organization

Many 2e students have difficulty with executive function skills, especially in their ability to set priorities, manage time, and organize their lives. Backward planning is a basic strategy that can help with time management and organizing events.

By providing management plans that outline steps and include clear timelines for completing their work, students can understand the idea of backwards planning. Such a plan lists individual tasks to be covered and provides target due dates and possible resources. Initially, these plans should be very detailed and target dates monitored carefully. It is a good idea to sit with students to get them started because frequently students simply do not know how to begin. (See Chapter 10 for a completed management plan.)

Although backward planning is an essential skill for all students, how the plan is organized and implemented should be personalized for individual students. Best strategies for organization and time management depend considerably on individual personality preferences. For example, Practical Managers and Learned Experts are more linear in how they organize their world (these are the students who like file folders). They benefit from to-do lists and outlines. They prefer quiet workspaces and are more comfortable with specific deadlines. Creative Problem Solvers and People Persons organize in nonlinear ways (think of stacks and piles of papers). They often prefer webbing out their ideas. They need more flexible management plans with a few firm deadlines along the way. Consider monthly calendars using sticky notes for tasks that can be can be moved around as needed. These students need space to spread out and keep their materials around them as they work. Table 12.4 reintroduces four students we highlighted in previous chapters and shows their organization and time management preferences relating to their personality styles.

Students enjoy experimenting with different ideas for organization and meeting deadlines. They can conduct their own "action research" to learn which strategies or combinations of strategies work best for them. We know that an imposed time management or organizational structure does not work as well as those designed by the students based on their style preferences.

Teach Stress Management, Conflict Resolution, and Anger Management Skills

Many of our students have emotional triggers that set them off, particularly in school settings. Meltdowns, bursts of anger, and an inability to get along with others create havoc in their lives and for those around them. Research has shown that teaching the skills of emotional intelligence actually can have a greater impact on emotional regulation than medication (Davidson & Begley, 2012). Table 12.5 includes a few suggestions for strategies that have been successful to help 2e students regulate emotion, resolve conflict, and manage their stress.

Teaching students how to reframe their perceptions of an event is another strategy to help students with emotional regulation. Here is an example from a discussion between a 2e student and the school counselor about creating a positive way of confronting stress:

Table 12.4

Students' Personality and Organization Preferences

Student	Personality Profile	Organization Tips Used When Working on Projects
Debra Project: "A Day in the Life of Jerusha Webster"	People Person, Learned Expert	• Used a shelf to organize piles of information for project. • Used webs for planning. • Used a monthly calendar with color-coded sticky notes to organize tasks and allow for flexibility within time frame. • Set broad deadlines to guide process with a firm deadline for completion.
Jimmy Project: Campaign to promote wearing bicycle helmets	Creative Problem Solver	• Kept materials and resources in a container. • Used a sticky note calendar so he could adjust the order of events and could physically discard note when task was done. • Had broad but firm deadlines.
Bill Project: Science research on "Photorhabdus luminescens: Inhibition of Pathogens & Its Possible Relationship to the Healing of Civil War Wounds that Glowed"	Learned Expert, Practical Manager	• Filed information in folders. • Created a detailed list of all tasks needed with specific deadlines for each. • Worked in a quiet and orderly space.
Kyle Project: Talking Computer Comedy Skit	Creative Problem Solver, Learned Expert	• Outlined for tasks • Created a flowchart on the computer. • Used online resources.

We have talked often about changing your response to stressful situations. The first step is to advocate for yourself and talk with your teacher. We will not make you do anything that you are not ready for. You are never in trouble if you need to leave class and stretch or walk or have a snack.

Can you agree not to say the words "I can't," "I won't," and "I hate"? Instead, from today forward, you can use the words, "I feel overwhelmed right now," "I feel scared about this class," or "I am afraid that I may not be successful."

Table 12.5
Strategies for Emotional Regulation

Strategy	Short Description	Skill	Resource
"I" Statements	Nonblaming statements that simply communicate how one person is affecting another; do not criticize; e.g., "When you tell me what I did right, I can do it again and I feel happy," or "When you say mean words to me, I can't get my work done and I feel frustrated."	Conflict Resolution: Communicating clearly about an interaction with another. The statements can be both positive and negative.	*Teaching Children to Care: Classroom Management for Ethical and Academic Growth, K–8* (Rev. ed.) by Ruth Sidney Charney (2015)
Action Wheels	Students can create an option wheel of actions that they can use to become regulated when upset, angry, or sad. The actions may be put on a wheel they can spin to select a strategy to help in the moment.	Mood management.	*Positive Discipline: The Classic Guide to Helping Children Develop Self-Discipline, Responsibility, Cooperation, and Problem-Solving Skills* by Jane Nelson (2006) (Her blog is https://www.positivediscipline.com/blog)
Deep Breathing	Learning to take deep breaths when anxious. There are many deep breathing techniques students can use to counteract anxious feelings. These skills should be practiced regularly so all students have them at their disposal during anxious moments.	Stress management.	The Mindful Classroom (https://themindfulclassroom.wordpress.com/2012/12/09/self-regulation-one-breath-at-a-time)

The more sensible strategies we can offer these students, the more likely they will be able to regulate their emotions. Remember that this is a slow process, so it is important to notice even incremental positive steps to self-regulation.

Use Authentic Contexts for the Development of Social Awareness, Social Skills, and Building Friendships

Some twice-exceptional students have difficulty making friends, understanding social context, and conversing with others due to their particular neurology. Often, these students participate in social skills training or attend social skills classes. We have found that embedding skill development into authentic contexts is particularly helpful for students who have little awareness of social skills. Here are some examples.

Use drama to build social awareness and social skills. Improvisation is a bona fide way to help students read the social context, anticipate emotional responses, and reply accordingly (Sciortino, 2016). All students at Bridges Academy take a drama class in which improvisation techniques help them respond socially and emotionally to unrehearsed situations. The effectiveness of using drama has been confirmed by a Vanderbilt University study funded by the National Institute of Health (Corbett et al., 2011). The results showed that a specially designed theater program had a significantly positive effect on social cognition, social interaction, and social communication in students with ASD.

Likewise, when social awareness and social skills are embedded into authentic learning experiences, students see the value of the skills and are more willing to practice them. For example, middle school students at Bridges Academy participated in a mock trial competition as part of their humanities class. Because they knew they would be appearing before a judge in a court of law, they were very receptive to lessons about making eye contact with the judge, the witnesses, and other "young attorneys." They learned how to listen carefully, ask questions when they did not understand a statement, and even how to dress appropriately for their appearance. Their drama teacher also taught them deep breathing techniques and how taking a sip of water could reduce their anxiety before the judge.

Create opportunities for students to forge friendships through common interests. Friendships happen when there is a reason for two individuals to want to spend time together. We have found that common interests are an effective starting point. For example, students may begin to interact with each other outside of class around their interests in video games. Minecraft, in particular, has students interact with each other as they visit each other's worlds and find commonalities to share. Such interests then lead to successful playdates, and, from these, a growing friendship may include going to a movie or just hanging out.

When there is a problem, Richard Lavoie (2005) explained that by using the "Social Skills Autopsy" approach, a 2e student can build social competencies (p. xlvii). Understanding that most social skill errors are not intentional (it is human to want to be liked), the basic principle of the "autopsy" is to help (nonjudgmentally) the child deconstruct the awkward situation and develop possible solutions. First, ask the student if he or she can identify the social error that just happened. If necessary, help interpret the situation. Then, together, discuss and role-play alternative social responses. Finally, create a scenario similar to the actual problem situation. This will allow the student to demonstrate his or her ability to respond, showing that he or she understands what is called for socially. If handled well, this strategy can be a fun and interesting way for students to improve their social confidence.

Provide ways for students to recover emotionally. Highly fragile, often emotionally charged 2e students require mechanisms to recover from outbursts, meltdowns, or shutdowns. Adults need to be sensitive to how the student is feeling and reacting at the moment and offer opportunities for them to regroup. One way to do this is to provide a safe place for the student to go where he or she can talk to someone, wash his or her face, or just sit quietly. For some, allowing time to switch focus and engage in something that is pleasant, such as playing with LEGO bricks, coloring, listening to music, or writing poetry, can bring calm feelings. For others, taking a walk or shooting baskets can be a settling activity. Once recovered, the student can suggest ways that he or she can then return to class.

When students cannot attend or participate in class activities after several reminders, it is a good idea to have a place to send them where they can think about why they are having a difficult time. Adults trained in helping students debrief what transpired monitor these "recovery rooms." Students are reminded of the essential agreement they signed and are encouraged to think of ways they can be in compliance.

Sometimes, students stop producing and/or become increasingly oppositional. When traditional strategies such as short-term breaks or consequences for behavior fail to make a difference, it may be time for what we call a TDO, or a talent development opportunity. Let's return to Olivia's story (Chapter 3). During her eighth-grade year, she was having difficulty completing her work, making friends in the new school, and was particularly stressed during physical education. Her sarcasm and refusal to participate, especially during P.E., resulted in her spending considerable time with the school counselor. She alternated between complaining about her peers and discussing her idea to paint a mural. She saw her classmates as prototypical monsters, each one with personality quirks and unique characteristics. Olivia argued that the perfect spot for the mural would be on the large blank wall in the counselor's office. After weeks of trying to convince the counselor to let her paint the mural, the counselor agreed—with the proviso that Olivia would submit a written proposal and present it to the school director. She jumped at this opportunity and spent a week working on the proposal with the assistance of the counselor.

The director actually liked the idea and thought Olivia's time would be better spent developing her artistic talent rather than disrupting P.E. class for the next several weeks. His willingness to allow time and space to create her mural was therapeutic for Olivia. She felt that the director trusted her and respected her idea. This proved to be a turning point for Olivia. Indeed, she became much more agreeable and even began to make some friends.

Note that the time for Olivia to paint the mural was not contingent on her behaving or producing in the classroom. This may seem contradictory to the more familiar strategy of pairing activities so that the less desirable task *precedes* a preferred task. This strategy is sometimes called Grandma's Rule, in deference to the often heard "You must finish your [some unpleasant vegetable], then you may have dessert." But, for students who are having a particularly difficult time, it is necessary to get them out of the deep hole they may have dug for themselves and instead give them a healthy dose of talent development. We have found that immersing them in an area of interest or talent can reduce anxiety and provide them with some hope for brighter days to come.

To conclude, these students spend a considerable time in school each day. If the learning environment does not support them and if these students don't feel appreciated and capable, their learning problems can grow to become severe emotional issues. Respecting the need for compatible, supportive intellectual, physical, and emotional environments for 2e students will contribute to their sense of well-being.

CHAPTER 13

When Learning Breaks Down

Modifications and Accommodations

As we pointed out in Chapter 5, learning follows a somewhat pre-dictable cognitive sequence. The sequence begins with a stimulus or event getting attention, and then the senses transfer the information into short-term storage where the brain's working memory begins to interpret, manipulate, and categorize information. In the best cases, the information eventually resides in long-term memory, where it can be retrieved and communicated as needed. For many 2e youngsters, these processes are not smooth, causing difficulty remembering, working with, and communicating information. Indeed, difficulties in the required areas of reading, writing, spelling, and mathematics keep these youngsters from thriving in school.

Many of these learning difficulties tend to remain through life. Therefore, a poor speller may need to rely on a proofreader or editor to check written work. Students who have difficulty memorizing math facts might need to ensure accuracy by using a calculator. Basic, repe-titious remediation for weaknesses is often not appropriate for them. Although remediation may make the learner a little more skillful, he or she will rarely become proficient in areas of weakness. At some point, we must decide when to use compensation techniques in favor of remedial strategies. Clarifying the targeted outcome can help guide this decision. For example, we should ask, "To what extent do we help children by teaching them to improve their handwriting before encour-aging them to put their thoughts on paper through technology?" Is the intended outcome authoring for communicating ideas or being able to produce readable handwriting?

What is the distinction between a disability and a handicap? Disabilities are physical states or conditions that result in impairment of functioning. Disabilities become handicaps when they interfere with the individual's ability to function in specific situations. We know that 2e learners can be capable and productive in some areas in school, as well as many areas outside school. They can learn, create, and perform well. When trying to meet some school or classroom requirements, however, they become handicapped because of the way they are asked to learn or perform. It is essential that we try to evaluate whether the environment is creating the handicap. Might a simple modification remove the student's roadblock to learning?

Consider the student who has an excellent understanding of mathematical principles but has great difficulty remembering math facts. What would be in the student's best interest—giving him or her 30 minutes a day of drill or allowing him or her to use a calculator? Will a small adjustment to the environment avoid handicapping this student's ability to succeed? Is it also possible that using a calculator to perform drill exercises might support the eventual remembering of the facts? At times, we must make modifications in the educational environment to accommodate specific learning needs. In our work, we use the term *modifications* to indicate the specific adjustments we can make to the learning environment to accommodate students' needs. The modifications allow these students *to compensate* for problematic weaknesses.

Effective compensation strategies are often unique to each individual (Mooney & Cole, 2000; Reis, Neu, & McGuire, 1995), for the success of any strategy depends on how well it fits with the student's learning strengths and patterns. For students like Olivia and Melanie, using art as a basis for writing was successful. In Melanie's case, she also relied on her friendships and social relationships for support in such activities as note taking and test review. Because she tested high as a People Person, this makes perfect sense for her. Olivia, a Learned Expert, was more analytical in how she processed information. She preferred grappling with concepts and explaining them through metaphor. Olivia also knew her debating skills were excellent (some of us call it arguing), so when allowed to choose a genre for writing, she liked to produce persuasive essays or opinion pieces.

For other students, technology may hold the key for their way of learning. Blaine found it difficult to attend to lectures, especially if the material was not novel or the pace of the lesson was slow. He found himself wanting more in-depth information about the topic than was currently being discussed. His teachers modified their lessons by allowing him to explore websites with advanced information about the topic during class discussions. He collected the most interesting facts and created fact sheets to share with classmates. For other students, a class discussion may be too fast-paced. Slow processing speed interferes with their ability to understand concepts. For them, using technology such as taping class lectures or using a laptop computer to take notes in class helps their particular brain wiring keep track of the conversations. Modifications that match the student's strengths obtain the best results.

To start this section, let's look at the specific areas where learning might be breaking down for 2e students and discuss modifications and accommodations that could be helpful. In Table 13.1 we present the most common areas of dysfunction and offer some practical tips and modifications for helping students compensate.

Focusing and Sustaining Attention

For bright minds to focus, information needs to be novel, personally relevant, or embedded within a meaningful context. When we previously discussed problems with attention and focus, we suggested that teachers try using entry points that fit with students' intellectual strengths and curiosities to engage them more fully in the curriculum and instruction. But, for 2e students whose brains may be wired differently, it is also important to consider the level of the content being taught. Does the lesson match readiness levels? Is the content of the lesson too easy or too difficult? Likewise, care should be taken to adjust the pacing of the lesson to align to a student's ability to learn new information. Finally, the quality of the responses should be sought rather than quantity for two reasons. First, the ability to sustain attention (once the novelty is gone) can be extremely difficult for these students. Second, because of slow processing speed, completing all of the work can be counterproductive. Consider fewer problems or more time to complete.

For many 2e students, sitting and listening invite inattention, but movement and active engagement can increase attention. Integrate movement into the curriculum. Allow them to walk and talk to organize their ideas and to think of ways they can initiate their work, as we described in the previous chapter.

Prompts can focus attention, such as "I need you to focus on this picture for a moment," or "Think about how long this assignment should take. I have allotted 5 minutes. Will that be enough time?" Let them hold a fidget, listen to music, or whatever these students believe will help them focus and sustain their attention over the course of the lesson.

Accessing Information With Limited Reading Skills

Bright students who have problems with decoding written content should have access to information in ways that minimize reading. Using inquiry methods and primary sources are exciting and sophisticated ways of learning. Instruction that incorporates entry points such as films, television documentaries, live drama, TED Talks, and well-reviewed websites are especially useful in conveying facts and new

Table 13.1
Modifications and Accommodations

Difficulty	Keys
Focusing and sustaining attention	• Employ environmental modifications • Use alternate entry points aligned to students' strengths and interests • Use technology • Try novelty • Allow attention sustainers: permitting gum chewing, listening to music using headphones, underlining or highlighting text when reading, doodling or playing with clay or silly putty while listening
Acquiring information with limited reading skills	• Use a multiple intelligences approach • Reverse the usual sequence, i.e., begin with experience • Teach through projects • Teach through the arts (drama, visual arts, poetry, etc.) • Use seminar instruction, lively discussion groups, simulations, and moral dilemmas • Use primary sources such as interviews, guest speakers, demonstrations • Engage students in discussion using supporting text • Take advantage of multimedia presentations • Use picture books • Employ teaching materials with a visual component • Provide books on tape • Use text-to-speech software
Organizing information	• Use advance organizers • Provided skeletal outlines • Use visual models and recipes • Teach and model webbing, storyboarding, using flowcharts • Provide software programs that help with writing and organizing • Use inductive teaching strategies
Remembering details and noncontextual materials	• Provide meaningful contexts for integrating facts and strategies • Use mnemonic devices • Use, and teach how to use, visual imagery • Allow students to use highlighter pens to mark important concepts (if rules permit it) • Encourage students to teach each other • Use word processor and laptop computer for note-taking • Provide student with a copy of the information that highlights key facts • Have students sequence activities after a lesson or event • Have students tape directions or information

Table 13.1, continued.

Difficulty	Keys
Remembering details and noncontextual materials, *continued.*	• Provide students with environmental cues and prompts (posted rules, steps for performing tasks, etc.) • Allow students to use resources in the environment to recall information (notes, textbooks, pictures, etc.) • Have students outline, summarize, or underline information to be remembered • Tell students what to listen for when being given directions or receiving information • Have students immediately repeat or paraphrase directions or information
Written expression (These suggestions assume that writing does not equate with paper-and-pencil tasks. When possible, students should complete writing tasks using a word processor.)	• Use artistic (visual and performing), scientific, and technological products to communicate knowledge • Use portfolio assessment of products and performances in addition to grading written products • Use technology (e.g., word processing programs with spelling and grammar check, electronic speller, word predictive software, organizational software) • Establish writing routine through ongoing discussion and practice • Extend time for completing written assignments or tests • Instruct students about using graphic organizers • Provide clear written expectations for writing tasks (rubrics) • Enlist writing prompts • Encourage students to proofread for only one type of error at a time • Use writing for real-world purposes

information to the student. Lectures, taped interviews, podcasts, books on tape, and text-to-speech software also provide students with alternate means of collecting information. Using field trips, demonstrations, and enthusiastic guest speakers can initiate and sustain learning in engaging ways.

Families, too, can provide these experiences for their youngsters. By informing parents of the topics you will be covering during the year, families may be able to arrange outings to a museum, play, or historic site related to the curriculum (and, in the best of circumstances, they might invite a classmate to participate along with their child). These outings can help 2e students acquire a more useful mental scaffolding to which they can link the new information covered in class. When these kinds of experiences *precede* the reading assignment, students can more easily decode the content because they already have some cognitive preparation from their prior experiences.

Picture books are particularly effective resources for students who are spatially oriented and prefer images to written words. High-quality picture books covering a wide range of topics exist for all age groups and can help introduce topics. Well-done illustrations can deliver a wealth of content and provide a context, making reading and comprehending the text easier. Students can explore original selections from Emily Dickinson, William Shakespeare, Robert Browning, Robert Frost, and others using picture books that artistically represent their work. History buffs can spend days pouring over visual accounts, such as maps of the Civil War battles. Graphic novels—many of which exist for nonfiction topics as well as fiction—can also serve as an effective format for presenting sophisticated content and greatly enhance reading enjoyment for 2e learners. The pictures present welcome invitations for inquiry and in-depth learning.

Accommodations to Address Deficits in Working Memory

It is not unusual for 2e students to have difficulty with working memory, which means it may take them longer to understand and interpret language. For some, the problem worsens during listening; with others, comprehending written language is more difficult. The ability to follow a lesson, decode symbols, encode, and manipulate the information mentally can also be problematic. Finally, deficits in working memory greatly affect production. Complex tasks that require a series of mental operations—organizing the information, thinking about meaning, and producing an intelligent response—are laborious at best. These students need strategies to help them keep track of their thinking.

Manipulating Information Mentally

Students need to be able to follow classroom discussions, take notes, and respond spontaneously when asked. When they are bombarded with information, having a way to focus and categorize the ideas can be helpful. For example, starting a lesson by sharing verbally and visually the lesson's purpose and how the information will be covered will help those students who need the structure defined for them. Likewise, providing a visual organizer such as an outline or flowchart showing the progression of the lesson supports working memory in making sense of the information. Another strategy is to use a PowerPoint presentation depicting the outline of the lecture. Pointing to the place in the outline that is being discussed at each moment allows students to keep track of the lesson. These strategies will also help students take notes—often a formidable task for 2e students. They are often confused about organizing the content into major topics and subtopics because they are unable to distinguish core content from peripheral material. Each fact can appear as a separate and equal entity, putting a sizable strain on their capacity to follow the discussion, isolate what is important, and write it down. If handwriting and spelling are not automatic, using even more mental energy to think about their handwriting and spelling makes note-taking nearly impossible and certainly not practical. Providing outlines ahead of time so students can highlight information, use visual symbols, or even record the lesson is preferable.

For similar reasons, it may be difficult for these students to participate in classroom discussions. By prompting 2e students ahead of time about the focus of the discussion, however, they can prepare their comments by jotting down some ideas that they would like to share with the class during discussions.

Visual organizers and verbal prompts can be very effective in helping these students follow a lesson, participate in discussions, and produce good work. The more we can do to help students with working memory deficits by not overloading them with too much information at once, the more likely they will be able process the information and expend their mental energy for thinking and responding.

Organizing for Production

In addition to having difficulty organizing and understanding information presented to them, many 2e students have trouble organizing information for products and presentations. These students are often holistic thinkers, and their ideas do not emerge in neat, sequential formats. When faced with planning a project or a piece of writing, these students simply do not know where to begin. Providing them with visual cues or having them create a model of their ideas, such as webs, storyboards, visual representations, and structured responsive formats, can help them organize their ideas for discussions, as well as for written products.

Webs or mind maps. These graphic organizers help students sort their ideas and sequence them into a logical written or oral response. Webbing begins by listing random and disconnected ideas on paper. We recommend using sticky notes or index cards so students can sort the ideas into groups. Labeling the groups helps to formulate the categories for the web. From this first web, students can generate new and more focused webs by adding details as needed (see Melanie's mind maps in Chapter 9). The web then is a visual map through which students can see the big idea and the supportive ideas. This map can then become a linear outline, as desired. The major subtopics become the Roman numerals of the outline, and the details listed under those headings become the alphabet letters of the outline. Of course, all of this can be done using software programs like Inspiration or Kidspiration (http://www.inspiration.com), or other mind mapping programs. There are also project management sites like Trello (https://trello.com) that greatly help students organize their search, create timelines, and keep information organized. We discuss more about technology later in this chapter.

Webs can be used effectively for planning a project as well as organizing the search. Debra, the young, fourth-grade historian introduced in Chapter 2, was inspired by an antique photograph album during a classroom interest center on historical research. She wanted to know much more about the family documented in the artifact but realized that answers could not be found in the available resources. The teacher encouraged her to consider what other kinds of questions she could explore and, as they talked, the teacher sketched out their ideas in a web format (see Figure 13.1).

After generating some tentative ideas, Debra evaluated the possibilities to see which one was the most appealing and feasible. The initial investigation included a trip to the Noah Webster House. Debra was captivated by the artifacts and historical lore all around her and thus began her original research. After carefully considering possible topics to be included, Debra developed a second web to help her plan her research, as shown in Figure 13.2. This format led to some research questions, an outline, and potential resources for finding information. Particularly useful is that through this process, the students get to focus the research and form the questions they wish to explore before reading up on the topic. Information gathering then can focus on one "bubble" at a time.

Other graphic organizers. Additional organizers include Venn diagrams, flowcharts, and many more easily accessible online options. Venn diagrams can be a great way to address the problem of comparing and contrasting particular topics. They require students to consider how classes of information relate to each other. Once the student establishes a picture of relationships, it becomes far easier to describe, especially for students whose strengths are in spatial intelligence. Likewise, flowcharts offer students a visual means of organizing information in order to get a clearer picture of relationships among facts, concepts, or events. This is especially critical for those students who have all of the facts but who have difficulty seeing the big picture. These organizers are helpful scaffolds for teachers to use to promote the understanding of concepts, relationships, and principles.

Storyboarding. One useful strategy for helping students organize a project or story is for them to create a storyboard. If they think like a filmmaker, they will depict the story as if they are seeing a movie in their heads. Each frame of the storyboard becomes a focus point to be developed later by adding details. Drawing a storyboard can also help with memory and sequencing. The storyboard pictured in Figure 13.3 sketches out some of the events leading up to the American Revolution. The student need not be artistic; stick figures with words here and there will suffice. As we mentioned before, any technique in which the student actively interacts with the content will enhance learning.

Visual representations, rubrics, formats. Providing a high-quality example to steer product development can help 2e students think about how they will communicate their ideas. Providing the scoring/grading rubric as a guide can help them

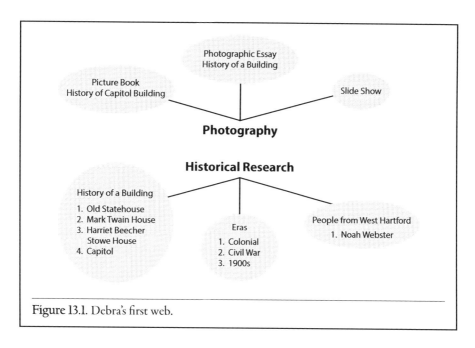

Figure 13.1. Debra's first web.

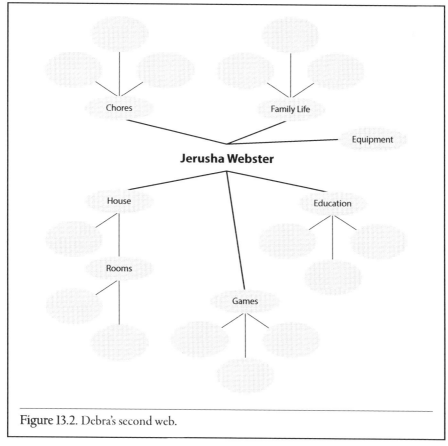

Figure 13.2. Debra's second web.

Figure 13.3. Storyboard of events leading up to American Revolution.

focus on the essential components and requirements of the assignment. A visual sketch of what the product should include is another option for students to understand what is expected.

Strategies for Remembering Details and Noncontextual Information

Some 2e students experience difficulties in storing and retrieving details. As a result, many are poor spellers, forget phone numbers, and never master their math facts.

Mnemonic Devices

One way to help these students with memory problems is to teach them how to invent mnemonics or funny ways to remember little details so easily lost. We remember some mnemonic devices from our own school days: The principal is your *pal*; Roy G. Biv cues the order of the colors of the rainbow. These are well-tested memory aids, but remember that the mnemonic strategy usually works best when the student invents a personal and original mnemonic (particularly when it brings a smile).

Guided Imagery

Another strategy is to use visual imagery where all senses are engaged and details provided to help encode students' contextual or episodic memories of events and details. For example, when teaching the water cycle in science to primary grade youngsters, we can use the following guided imagery experience to scaffold the details in encoding a rich schema.

> Close your eyes and picture a rainy day. Hear the rain. Feel it falling on your face. How does it feel? Are the droplets cold or warm

as they bounce off your cheeks? All of a sudden, a blast of wind carries you up, up to the grey cloud above. There, you meet Ronnie Raindrop who smiles at you. Watch him as he leaves the cloud and heads toward the ground below. What is Ronnie thinking as he tumbles to the earth? Can you hear the splash as he lands in the puddle? Can you still see him? The rain is stopping. Notice the sun peeking out behind the cloud. Can you feel its warmth spreading to the ground below? Notice Ronnie— or what is left of him— soaking up the sun, feeling warm and content. All of a sudden he feels as light as air. As a matter of fact, Ronnie has evaporated into the air! You can no longer see him as he swirls up toward the sky where he rests comfortably.

Then, have the students imagine other evaporated water droplets joining with Ronnie. Tell them to picture all of the raindrops holding hands, dancing and playing until there are so many that they form a cloud.

Ronnie moans that things are getting crowded and he feels bloated and damp. He is getting so heavy. Watch! He's falling, falling. Listen! Hear him call out, "Here I go again!"

Guided images help the students remember details gleaned from their multi-sensory experience. Visualization techniques like these and others are popular with meditation and mindfulness training.

Active Learning

Students themselves report that the most vivid memories come from information gained in a lively discussion, an experiment they conduct, or a simulation in which they have participated. In other words, the more active the learning activity is, the more likely information from it will be captured in long-term memory, especially if these experiences are followed by a verbal rehearsal or debriefing of what was learned. The information can also be captured in an online blog.

Overlearning

Generations of teachers have used drill and flashcards to help students remember math facts, spelling words, names, and dates. If you step back from this ritual, you might ask, which of these many facts are important enough to memorize, and how can I help students to *overlearn* them? The term *overlearning* describes the ongoing practice of skills seemingly mastered. For most learners, practice stops when the skills appear to be acquired. The problem is that a sense of minimum proficiency is not the same as automaticity. Automaticity in learning is the ability to respond quickly and efficiently—automatically—while mentally processing or physically performing a task. Automaticity results from experience, performing a task again and again and again. Think about learning how to ride a bike or drive a car. First attempts are difficult; we often talk to ourselves to keep all of the facts or steps in mind. Once we've practiced the task over and over, we find that we can perform it without thinking. For 2e students with memory problems, some tasks that others find pretty easy, such as sight recognition in decoding, memorizing math facts, forming letters of the alphabet, or spelling words, are not even close to becoming automatic.

Some of these students never accomplish automaticity, and thus their skills in note-taking, reading comprehension, and simple math manipulation are greatly compromised. In our culture, some of these skills are more important than others, like decoding printed letters, and especially letter-sound relationships. Math facts, too, are important, but they can be done with a calculator. Eventually, we should wonder where more time should be spent—practicing math facts to master them or developing good number sense? Spending time teaching these students *how* to think about numbers, *how* to estimate, and *how* to problem solve will provide the youngsters with strategies for figuring out solutions even if they have forgotten (or never learned) their math facts.

Using Technology to Compensate for Weak Basic Skills

Technology has become vitally important in enhancing learning for all children. But for students with learning differences, it is critical in helping them learn and produce. With technology, these students are able to access and organize information, increase accuracy in mathematics and spelling, and improve the visual quality of the finished product. In short, when these students complete assignments on the computer, they can likely produce work that will make them proud and perhaps even surprise observers. When 2e youngsters are denied access to tools such as technology, their disability begins to look like a real handicap.

In today's world, every student should be able to complete written assignments on a computer. Most students with writing problems who have been fortunate enough to have had computer access have shown remarkable improvement in writing fluency. They report a sense of empowerment. Not only does the finished product look neater, but these students also have a much easier time reading and revising drafts. In addition, many spell check programs recognize phonetic spelling, which is a big help to poor spellers. (This fact alone might be reason to teach bright students with spelling problems to spell phonetically so spell check can find their errors.) Using a computer bypasses a step for those students who have not developed automaticity in writing. No longer do they have to think about how to form letters while trying to keep a complex idea in mind; instead they simply touch a key or use "voice to text" programs to get their first drafts on "paper." One student we know, who had horrible handwriting, began doing his homework on the computer. Within a few weeks he became more willing to sit down to do his written assignments and subsequently put substantially more time and effort into his work. He composed more effective sentences and better organized paragraphs, and, as an unexpected byproduct, his restless behavior nearly evaporated.

Yes, technology provides powerful assistance for students with learning disabilities. According to Schwab Learning (2007), a branch of the Charles and Helen Schwab Foundation, "any item, piece of equipment, or system that helps bypass, work around, or compensate for a specific learning deficit" can be considered assistive technology (p. 2). These items range from low-tech options such as pencil grips, highlighting pens, and dictionaries, to high-tech items such as reading systems, voice-to-text software, and other programs that help students organize and outline their thinking and writing. We particularly like the book *Using Technology with Classroom Instruction That Works* (2nd ed., Pitler, Hubbell, & Kuhn, 2015), as it encourages teachers to use innovative strategies for integrating technology into classrooms for all children. With so many programs and apps that allow students to engage in learning in creative, productive ways, it behooves teachers and parents to become aware of the available possibilities—especially those that address the unique needs of 2e students.

Leppien and Thomas (2016) offered suggestions for particular apps they have found to be very successful for the 2e population (see Table 13.2).

When the curriculum is meaningfully challenging and teachers implement appropriate modifications, 2e students are far more likely to achieve success. Technical assistive devices, of course, are not magic. Specialists still need to use suitable remedial techniques to teach these students how to read, write, and spell. Reading programs that provide explicit instruction in phonological awareness, phonics, and decoding (Wilson Reading System, Orton-Gillingham. Approach, and the Lindamood-Bell Learning Systems) have met with great success for some 2e students. All of them use the idea of multisensory, phonetic-based instruction.

Table 13.2
Top Technology Tools

1. **Explain Everything** (http://explaineverything.com)—a design tool for annotating, animating, and creating narrative explanations and presentations. It serves as an interactive whiteboard and enables students to import documents, videos, and presentations. Students can use the recording function to record their writing and their voices about a key concept they are learning.

2. **Rev** (www.rev.com)—an app designed for both the iPhone and iPad as well as Android devices. Rev provides students with a way of communicating and sharing their thinking. It serves as a voice recorder that allows users to download and save recordings as well as to organize and edit speech-to-text transcriptions.

3. **Browsealoud** (www.texthelp.com/en-us/products/browsealoud)—software that reads and translates information aloud from places like websites and other online sources. Browsealoud facilitates access and participation for those who have visual or auditory impairments, engaging users with natural voices and in multiple languages.

4. **Evernote** (https://evernote.com)—an app for Apple and Windows products that provides a single workspace where users can write, collect thoughts, hold discussions, and present ideas. It gives students a means for organizing information as well as taking notes, annotating text, completing assignments, and creating school projects. In addition, Evernote syncs information to almost any device, enabling students to share their work.

5. **Padlet** (https://padlet.com)—a flexible app designed for the iPhone and iPad that functions as an open canvas for blogging and creating multimedia products. It enables users to attach videos, add audio recordings, insert photos, compose passages, or upload documents. The app lets students easily customize their Padlet creations, sharing and editing them among various contributors.

6. **Do it (Tomorrow)** (www.tomorrow.do)—an organizational app for Apple and Android devices which allows users to set reminders for daily tasks (but also makes it easy to push tasks off to tomorrow). The simple interface of Do it (Tomorrow) lets users view past tasks, delete tasks, delay tasks to another day, sync to-do lists to other devices, and backup information to the cloud. This app is handy for setting and maintaining short- and long-term goals.

7. **GoAnimate** (https://goanimate4schools.com)—an online resource that engages students in a safe environment and in a fun and interactive manner. The app enables students to produce videos, creating characters, scenes, and plots that illustrate their learning of content. In addition, it provides students with language skill practice and incorporates text-to-speech technology. Teachers can use the app to introduce lessons, create presentations, and check for understanding. The app is also a useful tool for educators using a "flipped classroom" model for delivering instruction online. With GoAnimate, they can produce animated videos, lectures, lessons, and assessments to enhance learning outside the classroom, reserving class time for collaborative work, concept mastery exercises, and experiments.

Table 13.2, continued.

8. **WordQ/SpeakQ** (www.goqsoftware.com/wordQspeakQ.php)—software resources that can be used together to provide students with help communicating their thinking and fixing writing mistakes. WordQ suggests word choices and also provides constructive feedback. SpeakQ allows students to dictate words into documents. When used in combination, the two apps have text-to-speech capabilities and help students with writing skills such as spelling, proofreading, and grammar.

9. **Announcify** (http://gdriv.es/announcify)—a text-to-speech app that reads out loud a variety of information, including calendar events, text messages, websites, or even whole documents. Students can customize it to their liking.

10. **Blabberize** (http://blabberize.com)—a website resource that allows students to animate any image to make it speak. The user just specifies the part of the image that should speak and then uploads the audio recording. This tool provides a great opportunity for students to both be creative and develop their language skills.

11. **Livescribe Pen** (www.livescribe.com)—an actual pen that captures everything the user hears and writes, and then transcribes it into a format suitable for Android and Apple devices. This organizational tool can help students keep track of assignments in a way that fits their learning style. A variety of Livescribe pens are available, including the Echo Smartpen, which transfers recordings into a PDF or audio file, and the Sky Smartpen, which transfers data into Evernote files.

12. **EDpuzzle** (https://edpuzzle.com)—an online tool that helps teachers and students share videos and audio files. The intention is to make learning more accessible and multisensory. EDpuzzle allows users to edit video and audio files, create quizzes, and share products through multiple social media outlets. In addition, it enables teachers to monitor the content experienced by students.

Note. From "Revealing the Strengths of 2e Students by Using Technology" by J. H. Leppien and T. M. Thomas, 2016, *2e Newsletter, 76,* pp. 3–4. Copyright 2016 by J. H. Leppien and T. M. Thomas. Reprinted with permission.

CHAPTER 14

A Community of Support

In previous chapters of this book, we concentrated on the characteristics of 2e learners and suggested strategies for how schools can best meet their educational needs. However, as implied throughout the book and evidenced in the case studies, 2e students often have social-emotional needs that even the best academic programs cannot meet completely. Realistically, we need to look beyond classroom teachers and enlist the support of others— parents, counselors, psychologists, educational therapists, and community agencies and resources.

Parents play a major role in advocating for their children and are often instrumental in having them properly identified and served. In addition, without a counselor or therapist in their corner, many of these students may not have achieved as they did. The psychological services these students received helped them understand their challenges and become proactive in getting the support they needed. We also recognize community organizations for their part in offering opportunities and environments in which these students can fit in socially and feel valued for their talents. Sports programs and scouting clubs are prime examples of social support networks that enhance the self-efficacy and self-esteem of 2e students. Through coordinated efforts, parents, counselors, therapists and community agencies can offer vital social and emotional reinforcement. The following story of Rose illustrates a successful collaboration.

Rose

An attractive, talented, and creative young girl, Rose enjoyed school. She excelled in elementary school, especially when she was learning about a favorite topic or when she had a positive relationship with her teacher. Even though her teachers were a little concerned with Rose's progress in reading, they considered her a fine student with many creative talents. But, when Rose entered middle school, her comfortable world started to crumble. She complained vaguely of problems with her teachers, saying she found them difficult to understand. The teachers' directions confused her, and she felt insecure expressing her opinions in front of others. Instead of enjoying activities or participating in class, she would escape to her books: Even though reading was challenging, it was less confusing than classroom interactions. Rose's parents were somewhat concerned that she was not paying attention in class, but they were pleased that she was reading. They grew alarmed, however, when they received the results of the sixth-grade state test: Rose scored far below grade level in reading, writing, and math. Her parents insisted on having a complete psychoeducational workup. The testing revealed that severe auditory processing problems were at the root of her difficulty with academic skills, and she was diagnosed as having a learning disability. Rose's advanced vocabulary and creative talents had disguised the problem during her elementary years, but the challenges of the middle school environment had proved to be too much.

With the test results in hand, Rose's parents tried repeatedly to convince the school to provide modifications to Rose's program. The school offered only minimal accommodations, and it was clear that they understood very little about what students who were simultaneously gifted and learning disabled might need. Rose quickly lost interest in school and no longer wanted to go. She became phobic about many things (catching a disease, being in a car wreck, etc.). With her self-esteem spiraling downward and signs of depression appearing, her parents opted to enroll her in a different educational setting, plus add regular counseling sessions. The school Rose and her parents chose was less structured than the public school, encouraged creative expression and thought, and emphasized the child's readiness to learn. For example, guest speakers frequently gave presentations on assorted topics from veterinary medicine to pottery making. Students decided which sessions to attend and how deeply—or whether—they would pursue a topic. Through special activities such as performance nights and art shows, the school also provided opportunities for students to display their creative talents.

Meanwhile, Rose's counselor encouraged her to explore her interests and ability areas. He suggested interesting ways for Rose to use her talent in writing and the arts for both therapeutic and talent development purposes. He encouraged her to keep a journal, create scrapbooks, and write her memoirs. These creative outlets were emotionally healing for her, and her parents consciously helped her find time to engage in them. Although writing was difficult, sometimes excruciating, Rose began to develop a love for putting down her thoughts and ideas.

The counselor also gave her tools to address her worries about social awkwardness. Rose confided,

> My counselor helped me see things differently. For instance, when I would be obsessing over some issue, he would ask me this question: "Rose, next year at this time will this still be important?"

In ninth grade, Rose decided to return to public school. Her auditory processing difficulties resurfaced immediately. She didn't comprehend or process much oral instruction during the school day and then would need to work for hours at home to complete her assignments. Her love of learning made her persevere even though it was difficult. Still, there were days when Rose was simply overwhelmed with schoolwork. Her mother would then step in and declare a "mental health day." This simple gesture gave Rose some breathing room from the regular demands of school and allowed her to finish some assignments, which in turn reduced her anxiety about keeping up with her peers. Her journal entries, short stories, and poetry also calmed her anxiety, and, of course, the byproduct was an impressive body of written material.

High school gave Rose the opportunity to focus seriously on her strength in the arts for the first time. She took sculpting and jewelry making and excelled. She spent every free moment in the workshop inventing, crafting, and polishing her pieces. Several of her glass sculptures were displayed in local art shows. Her art teachers told her about the Arts Academy (a magnet school) and encouraged her to apply. The Arts Academy provided a half-day program in conjunction with local high schools. Students attended academic classes in their local high schools in the morning and then spent 3 hours in the afternoon in classes at the magnet school. This option excited Rose, and she lost no time locating and completing the application forms. The application required evidence of creative talent, and Rose's portfolio won her a partial scholarship to the program. Her parents gladly contributed the remainder of the tuition because they understood the need for Rose to develop her talent and find like-minded peers who shared similar artistic talents. Attending the magnet school helped Rose regain her social-emotional balance:

> I enjoyed the great diversity of students from all walks of life. But I especially liked the environment because every student there *wanted* to be there. That's not the case at my regular school. Students at the Academy are passionate about their art. It makes a huge difference in the environment of the school where creativity is valued.

Although Academy teachers had very high expectations and the classes were challenging with a great deal of creative and analytic writing required, Rose's high school refused to give credits for Academy courses toward the language arts requirements for graduation. Rose felt that she could not put time and energy into two programs simultaneously, and so she chose to drop out of high school, but continue at the magnet school.

With her newly "found" free time, Rose sought out other experiences in the wider community to augment her education. She had the opportunity to go to El Salvador as part of a university service-learning project with which her father was associated. Rose joined a group of college students and worked alongside local villagers constructing a town meeting center. (Since then, Rose has returned to El Salvador twice more and raised several hundred dollars from high school groups to aid village projects.)

Fueled by a desire to help other communities, Rose discovered the Institute of International Living. This organization provides cultural experiences through service-learning projects across the globe. Rose applied for admission to a summer program after her junior year and was accepted with a partial scholarship. Rose chose a Brazilian experience that offered a weeklong stay with a local family to learn the culture, followed by a 4-week internship at a rainforest research station where she had an in-depth learning experience in ecology. Rose's self-chosen educational experiences were obviously much more expansive than anything available from her local high school. In these self-chosen experiences, her learning disabilities seemed almost nonexistent. In Brazil, her biggest challenge was learning Portuguese.

Rose also took advantage of local community resources. For example, she sampled classes in tai chi and liked them a lot. Her whole family had fun practicing this ancient martial art, and Rose benefited from its emphasis on self-discipline and the ability to focus. By now Rose had received her high school diploma—bypassing the system and taking the GED exam.

Rose's experience illustrates the supportive roles parents, counselors, and community can play in transforming a depressed and unmotivated youngster into a blossoming young adult. Rose's parents were her chief advocates—ensuring that Rose's difficulties were accurately identified and appropriately attended to. When the school fell short of meeting Rose's needs, her parents sought other options within the community that would offer more outlets for her abilities. They found a nontraditional setting that valued all students' gifts and talents. When she returned to public school, they supported her decision to continue in the arts magnet school and drop out of high school. They shared financial responsibilities with Rose to support outside educational offerings both at the magnet school and in her global wanderings. Finally, they sought out counseling to help address her depression. Rose's counselor encouraged her to explore who she was and helped her identify strengths and abilities, set meaningful goals, and trust her judgment. Rose herself sought out educational opportunities in the wider community that fit with her strengths and interests. By selecting and engaging in opportunities outside of school, she was able to find peer groups with whom she could identify. In these environments, Rose could see herself as a creative writer, artist, and social activist rather than a misfit in a culture that did not value those things that Rose values.

Social-Emotional Issues

As we have reiterated throughout the book, 2e students are often at risk for social-emotional difficulties because their high abilities and learning problems wear against each other. When such internal conflict induces social-emotional problems, it inhibits talent development. The usual result, of course, is dramatic underachievement (King, 2005; Olenchak & Reis, 2002). Ongoing frustrations and challenges generate negative patterns and reactions from students, families, and school personnel. Stereotyped perceptions and attitudes obstruct and often aggravate attempts at dealing with academic issues (Mendaglio, 1993b; Reis et al., 2014). Very few, if any, pay attention to the social-emotional outcomes of being twice-exceptional. Instead, the focus is generally on academic support and classroom management of the inappropriate behaviors associated with the learning disabilities or attention deficits.

To understand the kinds of support that would be helpful, we need to recognize the possible stressors they face and how the stressors affect social-emotional well-being. It is also important to appreciate that the behavioral manifestations of coping with stress are often natural reactions to an unfriendly environment. Fortunately, Rose's parents were aware of her needs. They saw the growing depression and her unwillingness to conform to school requirements as a cry for help. In response, they worked with Rose to construct an educational and psychological environment without the types of school demands that were exacerbating Rose's problems.

Unfortunately, 2e students are expected to function—and survive—in an unfriendly world where they are judged and judge themselves according to the ways they are not performing well. As a result, they may routinely experience extraordinary stress at school (Abeel, 2003; Baum & Olenchak, 2002; Foley Nicpon et al., 2011; Mooney & Cole, 2000). Such stress stimulates the fight-or-flight response. For example, Blaine (see Chapter 7) physically lashed out at his peers and teachers when he felt jammed into a psychological corner. He expressed his frustration and high stress level in a single question to his mother, "Why did God give me ADHD? I wish I would die so other kids would feel sorry for me."

In another instance, Samantha Abeel, a gifted writer with severe learning disabilities in math (dyscalculia) along with mild dyslexia (impeding spelling, grammar, and other production issues), opted to flee rather than fight. She withdrew from situations that were sources of stress. In her evocative memoir, *My Thirteenth*

Winter (2003), Samantha described the distress she felt during her first year at college, especially concerning social relationships:

> Once in awhile, my friends would decide they wanted to go out—to a dance on another campus or to a club in North Hampton or to a concert. Whenever I was invited, I always felt that familiar wave of insecurity and discomfort, and I would decline, making up an excuse for why I couldn't go. . . . Second semester my involvement in the social scene continued to deteriorate. . . . I was invited to parties and dances more frequently but my reactions were always the same—anxiety and insecurity—my excuses continued. I had a paper to write or I would go to the library at the last minute so my friends couldn't find me and make me come with them. I spent Friday and Saturday nights alone among the library stacks. Sometimes, when friends came by my room, I would pretend I wasn't there, ignoring their knocks. (p. 166)

Such issues rarely resolve themselves and often deteriorate over time. Freudenberger (1974) termed this downward spiral the "burnout cycle." Others have researched its signs and negative impact over time (Maslach & Jackson, 1981; Maslach & Leiter, 2015; Oosterholt, Maes, Van der Linden, Verbraak, & Kompier, 2015), especially regarding job-related stress. The same cycle, however, can apply to students who perceive school (and their lives) as stressful, and they show similar signs as those noted in adults. The burnout cycle begins when students find themselves in situations that are difficult, where they don't fit in, and the demands on them are not in harmony with their personal values and abilities. If the issues are not resolved, students may begin to act out—complain, cause trouble in class, play hooky, take extra time off, or turn in assignments late (or not at all). If the stress continues, students may begin to demonstrate the second phase of the burnout cycle—the physical manifestations. Here, the body responds to stressors by actually crying out physically. People report neck or back pain, stomach upset, diarrhea, headaches, eyestrain, a laundry list of physical ailments that are not imagined and are indicative of their emotional state. If no one addresses the causes of these symptoms, the sufferer heads for the final three phases of the cycle: "burning up, burning out, breaking down." In these phases, we see anxiety, severe depression, obsessive and compulsive behavior, or extreme inattentiveness and hyperactivity. When 2e students arrive at these last three phases, the social and emotional consequences are far more debilitating than the original academic problems (Baum, Renzulli, & Rizza, 2014; Meisgeier et al., 1978; Reis & Neu, 1994). According to Olenchak (1994), year after year of living through school-related frustration may then require in-depth individual support in which students explore the issues they face.

What interventions can interrupt the burnout cycle? How can we enlist the support of parents, counselors, therapists, and community resources to contribute to the healthy emotional development of these bright but challenged students? We outline the stressors these students face at different stages of development, the possible emotional and social consequences, and how these social-emotional issues could manifest themselves behaviorally during the burnout cycle in Table 14.1.

Parents, counselors, and therapists are key to helping 2e students manage or alleviate obvious stressors. Although they all can seek out supportive resources from the community, each party has something unique to offer.

How Parents Can Help

Parents play two major support roles for their twice-exceptional children. The first is advocacy. It's a primary responsibility to ensure that the school recognizes and attends to a child's needs. The second responsibility is furnishing home support of the child's talent development, academic, social, and emotional needs. At times, parents provide a shoulder to cry on, act as a confidant (as much as a parent can be), collaborate on homework, assume the role of resident problem-solver, and seek resources for any situation that presents itself. But, always, parents should see their role as opportunity-makers, where they find options and activities that both broaden the interests of their children and help them develop their abilities that can be overlooked in other settings, especially academic settings. Without such support, many 2e youngsters would fall apart. But there is a fine line, sometimes hard to discern, between protecting a child and overprotecting him or her. We have interviewed many parents about how they helped their 2e children grow to be socially, emotionally, and academically successful. The results of these inquiries show that parental roles change as students reach different stages or ages. Helping a student complete an assignment may work when the 7-year-old needs to read a story for homework, but it probably won't work with a depressed 17-year-old resisting parental assistance. Next, we explore how parental roles shift.

Elementary School

Advocacy role. Many times, parents are the first to recognize a problem as they see their once happy child become depressed, angry, or grow to dislike school. Some children become behavior problems and choose underachievement, developing perceptions of inadequacy, and poor self-efficacy. Parents must step in to make sure that the child's problem is identified and then that a suitable academic program can be put into place (see Chapter 11). The process begins with developing a positive relationship with the classroom teacher(s) and other school personnel. Discussing strategies that work at home and describing the times and circumstances when the

Table 14.1
Stressors, Emotional and Social Outcomes, and Behavioral Manifestations

Stage	Stressors	Emotional and Social Outcomes	Behavioral Manifestations
Elementary	Curriculum not aligned to child's strengths, styles, or interests Inability to learn academics Inability to make friends Inability to attend to tasks Unreasonable expectations of teachers and parents Fear of embarrassment and looking stupid in front of peers	Lowered sense of academic self-efficacy Negative perception of self worth Frustration Anxiety and depression	Complaints about school Physical ailments Avoidance behaviors Aggressive responses Inattention and hyperactivity Withdrawal
Middle School	Increased demand for self-regulation (time management, organization, and self-discipline) Increased demands for reading and writing proficiency Fitting with social milieu of the classroom Increased expectations of parents, teachers, and self	Perfectionism Sense of being overwhelmed Fear of failure and exposure of area of disability Fear of success Feelings of isolation and marginality Feelings of despair and learned helplessness Anxiety and depression	Underachievement Total commitment to achieving excellence to the exclusion of outside social activities Procrastination, avoidance of academic engagement Boredom with usual classroom fare Acting-out behaviors, immaturity
High School	High-stakes tests Written assignments and research papers Academic requirements for graduation Expectations for post-secondary opportunities Pressures to fit in and not appear different Expectations of self and others, especially in terms of future planning Relationships	Feeling overwhelmed Fear of failure Fear of success Anger Feelings of isolation, disconnectedness, and alienation Feelings of despair and learned helplessness Anxiety and depression	Absenteeism Underachievement Seeking out inappropriate peer groups Total commitment to achieving excellence to the exclusion of outside social activities Procrastination, avoidance of academic engagement Boredom and belief that school fare is irrelevant Self-medicate with drugs or alcohol

Note. By Susan Baum and Terry Neu.

child excels at home can be helpful in developing successful strategies for the classroom. If initial attempts to correct the situation are not successful, parents should ask for a complete psychoeducational evaluation. It is important to understand the legal rights afforded parents under IDEA (2004) legislation[8]. If necessary, parents should retain a child advocate familiar with the complexity of 2e students to help at school meetings.

Home support. Parents should be "partners in learning" with their children on homework assignments. Being a partner does not mean doing every problem (or even every other problem), but rather it means being aware of homework expectations in a gentle and supportive fashion. For example, parents may need to create a calm, low-stress, game-like environment for homework to take place and/or designate specific times—along with time *limits*—for homework. The best time is usually directly after dinner rather than right after school. Students need some downtime after school to play and relax. When they arrive home, a positive "meet and greet" routine is more healthy than a "let's get back to work" reminder. At that time of the day, parents should avoid talking about schoolwork. Rather, opening a give-and-take conversation with questions such as "What was fun today?" or "What did you notice that was interesting today?" sets a positive climate for communication. If the child arrives home upset, listening and providing hugs and snacks may soothe the situation. Parents need to use active listening and acknowledge that school can be difficult.

When helping with homework, parents should consider the child's preferred learning style. Some children need quiet places for study, and others need to be at the kitchen table with support nearby. Parents can allow their child to take regular and frequent short breaks. In addition, modeling time management techniques and teaching management skills show the child how to carve tasks into small, manageable parts. At times when school is too stressful, many parents can offer a "mental health day" and keep the child at home to regroup and reenergize, as described in Rose's story earlier. Jonathan Mooney (Mooney & Cole, 2000) explained how his mother implemented "mental health days" for him:

> Once a week I waited outside my second grade classroom and listened to my mom argue with Mrs. C. "You are destroying this kid. Look at him. He doesn't shower. He doesn't talk. He has been diagnosed with depression. He's only seven. Every time you terrorize him with those . . . spelling words, he wants to kill himself." (I worked for three hours a night on my spelling that year only to fail every test.) Mrs. C replies, "Kids have to learn how to spell. Those are the rules. There are no exceptions, Mrs. Mooney." So my

---

8   For more information regarding 2e students, we recommend the *2e Newsletter*, a wonderful resource for parents. The article "2e and IDEA: The right to assessment and service" by Mark Bade is in Volume 70, 2015.

mother created the exceptions: "mental health days." Anytime I had a spelling test, we went to the zoo. (p. 32)

Most importantly, parents must be enthusiastic about the child's abilities and interests. Showing authentic excitement, pride, and love sets the stage for them to feel good about themselves, to make friends, and to have prosocial adult role models. Providing enrichment activities outside of school and over the summer that enhance and develop the student's strengths, abilities, and interests can contribute to well-being far more than remedial classes in reading.

Middle School

All sorts of problems may surface for the first time during the middle school years. In addition, difficulties that seemed to have been solved at the elementary level may recur. Middle school classes require more reading, writing, organization, and time management. Students are vitally interested in fitting in socially and struggle to find a peer group with whom to identify. Many 2e students often try to hide their disability because they are afraid they won't fit in. For some, being perceived as being different is untenable. During this stage, these students often struggle between dependence on their parents and an increasing need for autonomy.

Parents may see their child begin to underachieve or his or her behavior worsen, as in the case of Bryan (Chapter 10), who became the class clown and took on bullying behaviors on the playground. Students whose expectations to excel in school magnify may give up their social life and extracurricular activities. On the other hand, students who perceive academic demands as too challenging may choose to stop trying, believing that failing for lack of trying is far preferable to putting forth effort and receiving a poor grade for it. Blaming failure on lack of effort may help protect self-esteem in the short term, but if the child gets caught in a cycle of failure/not trying/failure, feelings of helplessness may begin to surface in earnest.

School advocacy. Because of hormonal changes, rapid physical and psychological changes, and shifting social group patterns, early adolescence can be a time of social-emotional turmoil. As a result, parents have a more complex role to play. They must begin to relinquish some of the responsibility for advocacy to their child—expecting and assisting their child in self-advocacy. At the beginning of each year, parents should arrange a meeting with teachers, specialists, the counselor, and their child to review accommodations and negotiate a system in which the student can proactively work with the accommodations. Strategies that deliver an accommodation without drawing undue attention can greatly diminish the stress. For example, if students take exams in the resource room, they should be able to report directly to the resource room without first checking in with the classroom teacher. Another strategy for delivering an accommodation might be to let all students use laptops for writing assignments if they want to. We feel this is not only good for 2e students but is also appropriate for all learners.

Home support. At this stage, parents would be wise to avoid acting as a member of the homework police. If a child needs remedial support, hiring a tutor will enable parents to focus on the strengths of their child. Arranging a homework study session at home with a group of friends is one way to make sure that time is set aside for homework and projects. If the child asks for help with reading or editing, parents should pitch in. But at the same time, it is important not to allow the child to become overly dependent on assistance. Try to discriminate between what the child should be able to accomplish on his or her own and where he or she might appreciate or require help. These children need a flexible structure that offers plenty of authentic success opportunities and builds self-efficacy. Setting appropriate expectations and holding the student accountable will help develop self-regulation and confidence. Again parents must be careful that they are not imposing their own ways of doing things if their personality or learning styles do not align well to those of their children.

Parents might encourage their child to enroll in stress reduction activities such as yoga, karate, or tai chi—activities that may also help them develop self-discipline. Even better would be for parents to model stress reduction activities by learning to use them (or enroll in the activities together).

As much as their time and energies permit, parents can search out opportunities for enrichment and talent development in the wider community (e.g., clubs, sports, lessons, classes, etc.). It is critical that 2e children engage in activities with other talented peers who have similar strengths or interests. Friends with whom these students can feel comfortable are essential for social development. There are many outstanding summer residential programs for gifted students that will enrich and develop abilities and interests, as well as provide them with a social peer group[9].

Secondary Level

In high school, dually diagnosed students are bombarded with new challenges. Classes for bright youngsters usually demand proficiency in—and expect lots of—reading, listening, and note-taking. Students must complete long written assignments that involve synthesis and organization. High school is also filled with high-stakes exams, such as standardized tests, graduation exams, and entrance exams that add to the stress levels, because scores steer students' academic and career futures. Many 2e students are also worried about selecting an accommodating college or university and meeting real or perceived expectations for continuing their education. Finally, concerns about fitting in and developing social relationships continue to cause stress.

---

9   The National Association for Gifted Children maintains a list of summer programs at http://giftedandtalentedresourcesdirectory.com.

Stress that finds no release can result in students feeling depressed and overwhelmed. Some 2e students are still afraid to admit their learning challenges and struggle to maintain high levels of achievement. Others choose the path of least resistance and take low-level courses to avoid failure. If disabilities have been undiagnosed to this point, or the accommodations have been inappropriate or insufficient, 2e students can be confused and depressed—some severely—over their academic stumbling.

School advocacy. Parents and their children must continue to advocate for appropriate programs, including counseling. (In some instances, these students may require additional psychological or additional academic support outside of school.) Meeting the needs of 2e students requires flexible thinking and creative problem solving, and families should consider both in-school and out-of-school educational opportunities. Internships, independent study, and online courses can be motivating possibilities. Once considered shameful, families may consider letting these students drop out of high school with integrity. Students who do not finish high school, receive a diploma, or score well on the college entrance exams, can still continue their education at institutes of higher education. (We discuss these possibilities later in the chapter.)

Home support. It is vital that parents hold their child accountable for his or her behavior, even if it means letting him or her fail. Well-meaning parents who overprotect children by rescuing them from natural consequences are probably doing them a disservice. Students must learn to take responsibility for their decisions and behavior. If they continuously refuse to do their homework or refuse academic support, they will fail. Repeating classes or attending summer school may help these students comprehend the consequences of their behavior. If they cannot acquire minimal self-discipline before entering post-secondary education, the odds are very strong that they will fail during their first year.

The most important support a parent can provide is a positive, healthy relationship with their child. Expressing an interest in goals, aspirations, abilities, and experiences provides many openings for communication. Parents need to carefully listen to what their teen is saying, for real communication requires active listening and allowing various points of view. Also, parents must resist the urge to take away talent development activities to find more time to work on academics. Although this may seem practical, it can strip away the times when these adolescents feel best about themselves. Finally, it will be necessary for parents to seek professional help if their 2e teenager is experiencing severe levels of depression, debilitating confusion about the future, or generalized anxiety.

How Counselors Can Help

The support of a capable school counselor is essential to meeting the social-emotional needs of 2e students (Assouline, Nicpon, & Huber, 2006). Having an objective but empathetic professional, knowledgeable about the coexistence of gifts and talents with learning or attention difficulties, can ease tension and frustration. As Mendaglio (1993a) explained,

> Although the problem may be resident within the child, the intervention requires the designation of parents and teachers as clients of the counselor as well as they may inadvertently exacerbate the problem. (p. 137)

Olenchak (1994) extended this idea to include any adults who may be outside the school and family, but who are involved with the student (e.g., scout leaders, little league coaches). The counselor can suggest mitigating strategies to all adults who interact with these special students. The role of counselor-as-child-advocate includes providing a safe haven for the child, communicating the child's needs to teachers and others who work with the student, working with families, providing group counseling sessions for the student, locating community resources, and helping with post-secondary planning.

Providing a safe haven. We believe that 2e students need someone within the school to provide a safe haven for them, a place where they can retreat when they are feeling overwhelmed (Baum, Renzulli, & Rizza, 2014). When stress consumes them and emotions are fragile, it is crucial to have an empathetic adult to talk to. The counselor's office can also be a place to drop by to share news, both positive and negative.

Communicating students' needs. Advocacy also involves communicating the 2e student's needs and problems with anyone who interacts with the child. Consider what one counselor wrote to help with one student's transition to the next grade level:

> As Jordan's counselor, I wanted to take a few minutes to let you know a little about him. Jordan is a "twice-exceptional" student: he is very gifted intellectually (IQ between 140–180), [but has been diagnosed] with ADHD . . . [and] depression. . . . [He] is being served on an IEP with Linda B. in a resource room setting once a day. Jordan is a visual spatial learner. During lecture, he may appear off task, but he is usually multiprocessing. He does not need to . . . [give] you his undivided attention to . . . [pick] up concepts. In fact, looking around or doodling allows him to remain relatively

calm. Jordan has difficulty with processing speed. He needs more think time than most students to respond to questions. If he raises his hand to answer a question, please . . . call on him. However, please avoid calling on him spontaneously in class unless you are prepared to wait or offer clues to save him from discomfort. Jordan would benefit from frequent reminders about due dates and test dates. Please remind him to write them in his agenda. He has some difficulty with organization, so notebook checks might be useful. Jordan may take tests in Ms. B.'s room if needed, and the tests can be sent to her if he does not complete them in the classroom . . . He reads at well above the collegiate level in terms of vocabulary. However, his processing speed may interfere with his achievement unless accommodations are made. Jordan's previous experience in school has been difficult. Please provide as much encouragement as you can. His parents are very involved and you can email them anytime with concerns. You can also work through me or Ms. B. I hope we can make school a place this young man looks forward to coming to! Thanks.

Sincerely,
Jan D.

Working with families. The counselor can support families by helping them find positive ways to advocate for their children in school and provide appropriate support at home. Parents need to understand the unique characteristics of 2e students, the stressors their children are facing, as well as the social-emotional outcomes that result from these challenges. They also need to recognize that a child's maladaptive behaviors may spring from unresolved issues and stress. Counselors can involve parents in small-group meetings, parent workshops, or family counseling sessions with the student. It might be necessary to provide the family with names of family therapists if long-term therapy is indicated.

Providing group counseling sessions. In group sessions, counselors can help 2e youngsters understand and cope with the unique challenges they face. Group sessions send a clear message that these youngsters are not alone, that others share the same challenges and frustrations as they do (Mendaglio, 1993a):

When one finds that he or she is "not the only one," there is an immediate sense of relief particularly for gifted children with learning disabilities, a group with relatively low incidence within a school jurisdiction. (p. 137)

Members of the group can form a positive, prosocial group, especially for those youngsters who have felt marginalized. In addition, students may be more attentive to suggestions and observations their peers make than those adults make. It is the role of the counselor, however, to teach students how to use constructive feedback techniques.

Community Resources

The counselor can serve as an advocate for 2e students by finding opportunities for them to develop their abilities or by providing an environment for at least part of the school day in which these students can operate from a position of strength. Some of these opportunities may not be available through the school, and parents may need to step in to ensure their child can take advantage of special classes, clubs, and organizations. Table 14.2 outlines some possibilities.

Post-Secondary Education

Counselors play a key role in helping students plan for the future. It is vital that 2e students set career goals that complement their talents and interests. Once a student has some idea of the areas he or she might like to pursue, the next step is finding the right opportunities. Those pursuing post-secondary education must consider requirements for admission, the kinds of programs the school offers, and the availability of support for students with learning disabilities. For some students, mentorships or internships in areas of interest or talent may precede college entry. And, as high school counselor Anna Schaerf notes, "For other students, a gap year between high school and college to focus on social-emotional development or acquiring skills of daily life may be necessary" (personal communication, March 6, 2017). In fact, pursuing an internship directly after high school is often advantageous for students who are not quite ready for the college environment.

Many schools make accommodations in their entrance requirements for students with learning disabilities. Students with disabilities can apply for and be approved to use calculators on noncalculator mathematics sections, have more time on the test, and take the tests at home, online, in small groups, or use a scribe or reader. These adjustments have helped some 2e students score well and be more comfortable in the testing setting. However, some students don't test well and never will. Fortunately, many universities forgo usual requirements of admission testing and use other criteria such as essays, interviews, or portfolios. In fact, some students who fail to finish high school or earn a high school diploma can still attend college. Samantha, mentioned earlier in this chapter, finished high school but did not pass the exit exam in math. However, by the time she graduated high school, she was a published poet. Her collection of poems and her college essay recounting her journey in high school gained her admission to Mount Holyoke College. Because of her

Table 14.2
Community Resources

Resource	Description	Example
Local Talent Development	Community Arts Centers may have local theater groups, periodic musical performances, or art shows. Many of these centers offer individual or small-group instruction.	Singing the Clues (an individual instruction to help students master singing two pieces of their favorite Blues music) Introduction to Photography course
	Local Museums are wonderful resources that may also offer specialized courses of instruction in a related area.	A museum in New Haven, CT, highlights the engineering skills of Eli Whitney and offers after-school programs to encourage young inventors to build their own inventions.
	Societies and Organizations may offer training and opportunities to volunteer.	Audubon Society bird-watching tours
	Universities and Colleges often have special exhibits or programs open to the public.	Student projects for an Engineering Department Fair are placed on public display. An Anthropology Department demonstrates skills needed for archaeology digs.
National Competitions	Each year the number of nationally organized individual or small-group competitive programs increases. These programs encourage creative solutions and have benefited a number of the students we have worked with.	Odyssey of the Mind Future Problem Solving Destination Imagination Model U.N. International Science Fair Math Olympiad Young Writers projects America First (cooperation between students and industry to build robots for specific tasks) Battle Bots (student teams build robot that must accomplish a list of tasks)

Table 14.2, continued.

Resource	Description	Example
Clubs and Organizations	Part of the counseling process should include discovering student interests and strengths and matching students to organizations that provide talent development opportunities outside of school.	4-H of America Girl Scouts Boy Scouts Youth Orchestras and Choirs
Special Schools	There are situations in which the regular education setting is not working for a specific student. Such a situation is not the fault of an individual school district, but results from a mismatch between system resources and the needs of a specific GLD student. The Counselor must be aware of alternative placements to recommend to parents.	Within-District Special Programs: As mentioned in Chapter 11, several school districts have specialized programs to meet the needs of GLD students. Magnet Schools: In Rose's case, the area arts magnet school proved to be a haven for her talents. Most states have a magnet school system that provides specialized curriculum for secondary students that varies from aircraft mechanics to the culinary arts. Alternative Schools: A wide variety of private schools across the nation (as discussed in Chapter 10) provide the specialized environments GLD students need.
Mentorships and Internships	Some corporations and businesses encourage their employees to give back to the community, which may include providing mentoring opportunities and internships for local youth.	

Note. Compiled by Susan Baum and Terry Neu.

diagnosed learning disabilities, she had the option of being excused from required courses such as foreign language and math—areas she chose to avoid. Other 2e students quit high school and attend a community college in preparation for eventual university entrance.

To guide 2e students through the process of finding an appropriate institution of higher learning, Coleman (personal communication, February 23, 2017) has used these five questions with 2e college-bound students over the years and has found them to be useful. She says that students should ask themselves:

1. What areas of the curriculum are offered as majors, and do they meet with my interests?
2. What size campus will I feel comfortable with?
3. What are the students like? Will I fit in?
4. What extracurricular activities are available that I would be likely to participate in (sports, music, drama, fraternity/sorority, religious groups, etc.)?
5. What support services are available to help me with my learning disability?

Anna Schaerf (personal communication, March 6, 2017) includes additional questions to help with decision making:

1. What is the typical class size? (Most 2e students fare much better the smaller the class size.)
2. What are the entrance requirements?
3. What housing options are available? What types of housing supports can help me choose a room (roommate) and then deal with social-emotional conflicts that may arise?
4. What psychological and/or psychiatric supports do I need, and what is available on campus or in the surrounding community?
5. What are the production options available in classes? Is there homework daily? How are grades assessed? Are there opportunities for projects, oral presentations, or other products to be submitted for credit?

Final Thoughts

This book describes what we have learned studying and working with twice-exceptional students over the past 30 years. We know that for them to become successful adults they will need to believe in themselves and their abilities—and we are convinced that much will be gained by emphasizing these students' strengths and interests.

Twice-exceptional adults who are successful in their lives talk about how overcoming hurdles has made them confident and committed. In fact, many report that their challenges have actually enriched their lives. As the young poet Samantha Abeel (2003) commented,

> Over the years I have also come to view my learning disability as a rather strange and unusual gift. I believe it has allowed me to develop strengths I might not have otherwise developed. . . . We all come in unique packages with strengths and weaknesses, and somewhere there is a precious gift in all of us. I was blessed to have parents, mentors, and teachers who nurtured mine. No matter how difficult or complex the person in front of us may be, I have learned never to stop looking for his or her gift, as those around me never stopped looking for mine. (pp. 205–206)

To all of the 2e students like Samantha, we offer hope and wish them lifelong success.

References

Abeel, S. (2003). *My thirteenth winter: A memoir*. New York, NY: Orchard Books.

American Psychiatric Association. (1994). *Diagnostic and statistical manual of mental disorders* (4th ed.). Washington, DC: Author.

American Psychiatric Association. (2013). *Diagnostic and statistical manual of mental disorders* (5th ed.). Washington, DC: Author.

Anxiety and Depression Association of America. (2016). *Generalized Anxiety Disorder (GAD)*. Retrieved from https://www.adaa.org/understanding-anxiety/generalized-anxiety-disorder-gad

Asperger, H. (1944). Die "Autistischen Psychopathen" im Kindesalter. *European Archives of Psychiatry and Clinical Neuroscience, 117*(1), 76–136.

Asperger, H. (1979). Problems of infantile autism. *Communication, 13*, 45–52.

Assouline, S., Nicpon, M., & Huber, D. (2006). The impact of vulnerabilities and strengths on the academic experience of twice-exceptional students: A message to school counselors. *Professional School Counseling, 10*, 14–24.

Assouline, S. G., & Whiteman, C. S. (2011). Twice-exceptionality: Implications for school psychologists in the post–IDEA 2004 era. *Journal of Applied School Psychology, 27*, 380–402.

Baddeley, A. D. (1986). *Working memory*. Oxford, England: Clarendon Press.

Baddeley, A. D. (2001). Is working memory still working? *American Psychologist, 56*, 851–864. http://dx.doi.org/10.1037/0003-066X.56.11.851

Baldwin, L., Baum, S., Perles, D., & Hughes, C. (2015). Twice-exceptional learners: The journey toward a shared vision. *Gifted Child Today, 38*, 206–214.

Bandura, A. (1989). Human agency in social cognitive theory. *American Psychologist, 44,* 1175–1184.

Bandura, A. (1997). *Self-efficacy: The exercise of control.* New York, NY: Freeman.

Barkley, R. (2015). *Executive functioning and ADHD: Nature and assessment.* Retrieved from http://www.continuingedcourses.net/active/courses/course069.php

Bartol, T. M., Bromer, C., Kinney, J., Chirillo, M. A., Bourne, J. N., Harris, K. M., & Sejnowski, T. J. (2015). Nanoconnectomic upper bound on the variability of synaptic plasticity. *eLife,* 4:e10778. http://dx.doi.org/10.7554/eLife.10778

Baum, S. (1985). *Learning disabled students with superior cognitive abilities: A validation study of description behaviors* (Unpublished doctoral dissertation). University of Connecticut, Storrs, CT.

Baum, S. (1988). An enrichment program for gifted learning disabled students. *Gifted Child Quarterly, 32,* 226–230.

Baum, S. (2016). Building on what is right about our students. *2e Newsletter, 79,* 14–17.

Baum, S. M. (Ed.) (2004). *Twice-exceptional students and other special populations of gifted youngsters.* Essential readings in gifted education. Thousand Oaks, CA: Corwin Press.

Baum, S. M. (2009). Talent centered model for twice-exceptional students. In J. S. Renzulli, E. J. Gubbins, K. S. McMillen, R. D. Eckert, & C. A. Little (Eds.), *Systems and models for developing programs for the gifted and talented* (2nd. ed., pp. 17–47). Waco, TX: Prufrock Press.

Baum, S. M., Cooper, C. R., & Neu, T. W. (2001). Dual differentiation: An approach for meeting the curricular needs of gifted students with learning disabilities. *Psychology in the Schools, 38,* 477–490.

Baum, S. M., Cooper, C. R., Neu, T. W., & Owen, S. V. (1995). *Project High Hopes: Talent discovery assessment process user's guide.* Hamden, CT: Project High Hopes & Area Cooperative Educational Services.

Baum, S. M., Cooper, C. R., Neu, T. W., & Owen, S. V. (1997). *Evaluation of Project High Hopes* (Project R206A30159-95). Washington, DC: U.S. Department of Education.

Baum, S., & Kirschenbaum, R. (1984). Recognizing special talents in learning disabled students. *Teaching Exceptional Children, 16,* 92–98.

Baum, S., & Nicols, H. J. (2015*). Quick personality indicator.* Studio City, CA: 2e Center for Research and Professional Development at Bridges Academy.

Baum, S., Novak, C., Preuss, L., & Dann, M. (2009). The 2e profile: Multiple perspectives. *2e Newsletter, 36,* 13–18.

Baum, S. M., & Olenchak, F. R. (2002). The alphabet children: GT, ADHD, and more. *Exceptionality, 10,* 77–91.

Baum, S. M., Owen, S. V., & Dixon, J. (1991). *To be gifted and learning disabled: From identification to practical intervention strategies.* Mansfield Center, CT: Creative Learning Press.

Baum, S. M., Owen, S. V., & Oreck, B. A. (1996). Talent beyond words: Identification of potential talent in dance and music in elementary students. *Gifted Child Quarterly, 40,* 93–102.

Baum, S., Owen, S., & Oreck, B. (1997). Transferring individual self-regulation processes from arts to academics. *Arts Education Policy Review, 98*(4), 32–39.

Baum, S. M., Renzulli, J. S., & Hébert, T. (1995). *The prism metaphor: A new paradigm for reversing underachievement* (CRS 95310). Storrs, CT: National Research Center on the Gifted and Talented.

Baum, S. M., Renzulli, S., & Rizza, M. G. (2014). The twice-exceptional adolescents: Who are they? What do they need? In F. A. Dixon & S. M. Moon (Eds.), *The handbook of secondary gifted education* (2nd ed., pp. 155–184). Waco, TX: Prufrock Press.

Baum, S., Schader, R., Dismuke, S., & Sly, R. (2012). *Reflective RTI: Rationale and resources to create instructional plans for the 2e learner.* Studio City, CA: 2e Center for Research and Professional Development at Bridges Academy.

Baum, S. M., Schader, R. M., & Hébert, T. P. (2014). Through a different lens: Reflecting on a strengths-based, talent-focused approach for twice-exceptional learners. *Gifted Child Quarterly, 58,* 311–327.

Baum, S., Viens, J., & Slatin, B. (2005). *Multiple intelligences in the elementary classroom: A teacher's toolkit.* New York, NY: Teachers College Press.

Berg, C. (2003). *How to aim a bouncing brain.* Boston, MA: Sandberg.

Bloom, B. S. (1985). *Developing talent in young people.* New York, NY: Ballantine.

Blucher, R., & Wayland, S. (2015). Supporting 2e students in Prince George's county. *2e Newsletter, 71,* 3–9.

Blume, H. (1998). Neurodiversity: On the neurological underpinnings of geekdom. *The Atlantic.* Retrieved from https://www.theatlantic.com/magazine/archive/1998/09/neurodiversity/305909

Bridges Academy. (2013). *The 2e Center for Research and Professional Development* [PowerPoint slides].

Brody, L. E., & Mills, C. J. (1997). Gifted children with learning disabilities: A review of the issues. *Journal of Learning Disabilities, 30,* 282–296.

Brooks, R., & Goldstein, S. (2012). *Raising resilient children with autism spectrum disorders: Strategies for maximizing their strengths, coping with adversity, and developing a social mindset.* New York, NY: McGraw-Hill.

Budding, D. E., & Chidekel, D. (2012): ADHD and giftedness: A neurocognitive consideration of twice exceptionality. *Applied Neuropsychology: Child, 1,* 145–151. doi:10.1080/21622965.2012.699423

Center for Disease Control. (2016). *Checklist: Signs and symptoms of attention-deficit/hyperactivity disorder (ADHD)*. Retrieved from https://www.cdc.gov/ncbddd/adhd/checklist.html

Center on the Developing Child, Harvard University. (2017). *Executive function and self-regulation*. Retrieved from http://developingchild.harvard.edu/science/key-concepts/executive-function

Checkley, K. (1997). The first seven . . . and the eighth: A conversation with Howard Gardner. *Educational Leadership, 55*(1), 8–13.

Clinkenbeard, P. (1994, April). Motivation and the gifted student. *AEGUS Newsletter,* 4–5.

Cohen, N. J., & Squire, L. R. (1980). Preserved learning and retention of pattern analyzing skill in amnesia: Dissociation of knowing how and knowing that. *Science, 210,* 207–209.

Cohen, S. S., & Vaughn, S. (1994). Gifted students with learning disabilities: What does the research say? *Learning Disabilities: A Multidisciplinary Journal, 5,* 87–94.

Coleman, M. R., & Hughes, C. E. (2009). Meeting the needs of gifted students within an RtI framework. *Gifted Child Today, 32*(3), 14–17.

Conners, C. K. (1997). *Conners' rating scales—revised.* Toronto, ON: Multi-Health Systems.

Corbett, B. A., Gunther, J. R., Comins, D., Price, J., Ryan, N., Simon, D., . . . & Rios, T. (2011). Brief report: Theatre as therapy for children with autism spectrum disorder. *Journal of Autism and Developmental Disorders, 41,* 505–511. doi:10.1007/s10803-010-1064-1

Cramond, B. (1994). Attention deficit-hyperactivity disorder and creativity—What is the connection? *Journal of Creative Behavior, 28,* 193–209.

Crim, C., Hawkins, J., Ruban, L., & Johnson, S. (2008). Curricular modifications for elementary students with learning disabilities in high-, average-, and low-IQ groups. *Journal of Research in Childhood Education, 22,* 233–245. doi:10.1080/02568540809594624

Cruickshank, W. M. (1966). *The teacher of brain-injured children: A discussion of the bases for competency.* Syracuse, NY: Syracuse University Press.

Cruickshank, W. M. (1967). *The brain-injured child in home, school, and community.* Syracuse, NY: Syracuse University Press.

Cruickshank, W. M. (1977). Myths and realities in learning disabilities. *Journal of Learning Disabilities, 10,* 51–58.

Cruickshank, W. M., Bentzen, F. A., Ratzeburg, G. H., & Tannhauser, M. T. (1961). *A teaching method for brain-injured and hyperactive children.* Syracuse, NY: Syracuse University Press.

Csikszentmihalyi, M. (1990). *Flow: The psychology of optimal experience.* New York, NY: HarperCollins.

Csikszentmihalyi, M. (1997). *Finding flow: The psychology of engagement with everyday life*. New York, NY: Basic Books.

Csikszentmihalyi, M., Rathunde, K., & Whalen, S. (1996). *Talented teenagers: The roots of success and failure*. New York, NY: Cambridge University Press.

Dabrowski, K., & Piechowski, M. M. (1977). *Theory of levels of emotional development* (Vols. 1 & 2). Oceanside, NY: Dabor Science.

Davidson, R. J., & Begley, S. (2012). *The emotional life of your brain: How its unique patterns affect the way you think, feel, and live—and how you can change them.* New York, NY: Hudson Street Press.

Delcourt, M. (1998). *What parents need to know about recognizing and encouraging interests, strengths, and talents of gifted elementary school children: Practitioners' guide*. Storrs, CT: National Research Center on the Gifted and Talented.

Delis, D. C. (2012). *Delis—Rating of executive function*. Bloomington, MN: Pearson.

Dixon, J. P. (1983). *The spatial child*. Springfield, IL: Charles C. Thomas.

Duckworth, A. (2016). *Grit: The power of passion and perseverance*. New York, NY: Scribner.

Dweck, C. S. (2000). *Self-theories: Their role in motivation, personality, and development*. Philadelphia, PA: Psychology Press.

Dweck, C. S. (2012). Mindsets and malleable minds: Implications for giftedness and talent. In R. F. Subotnik, A. Robinson, C. M. Callahan, & E. J. Gubbins (Eds.), *Malleable minds: Translating insights from psychology and neuroscience to gifted education* (pp. 97–208). Storrs, CT: National Research Center on the Gifted and Talented.

Dweck, C. S., Mangels, J. A., & Good, C. (2004). Motivational effects of attention, cognition, and performance. In D. Y. Dai, & R. J. Sternberg (Eds.), *Motivation, emotion, and cognition: Integrated perspectives on intellectual functioning and development* (pp. 41–55). Mahwah, NJ: Erlbraum.

Eberle, R., & Stanish, R. (1996). *CPS for kids: A resource book for teaching creative problem-solving to children*. Waco, TX: Prufrock Press.

Education for All Handicapped Children Act of 1975, Pub. Law 94-142 (November 29, 1975).

Eide, B., & Eide, F. (2011). *The dyslexic advantage: Unlocking the hidden potential of the dyslexic brain*. New York, NY: Hudson Street Press.

Emerick, L. J. (1992). Academic underachievement among the gifted: Students' perceptions of factors that reverse the pattern. *Gifted Child Quarterly, 36,* 140–146.

Foley Nicpon, M., Allmon, A., Sieck, R., & Stinson, R. D. (2011). Empirical investigation of twice-exceptionality: Where have we been and where are we going? *Gifted Child Quarterly, 55,* 3–17.

Freudenberger, H. J. (1974). Introduction and acknowledgment. *Journal of Social Issues, 30,* 1–7. doi:10.1111/j.1540-4560.1974.tb00689.x

Gallagher, J. J., & Gallagher, S. A. (1994). *Teaching the gifted child* (4th ed.). Boston, MA: Allyn & Bacon.

Gardner, H. (1983). *Frames of mind: The theory of multiple intelligences*. New York, NY: Basic Books.

Gardner, H. (1993). *Multiple intelligences: New horizons in theory and practice*. New York, NY: Basic Books.

Gardner, H. (1999). *Intelligence reframed: Multiple intelligences for the 21st century*. New York, NY: Basic Books.

Gardner, H. (2000). Extraordinary deviations. In K. Kay (Ed.), *Uniquely gifted: Identifying and meeting the needs of the twice-exceptional student* (pp. 195–196). Gilsum, NH: Avocus.

Getzels, J., & Jackson, P. (1962). *Creativity and intelligence: Explorations with gifted students*. New York, NY: Wiley.

Gifted and Talented Children's Education Act of 1978, §901, 20 U.S.C. 3311.

Gifted Development Center. (n.d.). *Twice-exceptional: K–12 planning for the twice-exceptional (2e) child*. Retrieved from http://www.gifteddevelopment.com/about-our-center/our-services/k-12-educational-planning/twice-exceptional

Goertzel, V., & Goertzel, M. (1962). *Cradles of eminence: A provocative study of the childhoods of over 400 famous twentieth-century men and women*. Boston, MA: Little Brown.

Goldstein, S., Naglieri, J. A., Princiotta, D., & Otero, T. M. (2014). Introduction: A history of executive functioning as a theoretical and clinical construct. In S. Goldstein, & J. A. Naglieri (Eds.), *Handbook of executive functioning* (pp. 3–12). New York, NY: Springer.

Goleman, D. (1995). *Emotional intelligence: Why it can matter more than IQ*. New York, NY: Bantam Books.

Grandin, T. (2006). *Thinking in pictures: My life with autism* (Rev. ed.). New York, NY: Vintage Books.

Grandin, T., & Panek, R. (2013). *The autistic brain: Thinking across the spectrum*. New York, NY: Houghton Mifflin Harcourt.

Gregorc, A. F. (1982). *An adult's guide to style*. Maynard, MA: Gabriel Systems.

Guilford, J. P. (1959). Three faces of intellect. *American Psychologist, 14,* 469–479

Guilford, J. P. (1968). *Intelligence, creativity, and their educational implications*. San Diego, CA: Knapp.

Hallahan, D. P., & Mercer, C. D. (2001). *Learning disabilities: Historical perspectives. Executive summary*. Paper presented at the Learning Disabilities Summit: Building a Foundation for the Future, Washington, DC.

Hildreth, G. H. (1966). *Introduction to the gifted*. New York, NY: McGraw-Hill.

Hollingworth, L. S. (1923). *Special talents and defects: Their significance for education*. New York, NY: Macmillan.

Immordino-Yang, M. H. (2016). *Emotions, learning, and the brain: Exploring the educational implications of affective neuroscience.* New York, NY: Norton.

Individuals with Disabilities Education Improvement Act, Pub. Law 108-446 (December 3, 2004).

Joyce, B., Weil, M., & Calhoun, E. (2014). *Models of teaching* (9th ed.). Upper Saddle River, NJ: Pearson.

Jung, C. G. (1939). *The integration of the personality.* New York, NY: Farrar & Rinehart.

Kanner, L. (1943). Autistic disturbances of affective contact. *Nervous Child, 2,* 217–250.

Kaufman, F. (1991). *The courage to succeed: A new look at underachievement.* Keynote address at the annual conference of the Association for the Education of Gifted Underachieving Students, University of Alabama, Tuscaloosa, AL.

Kaufman F., Kalbfleisch M. L., Castellanos F. X. (2000). *Attention deficit disorders and gifted students: What do we really know?* (RBDM0105). Storrs, CT: National Research Center on the Gifted and Talented, University of Connecticut.

Kaufman, S. (2013). *Ungifted: Intelligence redefined.* New York, NY: Basic Books.

Kessler, E., & Schneider, M. (n.d.). *IEP planning: Accommodations & modifications.* Retrieved from http://www.smartkidswithld.org/getting-help/the-abcs-of-ieps/iep-planning-accommodations-modifications

Kirk, S. A. (1962). *Educating exceptional children.* Boston, MA: Houghton Mifflin.

Klingberg, T. (2010). Training and plasticity of working memory. *Trends in Cognitive Science, 14,* 317–324.

King, E. W. (2005) Addressing the social and emotional needs of twice-exceptional students. *Teaching Exceptional Children, 38,* 16–20.

Lavoie, R. (2005). *It's so much work to be your friend: Helping the child with learning disabilities find social success.* New York, NY: Touchstone.

Learning Disabilities Association of America. (2017). *Types of learning disabilities.* Retrieved from https://ldaamerica.org/types-of-learning-disabilities

Leppien, J., & Thomas, T. (2016). Revealing the strengths of 2e students by using technology. *2e Newsletter, 76,* 3–4.

Levine, M. (2002). *A mind at a time.* New York, NY: Simon & Schuster.

Levy, L. (2014). How stress affects the brain during learning. *Edudemic.* Retrieved from http://www.edudemic.com/stress-affects-brain-learning

Loftus, E. F. (1996). *Eyewitness testimony: With a new preface.* Cambridge, MA: Harvard University Press.

Loftus, E. F., & Palmer, J. C. (1974). Reconstruction of automobile destruction: An example of the interaction between language and memory. *Journal of Verbal Learning and Verbal Behavior, 13,* 585–589.

Lovecky, D. V. (2004). *Different minds: Gifted children with AD/HD, Asperger syndrome, and other learning deficits.* Philadelphia, PA: Kingsley.

Lovett, B. J., & Lewandowski, L. J. (2006). Gifted students with learning disabilities: Who are they? *Journal of Learning Disabilities, 39,* 515–527. doi:10.1177/00222194060390060401

MacKinnon, D. W. (1965). Personality and realization of creative potential. *American Psychologist, 27,* 717–727.

Maker, C. J. (1977). *Providing programs for the gifted handicapped.* Reston, VA: Council for Exceptional Children.

Maslach, C., & Jackson, S. E. (1981). The measurement of experienced burnout. *Journal of Occupational Behavior, 2,* 99–113. doi:10.1002/job.4030020205

Maslach, C., & Leiter, M. P. (Eds.). (2015). It's time to take action on burnout. *Burnout Research, 2,* iv–v. doi:10.1016/j.burn.2015.05.002

Maslow, A. H. (1958). A dynamic theory of human motivation. In C. L. Stacey, & M. DeMartino (Eds.), *Understanding human motivation* (pp. 26–47). Cleveland, OH: Howard Allen.

Mayo Clinic Staff. (2017). *Diseases and conditions: Generalized anxiety disorder: Symptoms.* Retrieved from http://www.mayoclinic.org/diseases-conditions/generalized-anxiety-disorder/basics/symptoms/con-20024562

McCoach, D. B., Kehle, T. J., Bray, M. A., & Siegle, D. (2001). Best practices in the identification of gifted students with learning disabilities. *Psychology in the Schools, 38,* 403–411. doi:10.1002/pits.1029

Medina, J. (2008). *Brain rules: 12 principles for surviving and thriving at work, home, and school.* Seattle, WA: Pear Press.

Meisgeier, C., Meisgeier, C., & Werblo, D. (1978). Factors compounding the handicapping of some gifted children. *Gifted Child Quarterly, 22,* 325–331.

Mendaglio, S. (1993a). Counseling gifted learning disabled: Individual and group counseling techniques. In L. K. Silverman (Ed.), *Counseling the gifted and talented* (pp. 131–149). Denver, CO: Love.

Mendaglio, S. (1993b). Sensitivity: Bridging affective characteristics and emotions. *Journal of Secondary Gifted Education, 5,* 10–13.

Minner, S. (1990). Teacher evaluations of case descriptions of LD gifted children. *Gifted Child Quarterly, 34,* 37–39.

Mooney, J., & Cole, D. (2000). *Learning outside the lines: Two ivy league students with learning disabilities and ADHD give you the tools for academic success and educational revolution.* New York, NY: Fireside.

National Association for Gifted Children. (2010). *Redefining giftedness for a new century: Shifting the paradigm* [Position statement]. Washington, DC: Author.

National Center for Learning Disabilities. (2007). *Learning disabilities checklist.* New York, NY: Author.

National Center on Response to Intervention. (2010). *Essential components of RTI—A closer look at response to intervention.* Retrieved from http://www.rti4success.org/sites/default/files/rtiessentialcomponents_042710.pdf

National Education Association. (2006). *The twice-exceptional dilemma.* Washington, DC: Author.

Neihart, M. (2000). Gifted children with Asperger's syndrome. *Gifted Child Quarterly, 44,* 222–230.

Nelson, K. C. (1989). Dabrowski's theory of positive disintegration. *Advanced Development, 1,* 1–14.

Nicols, & Baum, S. (2003). *A toolkit for teens: Helping adolescents manage their stress.* Washington, DC: Office of Overseas Schools, United States Department of State.

Oak Foundation. (n.d.). *Oak Foundation: Learning differences programme* [PowerPoint slide]. Retrieved from http://www.collegestar.ecu.edu/lib/documents/slc13-posters/ppt/slc13_oak.ppt

Olenchak, F. R. (1994). Talent development: Accommodating the social and emotional needs of secondary gifted/learning disabled students. *Journal of Secondary Gifted Education, 5*(3), 40–52.

Olenchak, F. R., & Reis, S. M. (2002). Gifted students with learning disabilities. In M. Neihart, S. M. Reis, N. M. Robinson, & S. M. Moon, *The social and emotional development of gifted children: What do we know?* (pp. 177–192). Waco, TX: Prufrock Press.

Oosterholt, B. G., Maes, J. H., Van der Linden, D., Verbraak, M. J., & Kompier, M. A. (2015). Burnout and cortisol: Evidence for a lower cortisol awakening response in both clinical and nonclinical burnout. *Journal of Psychosomatic Research, 78,* 445–451.

Oreck. B., Baum, S., & McCartney, H. (2000). *Artistic talent development for urban youth: The promise and the challenge.* Storrs, CT: University of Connecticut, National Research Center on the Gifted and Talented.

Packer, L. E. (2017). *Overview of executive dysfunction.* Retrieved from http://www.schoolbehavior.com/disorders/executive-dysfunction/overview-of-executive-dysfunction

Pereles, D. A., Omdal, S., & Baldwin, L. (2009). Response to intervention and twice-exceptional learners: A promising fit. *Gifted Child Today, 32*(3), 40–51.

Piechowski, M. M. (1991). Emotional development and emotional giftedness. In N. Colangelo & G. A. Davis (Eds.), *Handbook of gifted education* (pp. 285–306). Boston, MA: Allyn & Bacon.

Piechowski, M. M., & Colangelo, N. (1984). Developmental potential of the gifted. *Gifted Child Quarterly, 28,* 80–88.

Pinker, S. (1997). *How the mind works.* New York, NY: Norton.

Posner, M. I. (1975). Psychobiology of attention. In M. S. Gazzaniga & C. Blakemore (Eds.), *Handbook of psychobiology* (pp. 441–480). New York, NY: Academic Press.

Pribram, K. H. (1973). The primate frontal cortex—Executive of the brain. In K. H. Pribram & A. R. Luria (Eds.), *Psycholophysiology of the frontal lobes* (pp. 293–314). New York, NY: Academic Press.

Reis, S. M., Baum, S. M., & Burke, E. (2014). An operational definition of twice-exceptional learners: Implications and applications. *Gifted Child Quarterly, 58,* 217–230.

Reis, S. M., & Neu, T. W. (1994). Factors involved in the academic success of high ability university students with learning disabilities. *Journal of Secondary Gifted Education, 5*(3), 60–74.

Reis, S. M., Neu, T. W., & McGuire, J. (1995). *Talents in two places: Case studies of high ability students with learning disabilities who have achieved* (Research Monograph No. 95114). Storrs, CT: University of Connecticut, National Research Center on the Gifted and Talented.

Reis, S. M., Renzulli, J. S., & Burns, D. E. (2016). *Curriculum compacting: A guide to differentiating curriculum and instruction through enrichment and acceleration* (2nd ed.). Waco, TX: Prufrock Press.

Reis, S. M., Westberg, K. L., Kulikowich, J., Calliard, F., Hébert, T., Plucker, J. . . . Smist, J. M. (1993). *Why not let high ability students start school in January? The curriculum compacting study* (Research Monograph 93106). Storrs, CT: National Research Center on the Gifted and Talented, University of Connecticut.

Renzulli, J. S. (1976). The enrichment triad model: A guide for developing defensible programs for the gifted and talented. *Gifted Child Quarterly, 20,* 303–306.

Renzulli, J. S. (1978). What makes giftedness? Re-examining a definition. *Phi Delta Kappan, 60,* 180–184, 261.

Renzulli, J. S. (2005). The three-ring conception of giftedness: A developmental model for creative productivity. In R. J. Sternberg & J. E. Davidson (Eds.), *Conceptions of giftedness* (2nd ed., pp. 246–279). New York, NY: Cambridge University Press.

Renzulli, J. S., & Reis, S. M. (2014). *The schoolwide enrichment model: A how-to guide for talent development* (3rd ed.). Waco, TX: Prufrock Press.

Renzulli, J. S., Smith, L. H., White, A. J., Callahan, C. M., Hartman, R. K., Westberg, K. L. Gavin, M. K., . . . & Sytsma Reed, R. E. (2010). *Scales for rating the behavioral characteristics of superior students: Technical and administration manual* (3rd ed.). Waco, TX: Prufrock Press.

Roe, A. (1953). *The making of a scientist.* New York, NY: Dodd Mead.

Sabatino, C., & Wiebe, C. (in press). Bridges Academy: A strength-based model for 2e education. In S. Kaufman, *Twice-exceptional: Supporting and educating bright and creative students with learning difficulties.* New York, NY: Oxford University Press.

Schiff, M. M., Kaufman, A. S., & Kaufman, N. L. (1981). Scatter analysis of WISC-R profiles for learning disabled children with superior intelligence. *Journal of Learning Disabilities, 14,* 400–404. doi:10.1177/002221948101400711

Schlicter, C. H. (2009). Talents unlimited: Skills instruction for all children. In J. S. Renzulli, E. J. Gubbins, K. S. McMillen, R. D. Eckert, & C. A. Little (Eds.), *Systems and models for developing programs for the gifted and talented* (2nd. ed., pp. 433–456). Waco, TX: Prufrock Press.

Schneps, M. H. (2014). The advantages of dyslexia: With reading difficulties can come other cognitive strengths. *Scientific American.* Retrieved from https://www.scientificamerican.com/article/the-advantages-of-dyslexia

Schwab Learning. (2007). *Assistive technology: A parent's guide.* Retrieved from http://www.disabilityrightsca.org/pubs/Assistive_Technology_Parents_Guide.pdf

Sciortino, P. (2016, July). Improvisational play: Social/emotional learning for 2e students. *2e Newsletter, 77.*

Section 504 of the Rehabilitation Act, 29 U.S.C. Section 706 et. Seq. (1973).

Seligman, M. E., & Csikszentmihalyi, M. (Eds.). (2000). Happiness, excellence, and optimal human functioning [Special issue]. *American Psychologist, 55,* 5–183.

Senf, G. M. (1983). The nature and identification of learning disabilities and their relationship to the gifted child. In L. H. Fox, L. Brody, & D. Tobin (Eds.), *Learning disabled/gifted children* (pp. 7–49). Austin, TX: PRO-ED.

Silberman, S. (2015). *NeuroTribes: The legacy of autism and the future of neurodiversity.* New York, NY: Random House.

Silver, H. F., & Hanson, J. R. (1996). *Learning styles and strategies* (2nd ed.). Woodbridge, NJ: Silver Strong.

Silver, H. F., Hanson, J. R., & Chu, J. (1982). *Teaching styles and strategies.* Woodbridge, NJ: Silver Strong.

Silver, H., Strong, R., & Perini, M. (1997). Integrating learning styles and multiple intelligences. *Educational Leadership, 55,* 22–27.

Silverman, L. K. (1989). Invisible gifts, invisible handicaps. *Roeper Review, 12,* 37–41. http://dx.doi.org/10.1080/02783198909553228

Silverman, L. K. (1993). The gifted individual. In L. K. Silverman (Ed.), *Counseling the gifted and talented* (pp. 3–28). Denver, CO: Love.

Singer, J. (1998). *Odd people in: The birth of community amongst people on the Autism Spectrum: A personal exploration of a new social movement based on neurological diversity* (Honours dissertation). University of Technology, Sydney, Australia.

Sternberg, R. J. (1988). Mental self-government: A theory of intellectual styles and their development. *Human Development, 31,* 197–224.

Sternberg, R. J. (1995). *A triarchic approach to giftedness.* Storrs, CT: University of Connecticut, National Research Center on the Gifted and Talented.

Sternberg, R. J. (1997). What does it mean to be smart? *Educational Leadership, 54*(6), 20–24.

Sternberg, R. J., & Davidson, J. E. (Eds.). (2005). *Conceptions of giftedness* (2nd ed.). New York, NY: Cambridge University Press.

Strauss, A. A., & Lehtinen, L. E. (1947). *Psychopathology and education of the brain-injured child* (Vol. 1). New York, NY: Grune & Stratton.

Subotnik, R. F., Olszewski-Kubilius, P., & Worrell, F. C. (2011). Rethinking giftedness and gifted education: A proposed direction forward based on psychological science. *Psychological Science in the Public Interest, 12,* 3–54.

Tannenbaum, A. J. (1983). *Gifted children: Psychological and educational perspectives.* New York, NY: Macmillan.

Terman, L. (1959). *Genetic studies of genius: The gifted group at mid-life.* Stanford, CA: Stanford University Press.

Terman, L., & Oden, M. (1947). *Genetic studies of genius: Mental and physical traits of a thousand gifted children* (Vol. 1.). Stanford, CA: Stanford University Press.

Thompson-Schill, S. L., Ramscar, M., & Chrysikou, E. G. (2009). Cognition without control: When a little frontal lobe goes a long way. *Current Directions in Psychological Science, 18,* 259–263. doi:10.1111/j.1467-8721.2009.01648

Title V, Part D. [Jacob K. Javits Gifted and Talented Students Education Act of 1988], Elementary and Secondary Education Act of 1988 (2002), 20 U.S.C. sec. 7253 et seq.

Triesman, A. M. (1964). Monitoring and storage of irrelevant messages in selective attention. *Journal of Verbal Learning and Verbal Behavior, 3,* 449–459.

U.S. Department of Education. (1993). *National excellence: A case for developing America's talent.* Washington, DC: Office of Educational Research and Improvement.

U.S. Department of Education. (n.d.) *Building the Legacy: IDEA 2004: Additional procedures for evaluating children with specific learning disabilities (SLD).* Retrieved from http://idea-b.ed.gov/explore/view/p/,root,regs,preamble1,prepart1,D,72,.html

VanTassel-Baska, J. (1992). *Planning effective curriculum for gifted learners.* Denver, CO: Love.

Vaughn, S. (1989). Gifted learning disabilities: Is it such a bright idea? *Learning Disabilities Focus, 4,* 123–126. doi:10.1177/002221948902200401

Wallach, M. A. (1976). Tests tell us little about talent: Although measures of academic skills are widely used to determine access to contested educational opportunities, especially in their upper ranges they lack utility for predicting professional achievement. *American Scientist, 64,* 57–63.

Wallraff, B. (1998). Other than normal. *Atlantic Unbound: From the Word Fugitives archive.* Retrieved from http://www.theatlantic.com/past/docs/unbound/fugitives/notnormal.htm

Webb, J. T., Amend, E. R., Webb, N. E., Goerss, J., Beljan, P., & Olenchak, F. R. (2005). *Misdiagnosis and dual diagnoses of gifted children and adults: ADHD, bipolar, OCD, Asperger's, depression, and other disorders.* Scottsdale, AZ: Great Potential Press.

Webb, J. T., Gore, J. L., Amend, E. R., & DeVries, A. R. (2007). *A parent's guide to gifted children.* Tuscon, AZ: Great Potential Press.

WebMD. (2017). *Autism - symptoms.* Retrieved from http://www.webmd.com/brain/autism/autism-symptoms#1

Wechsler, D. (1974). *Wechsler intelligence scale for children—Revised (WISC-R).* New York, NY: Psychological Corporation.

Wechsler, D. (1991). *Wechsler intelligence scale for children* (3rd ed.). New York, NY: Psychological Corporation.

Wechsler, D. (2003). *Wechsler intelligence scale for children* (4th ed.). New York, NY: Psychological Corporation.

Wechsler D. (2014). *Wechsler intelligence scale for children* (5th ed.). Bloomington, MN: Pearson.

West, T. (1997). *In the mind's eye: Visual thinkers, gifted people with dyslexia and other learning difficulties, computer images and the ironies of creativity* (Updated Ed.). New York, NY: Prometheus Books.

Whitmore, J. R. (1980). *Giftedness, conflict, and underachievement.* Boston, MA: Allyn & Bacon.

Williams, K. (2013). *Mentorship and gifted youth* [Web log post]. Retrieved from http://educationaladvancement.org/mentorship-and-gifted-youth

Willis, J. (2007). The neuroscience of joyful education. *Educational Leadership, 64.* Retrieved from http://www.ascd.org/publications/educational-leadership/summer07/vol64/num09/The-Neuroscience-of-Joyful-Education.aspx

Winner, E. (1996). *Gifted children: Myths and realities.* New York, NY: Basic Books

Witty, P. A. (1958). Who are the gifted? In N. B. Henry (Ed.), *Education of the gifted. The 57th yearbook of the National Society for the Study of Education* (Part II, pp. 41–63). Chicago, IL: University of Chicago Press.

Wright, P. W., & Wright, P. D. (2007). *Is a child with ADD/ADHD eligible for special education?* Retrieved from http://www.wrightslaw.com/advoc/ltrs/eligibility_add.htm

Yell, M. L., Shriner, J. G., & Katsiyannis, A. (2006). Individuals with disabilities education improvement act of 2004 and IDEA regulations of 2006: Implications for educators, administrators, and teacher trainers. *Focus on Exceptional Children, 39*(1), 1–24.

Zimmerman, B. J. (1989). A social cognitive view of self-regulated academic learning. *Journal of Educational Psychology, 81,* 329–339.

Zimmerman, B. J. (2002). Becoming a self-regulated learner: An overview. *Theory Into Practice, 41,* 64–70.

Zirkel, P. A., & Krohn, N. (2008). RTI after IDEA: A survey of state laws. *Teaching Exceptional Children, 40,* 71–73.

Appendices

Appendix A

Project High Hopes Program Description

Project High Hopes[10], a 3-year talent development program was a gifted program for twice-exceptional students in Connecticut and Rhode Island funded by the Javits Act program. The purpose of this program was to identify and nurture artistic, scientific, or engineering talents in students with special needs. The project served 130 students in grades 5 through 8 at nine sites in Connecticut and Rhode Island, including six public schools, a private school for the learning disabled, and two schools for the deaf. Of the 130 students, 72 (55.4%) attended a special school, 19 (14.6%) received resource room services in their school, and 39 (30%) were mainstreamed within the regular school setting. Selected students came from the special education population at each site who had been identified as having one or more of the following: learning disabilities, attention deficits, emotional and behavioral disorders, pervasive developmental disorders, or hearing impairments.

The sequence of activities followed typical talent development models (Bloom et al., 1985; Csikszentmihalyi, Rathunde, & Whalen, 1996; Renzulli, 1977). The first step was to expose students to a variety of domains in order to uncover talent potential. Once students were identified as talented within a particular domain, they participated in talent development activities within that domain. These lessons taught students the skills of the discipline through authentic activities and learning experiences. During the final stage, activities encourage students to further their abilities by becoming creative producers within their talent areas.

---

10   Project High Hopes: Identifying and Nurturing Talent in Students with Special Needs (1993–1996) was funded by the Jacob K. Javits Gifted and Talented Students Education Act. Contributions to this program description were made by Carolyn Cooper, project administrator, and Terry Neu, project coordinator.

Activities during the first year involved the domains of visual and performing arts, biological science, physical science, and engineering design. These activities were part of the Talent Discovery Assessment Process as described (see Chapter 8) and served as audition sessions where students' potential talent in these domains could surface.

During the second year of the project, activities focused on teaching students the skills and methods of the discipline of their talent. Renzulli's Enrichment Triad Model (1977) guided the skill development curriculum. Activities elicited specific cognitive, creative, and affective behaviors characteristic of practicing professionals in each discipline. Content specialists, such as zoologists, botanists, a biological illustrator, physicists, engineers, visual artists, and actors, taught biweekly, 90-minute lessons that engaged students in learning authentic skills of those professionals. During each session, students were engaged in authentic content and advanced-level skills. For example, over the course of several engineering sessions, students learned how to use a transit to measure the gradations of their auditorium. From these measurements, they constructed a topographic map and then a scale model. In biology, students assumed the role of scientist as they discovered what constitutes an owl's diet. They carefully dissected owl pellets and, using anatomy charts, identified parts of skeletal structures of the owl's prey. One group of students reconstructed an entire vole skeleton, learning about the structure of the food chain and the carrying capacity of the owl in the process. By comparing and contrasting the skeletal remains, students determined important facts about what the owls had consumed, and probing questions led to higher-level extrapolation, inference, and deduction.

The next phase of the project helped students apply their new skills in an interdisciplinary context. Project High Hopes conducted an extremely successful one-week summer residential program on the campus of the American School for the Deaf in West Hartford, CT. Twenty-seven identified students worked in research and development (R&D) "companies" to solve a genuine problem associated with the pond there. This intense problem-based learning experience gave these middle school students a rare educational opportunity to become bona fide real-world problem-solvers. The students were assigned to interdisciplinary teams comprising engineers, scientists, artists, and actors to collaborate on the problem. Their goal was to develop a proposal containing a creative solution for reconstructing the pond. Students worked in an advanced laboratory environment in which specially selected and highly qualified teacher-facilitators coached the individual research and development companies in the creative problem solving process. When needed, content-area specialists (mentors) in the four domains—engineering, performing arts, science, and visual arts—furnished technical advice on tools, techniques, and materials used by practicing professionals in those specific domains. Both teacher-facilitators and mentors taught students to capitalize on their talents and strengths to create a relevant proposal with supporting products, data, and budget considerations.

For 3 days, student R&D companies were fully focused on the creative problem solving process. Which species of animal life had once inhabited the pond? What degree of stress had the existing bridges tolerated? Student companies then began to finalize plans for their presentations to the Board of Directors and eagerly sought advice from the mentors as to how to polish their presentations creatively and professionally.

At the Presentations Forum, held on the final day of the week, each R&D company presented its proposal to a simulated Board of Directors for the school. In addition, another 300 people sat in the audience. The students introduced themselves as the professionals they had become in the course of the week's work; "I'm Joseph, and I'm the botanist in this firm!" one proclaimed to the audience.

Each company presented its proposed solution for reconstructing the pond using an innovative approach that reflected the creative problem solving techniques the students had been using all week. Because the activity was purposeful and was intended to influence a real audience, students sought out feedback and perfected their presentations. The students remained focused on their tasks over the course of the week. Often they ignored scheduled free time to continue working on their projects. Students who had few social skills bonded around similar interests and purposes. On the final day, there was no doubt in anyone's mind that each of these youngsters was highly talented. For the week, they seem to have left their disabilities at home.

During the final year of the project, students engaged in activities where they could continue to solve problems and develop their talents at levels commensurate with talented peers without disabilities. These students, who had been regarded as losers in fifth and sixth grade, were gaining entrance into the districts' traditional gifted programs and advanced science and art classes. Table A.1 summarizes these students' accomplishments as they evolved from students with special needs to students with gifts and talents. Some had entered art contests, others auditioned for roles in their school plays, and some entered advanced science classes. One young woman conducted a study on animal behavior and won a commendation at a science fair competition.

During the talent development lessons, Project High Hopes staff had the opportunity to observe the students succeeding. Learning was active, mentors guided rather than lectured, reading and writing were minimized, and clear expectations, carefully defined tasks, and rigid deadlines guided the process. Because the problem was real and purposeful and the students were working in their talent areas, students appeared motivated, in control of their learning, and confident in their abilities. More specifically, they displayed a variety of self-regulatory behaviors known to underlie learning and achievement (Zimmerman, 1989; Duckworth, 2016).

Table A.1

Project High Hopes Student Accomplishments

Domain	Opportunity	Results
Engineering	Odyssey of the Mind competitions	Five teams participated in Connecticut; two second-place awards and one third-place award.
Engineering	Egg-drop competition	Two students had award-winning entires in the school's egg drop contest.
Performing Arts	Auditions for school plays	Five students were selected by an audition process for leading roles in their schools' productions.
Visual Arts	Student regional juried art shows	Ten students had art work selected in juried competitions in Massachusetts, Rhode Island, and Connecticut.
Visual Arts	District gifted art program	Three students selected for advanced art class.
Science	Science fair competitions	Seven students entered science fairs and one received a written commendation for high quality.
Science	Physics Day Competition	Twelve students participated in district science completion. Nine received recognition for their problem-solving ability.
Science	Acceptance to advanced science classes	Two students accepted into their districts' advanced science class for gifted students.

Appendix B

WISC Changes

WISC-III	Verbal	Verbal Comprehension	Information Similarities Vocabulary Comprehension
		Freedom From Distractibility	Arithmetic Digit Span
	Performance	Perceptual Organization	Picture Completion Picture Arrangement Block Design Object Assembly
		Processing Speed	Coding Symbol Search
WISC-IV	Verbal	Verbal Comprehension	Information Similarities Vocabulary Comprehension
		Working Memory	Arithmetic Digit Span *Letter-Number Sequencing*
	Performance	Perceptual Organization	Picture Completion Block Design *Matrix Reasoning*
		Processing Speed	Digit Symbol Coding Symbol Search

WISC-V	Verbal Comprehension	Information Similarities Vocabulary Comprehension
	Visual Spatial	Block Design *Visual Puzzles*
	Fluid Reasoning	*Matrix Reasoning* *Figure Weights* *Picture Concepts* *Arithmetic*
	Working Memory	Digit Span *Picture Span* Letter-Number Sequencing
	Processing Speed	Coding Symbol Search *Cancellation*

Note. Features new to the WISC-IV or WISC-V appear in italics. (Adapted from Wechsler, 1991, 2003, 2014.)

Appendix C

Reflective RTI

INFORMATION COLLECTION FOR
REFLECTIVE RTI™

DATE: ....

Student Name: ....

Date of Birth: ....

Current Grade: ....

Current Teacher: ....

    Phone: ....

    Email: ....

Receiving Special Services?   Yes   No
    If yes, what? ....

Special Services contact information: ....

....

    Phone: ....

    Email: ....

Mother: ....

    Phone: ....

    Email: ....

Father: ....

    Phone: ....

    Email: ....

1. Reason(s) for Plan
(Include no more than three presenting issues for this Reflective RTI plan.)
1.
2.
3.

Baum, Schader, Dismuke, & Sly (2012)

2. — Behaviors and Challenges (Summarize behaviors and challenges observed at home, in the classroom, and during extracurricular situations.)	3. — Taking Stock (Summarize interests, strengths, learning preferences, and experiences from screening instruments such as MY LEARNINGPRINT™, as well as pertinent results from testing and classroom performance.)	
School:	*Expressed Interests:*	
	Strengths:	
Home:	*Learning Preferences:*	
	Relevant Experiences:	
Extracurricular Activities:	*Testing Results:*	
	Other Performance Indicators:	

4. — Times of Personal Best	5. — Expectations
(When, and under what circumstances, are the presenting issues _least_ observable? When are the good times? Include observations from teacher(s), parents, and the student.)	(Frame the hopes and dreams for a school year...but also document any long-term aspirations that may be mentioned from the perspective of teacher(s), parents, and student.)
Input from teacher(s):	_Input from teacher(s):_
Input from parents:	_Input from parents:_
Input from student:	_Input from student:_

6. -- Summary (what have we learned about this child)

This student is at his/her personal best when:

This student has strong interest and abilities in:

He/She has mastered the regular curriculum except:

He/She has difficulty with:

By the end of this school year, it would be important for this student to:

7. -- Questions and Working Hypotheses (creating innovative strategies that can reach this child)

Knowing these things (above), what do we need to address for success?

Looking at times of personal best along with strengths and interests, what can deduce about how this child learns best?

What opportunities are there to work in strength and ability areas every day?

• Inside the curriculum:

• Outside the curriculum:

How might his/her interests and abilities be helpful in opening doors to address the challenges?

• Inside the curriculum:

• Outside the curriculum:

Other things to consider: Could it be that the curriculum isn't challenging?   Yes   No   Is the curriculum relevant?   Yes   No
Could there be missing skills? (If so, what..)
Might the curriculum be too abstract?   Yes   No   Could the pace be too slow?   Yes   No
Could there be a hidden reading difficulty?   Yes   No   Is the classroom set-up appropriate?   Yes   No

Now, refer to the research-based strategies sheet and collaboration log, as you build a Reflective RTI

Note. From *Reflective RTI: Rationale and Resources to Create Instructional Plans for the 2e Learner* (pp. 1–4), by S. Baum, R. Schader, S. Dismuke, and R. Sly, 2012, Studio City, CA: 2e Center for Research and Professional Development at Bridges Academy. Copyright 2012 by S. Baum, R Schader, S. Dismuke, and R. Sly. Reprinted with permission.

Appendix D

Presenting Behaviors Checklist

REFLECTIVE RTI™: OBSERVATION RATING SHEET

Student Name:...

Rater: ....

Relationship to Student: ....

DATE: ....

Observation	Measure of Severity or Frequency						
	Indicate on a scale of 1 to 7 with "1" being not a severe problem, or one that is observed infrequently and "7" indicating a severe problem, or one that is observed frequently.						
Academic:							
1. Has difficulty completing work	1	2	3	4	5	6	7
2. Has advanced vocabulary	1	2	3	4	5	6	7
3. Has difficulty with written production	1	2	3	4	5	6	7
4. Shows difficulty with reading	1	2	3	4	5	6	7
5. Generates creative responses	1	2	3	4	5	6	7
6. Shows difficulty with math	1	2	3	4	5	6	7
7. Doesn't turn in homework	1	2	3	4	5	6	7
8. Very knowledgeable about specific topics	1	2	3	4	5	6	7
9. Asks many questions	1	2	3	4	5	6	7
10. Other_____	1	2	3	4	5	6	7
11. Other_____	1	2	3	4	5	6	7
12. Other_____	1	2	3	4	5	6	7
Emotional/Behavioral:							
13. Is anxious	1	2	3	4	5	6	7
14. Is non-cooperative	1	2	3	4	5	6	7
15. Lacks motivation	1	2	3	4	5	6	7
16. Is easily bored	1	2	3	4	5	6	7
17. Is easily frustrated	1	2	3	4	5	6	7
18. Has difficulty sitting still	1	2	3	4	5	6	7
19. Responds positively to challenge	1	2	3	4	5	6	7
20. Feelings are hurt easily	1	2	3	4	5	6	7
21. Is concerned with fairness and justice	1	2	3	4	5	6	7
22. Is perfectionistic	1	2	3	4	5	6	7
23. Has high degree of energy	1	2	3	4	5	6	7
24. Other_____	1	2	3	4	5	6	7
25. Other_____	1	2	3	4	5	6	7

additional items on back   Baum, Schader, Dismuke, & Sly (2012)

REFLECTIVE RTI: OBSERVATION RATING SHEET (PG. 2)

Observation	Measure of Severity or Frequency						
	Indicate on a scale of 1 to 7 with "1" being not a severe problem, or one that is observed infrequently and "7" indicating a severe problem, or one that is observed frequently.						
Cognitive:							
26. Has difficulty remembering things	1	2	3	4	5	6	7
27. Has difficulty following directions	1	2	3	4	5	6	7
28. Has trouble making decisions and/or planning	1	2	3	4	5	6	7
29. Has trouble transitioning	1	2	3	4	5	6	7
30. Shows curiosity	1	2	3	4	5	6	7
31. Has difficulty sustaining attention	1	2	3	4	5	6	7
32. Is disorganized	1	2	3	4	5	6	7
33. Has difficulty working independently	1	2	3	4	5	6	7
34. Grasps concepts quickly	1	2	3	4	5	6	7
35. Has prodigious memory	1	2	3	4	5	6	7
36. Other_____	1	2	3	4	5	6	7
37. Other_____	1	2	3	4	5	6	7
Social:							
38. Has few friends	1	2	3	4	5	6	7
39. Has limited social skills	1	2	3	4	5	6	7
40. Is not socially aware	1	2	3	4	5	6	7
41. Takes charge in groups	1	2	3	4	5	6	7
42. Shows bullying behaviors	1	2	3	4	5	6	7
43. Has empathy	1	2	3	4	5	6	7
44. Prefers company of older companions	1	2	3	4	5	6	7
45. Other_____	1	2	3	4	5	6	7
46. Other_____	1	2	3	4	5	6	7

Review any items that received ratings of "1" or "2" and "6" or "7"	
Academic	
Emotional / Behavioral	
Cognitive	
Social	

Baum, Schader, Dismuke, & Sly (2012)

Note. From *Reflective RTI: Rationale and Resources to Create Instructional Plans for the 2e Learner* (pp. 5–6), by S. Baum, R. Schader, S. Dismuke, and R. Sly, 2012, Studio City, CA: 2e Center for Research and Professional Development at Bridges Academy. Copyright 2012 by S. Baum, R Schader, S. Dismuke, and R. Sly. Reprinted with permission.

Appendix E

Sample Structured Interview Form

1. Describe this child's interests.	

2. Have you observed situations in which this child:	
• becomes totally absorbed in a particular subject area?	Yes / No *(If yes, please explain.)*
• has discussed adult topics such as politics, religion, or current events?	Yes / No *(If yes, please explain.)*
• becomes self-assertive, stubborn, or aggressive.	Yes / No *(If yes, please explain.)*
• avoided tasks?	Yes / No *(If yes, please explain.)*
• was particularly curious?	Yes / No *(If yes, please explain.)*
• was highly imaginative?	Yes / No *(If yes, please explain.)*
• was humorous or seemed to be aware of nuances of humor?	Yes / No *(If yes, please explain.)*

Note. Adapted from *Scales for Rating the Behavioral Characteristics of Superior Students* (3rd ed., pp. 37–51), by J. S. Renzulli et al., 2010, Waco, TX: Prufrock Press. Copyright 2010 by Prufrock Press. Adapted with permission.

Appendix F

Project High Hopes Identification Activities[11]

Three-Dimensional Arts[12]

Introduction:

This activity is designed to identify young artists with three-dimensional skills. Two lessons are described which tap students' spatial skills and give the observer opportunities to record behaviors in this domain.

Behaviors to be Observed:

- Balance.
- Form (dimensionality).
- Clear communication of intent.
- Unified design (parts to whole, inclusion/exclusion).
- Experiments with ideas, materials, or techniques.
- Combines disparate parts to create unique solution.
- Uses detail to show complexity of ideas.
- Uses tools and materials effectively.
- Accepts and incorporates other's feedback.
- Is able to talk about work.

---

11   Project High Hopes is a Javits Act Program #R206R00001.
12   Compiled and developed by Anders Bachman, freelance artist and consultant.

Organization for Learning:

The environment should have desk top space for each student, preferable arranged in a circle with an inlet to the center, or as a second choice, in small clusters. Each desk top should be covered with a piece of cardboard to protect it from the wire and to facilitate cleaning up.

Activity Title: Creating Structures with Wire

Time Frame: 45 minutes
Materials:

- 2′, 3′, or 4′ piece of wire (pliable)
- one pair of needle-nose pliers
- one pair of regular pliers per student

Procedures:

The objective of this activity is to elicit three-dimensional thinking using a medium gauge wire to create your favorite food. We are going to explore a little piece of our imagination and practice catching our images. What's fun about his for me is that both the images which you will each create today will be different from everyone else's. None of them will be right or wrong. We can all have some fun.

Imagine your favorite food sitting on the table in front of you. My favorite food is an apple. It's easy for me to create an example using it.

Example: Imagine a firm green apple. On the surface of this apple we are using a thin black magic marker to draw a continuous line which explores the surface of our apple, up and down the sides, over the bumps on the bottom, and up and around the stem. Maybe there is still a leaf attached to the stem, we'll explore it also. Imagine what the apple looks like now with a thin black line meandering around on its surfaces. Magically our thin black line turns into a stiff wire, and just as magically our apple disappears, leaving the stiff wire behind, describing its surfaces. Try to use this idea as a starting point or springboard when creating your wire object. Remember, you can pick any food. It doesn't have to be an apple.

One more thing, be careful of the tools. Make sure that the pliers do not get anything in their working parts, and make sure that the end of your wire is not bothering someone else. At the end of our session, after we clean up, we can have a short show and tell. We will begin cleaning up at _____.

Drama Activities[13]

Introduction:

The exercises are designed to produce many different behaviors, and there seems to be enough overlapping of intended behaviors to ensure each student a fair chance at exhibiting the greatest range of behaviors over the entire session.

Please realize although the two Performing Arts sessions are designed to identify gifts in movement and the dramatic arts, the two disciplines share much common ground in their beginning stages. The exercises outlined below are designed to provide the students with the widest possible range of verbal and physical stimuli in order to produce the desired behaviors.

Behaviors to be Observed:
- Uses facial expressions.
- Uses expressive voice.
- Uses body language.
- Shows clear communication of intent.
- Creates elaborate movements, characters, or skits.
- Accepts and incorporates others' feedback.

Organizing for Learning:

You will need a large, open room or an average classroom with desks, tables, etc., cleared. All corners, piles of desks, etc. should be cushioned (ideally with gym mats, foam rubber, etc.) in smaller rooms. The students should wear clothes suitable for sitting on the floor and comfortable footwear (students may be asked to remove shoes for easier movement and to prevent injury). Finally, ice-packs and a first aid kit should be in the room for minor injuries.

Activity Title: Explosions

Time Frame: 5 minutes
Materials:
- Ice pack or alternative medical care in case of emergency.

Procedures:

Students will walk around the room, leaving plenty of space between themselves and others. At a signal (handclap or flick of the lights) they will "explode out of the walk and into a freeze. After two rounds, the students will be instructed to mime performing a task from their freeze position (example: arms akimbo, fists on top

---

13   Compiled and developed by Jason LaRosa, Eastern Connecticut State University.

of each other, and legs parallel in an open stance could become swinging a baseball bat). The task should be sustainable long enough for the instructor and observers to see it.

Activity Title: Machines

Time Frame: 10 minutes
Materials:
- Ice pack or alternative medical care in case of emergency.

Procedures:

One student starts a motion, another student joins in with a complementary motion, other students fill in with motions complementing the positive and negative space created by the first two students. The result of this exercise should be a creation of automated motion created by bodies working in harmony.

Activity Title: Hello!

Time Frame: 5 minutes
Materials:
- Ice pack or alternative medical care in case of emergency.

Procedures:

The leader will provide a brief introduction of himself, identify a space where he and the students will be performing the activities, and outline the activities.

The group and leader stand in a circle. The leader addresses each student with "Hello" punctuated with a wave and certain attitude. Once the leader addresses each student, he will change the wave and the attitude and repeat. The activity will end after four rounds or after each student who desires to lead a round has done so.

Activity Title: First Thing In the Morning

Time Frame: 15 minutes
Materials:
- Ice pack or alternative medical care in case of emergency.

Procedures:

This is a mime exercise. The leader will explain that we will demonstrate what we do first thing in the morning and will encourage the students to try the exercise and guess each other's activities. If possible, the instructor should find out what each student will be demonstrating so he can help revise each student's work for clarity and detail.

Engineering and Design[14]

Introduction:

Engineering has been considered a strength area of the spatial child. Students with strong spatial skills seldom have instruction modified to elicit this strength area. This activity has been designed to capitalize on spatial strengths by presenting a problem faced by Leonardo da Vinci. As Leonardo approached this problem through the use of testing models, students will follow his example as they explore basic concepts in engineering and design. Little or no verbal directions are needed, as students use visual cues to actually construct the original model, then test and modify to increase the distance achieved by their car. There area multiple possible solutions generated by students to this problem.

Behaviors to be Observed:
- Actively manipulates materials.
- Tries to predict outcomes.
- Understands the main concepts of today's topic.
- Product shows clarity of thought and focused plan of action.
- Puts materials together in a unique way.
- Explains the logic of alternative solutions.
- Shows problems solving by pursuing and unprompted investigation.

Organization for Learning:

Set up a materials table. Arrange work tables in a manner which allows the students to move to different locations with ease. Make sure there is easy access to a hallway or other area in which the completed vehicles have plenty of room to run.

Activity Title: Building Rubber Band Powered Vehicles, da Vinci Style

Time Frame: 70 minutes
Materials (list per student):
- 2 axles
- 2 front wheels
- 2 rear wheels
- 4 eye screws
- small nails
- 1 12 x 3/4 x4 soft wood board
- hammer
- large rubber bands

---

14   Compiled and developed by Bill Brown, Director, Eli Whitney Museum and Workshop.

Procedures:

Students will be introduced to the work of Leonardo da Vinci. da Vinci had conceived of a spring-powered vehicle using the mechanisms commonly found in wind-up clocks. Show students the drawing and ask students, "What do you think this is? How might it work?" Demonstrate the spring power used to run a clock and ask for student feedback. Show students a mock up of Leonardo's cart which has been altered to run on rubber bands. Wind up the cart and let it travel across a table or floor. Ask students for the noted differences they notice between the design of the cart and automobiles they are familiar with. Take out enough parts to assemble a demo four-wheeled car. Model the construction technique with a limited amount of teacher talk.

Key Points for Students to Observe:
- using a nail to start the eye screw hole
- placement of the wheels on the axles
- anchoring a nail on the front to attach the rubber bands (without smashing an axle)
- attaching a rubber band to the back axle
- winding up the back wheel

Allow time for students to complete their model. Emphasize that they will need to make adjustments to increase their car's distance after they test their model each time. While students are constructing their model, mark off a testing track at five foot intervals. A tiles floor with 12" tiles is ideal, but if this is not available, use masking tape to mark off appropriate intervals. Typically, students finish their prototypes at different times. As students finish, have them test their vehicle on the track. Make sure to keep accurate records for each test they conduct. Also, be sure to debrief each student after each test and elicit students' alterations for extended runs.

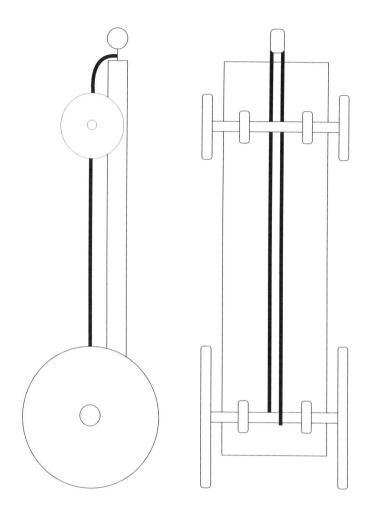

Zoology[15]

Introduction:

Reptiles and amphibians have always held a certain fascination for some students. This lesson is designed to draw out the naturalist by sing common salamanders, frogs, lizards, and turtles. Through the careful use and examination of live specimens student behaviors that are highly valued in science such as observation, comparison, and contrasting skills can be identified in students.

---

15   Compiled and developed by Julie Henry, Department of Ecology and Evolutionary Biology, University of Connecticut.

Behaviors to be observed:
- Displays curiosity by asking relevant questions.
- Shows a lot of knowledge related to today's topic.
- Actively manipulates materials.
- Communicates clearly the results of the project.
- Systematically tests hypothesis.
- Tries to predict outcomes.
- Represents ideas in the form of a model.
- Finds means of overcoming obstacles in problem solving.

Organization for Learning:

The room should have long tables for specimen display and for student work areas. Be sensitive to some students' fear of reptiles and amphibians. Caution: some specimens should not be held by students. The specimens should be arranged in individual tanks that can be manipulated for observation.

Activity Title: Comparing and Contrasting Reptiles and Amphibians

Time Frame: 55 Minutes
Materials:
- Terrarium (-ia)
- Salamander(s)
- Lizard(s)
- Turtle
- Frog
- Drawing paper and pencils with erasers (paper can be divided up into sections and prelabled)
- Photographs or slides of child, dog, bird, reptile, amphibian, fish

Procedures:
1. First, ask children what pets they have to see if they have an image in their experience to relate to. Children will probably have additional or different answers to the ones listed. Talk about these answers. Compare animals listed above, starting with the most complicated and progressing to least complicated. Ask students: What are the similarities? What are the differences?
2. Observation of two very different amphibian/reptiles . . . such as turtle and frog. Looking at the two will allow them to feel comfortable about making contrasts and will provide a warm-up for the next exercise. As we look at the animals we will talk about the same body parts and exercise 3.

3. Observation of salamander and lizard. Draw and talk about the following for each organism:

    Head: eyes, ears, mouth, nostrils
    Limbs: leg, feet, toes, claws, tail
    Body: movement, limb placement
    Skin: texture, color, etc.
    Behavior
    Habitat

4. Compare and contrast the salamander and the lizard. Some points probably will have been made earlier, but they can be repeated for emphasis. At this point, reptiles and amphibians can again be a topic to talk about (adaptations to land etc.). Children's experience with these organisms can be solicited at this time.

About the Authors

Susan Baum, Ph.D., is the director of the 2e Center for Research and Professional Development at Bridges Academy. Professor emeritus from the College of New Rochelle, Susan is well known for her seminal research and publications in 2e education.

Robin Schader, Ph.D., is a trustee of Bridges Academy, a school for twice-exceptional students, and serves on the executive board of the 2e Center for Research and Professional Development. Formerly, she served as the Parent Resource Advisor for the National Association for Gifted Children.

After 30 years teaching Educational Psychology at the University of Connecticut, **Steve Owen, Ph.D.,** became a biostatistician at the University of Texas. After a decade, he retired to Northern California.

Index